Tea ing Mathematics in S ondary Schools

The Open University *Flexible* Postg uate Certificate of Education

The re s and the companion volumes in the *flexible* PGCE series are:

Aspe *Teaching and Learning in Secondary Schools: Perspectives on practice*

Teac *Learning and the Curriculum in Secondary Schools: A reader*

Aspects *of Teaching Secondary Mathematics: Perspectives on practice*

Teaching Mathematics in Secondary Schools: A reader

Aspects of Teaching Secondary Science: Perspectives on practice

Teaching Science in Secondary Schools: A reader

Aspects of Teaching Secondary Modern Foreign Languages: Perspectives on practice

Teaching Modern Foreign Languages in Secondary Schools: A reader

Aspects of Teaching Secondary Geography: Perspectives on practice

Teaching Geography in Secondary Schools: A reader

Aspects *of Teaching Secondary Design and Technology: Perspectives on practice*

Tea ng *Design and Technology in Secondary Schools: A reader*

Asp *of Teaching Secondary Music: Perspectives on practice*

Teaching Music in Secondary Schools: A reader

A e subjects are part of the Open University's initial teacher education course, the *flexible* PGCE, and constitute part of an integrated course designed to develop critical understanding. The set books, reflecting a wide range of perspectives, and discussing the complex issues that surround teaching and learning in the twent century, will appeal to both beginning and experienced teachers, to mentors, tutors, advisers and other teacher educators.

If you would like to receive a *flexible* PGCE prospectus please write to the Course Reservations Centre at The Call Centre, The Open University, Milton Keynes MK7 6ZS. Other information about programmes of professional development in education is available from the same address.

Teaching Mathematics in Secondary Schools
A reader

Teaching Mathematics in Secondary Schools: A reader introduces and explores a broad range of contemporary issues and key ideas and will provide a useful background for those teaching and training to teach this core subject.

This book is concerned with exploring the bigger picture of mathematics education. Divided into seven sections to help structure reading, it covers:

- How students learn and develop as mathematics teachers
- The changing view of mathematics as a school subject
- Ideas about learning mathematics – how learning can be improved and how to generate 'magical moments' for learners
- Ideas about teaching mathematics – making mathematics classrooms exciting and challenging
- Ideas about assessing learning in mathematics – how the decisions we make influence the outcomes of our assessment
- Social and contextual issues – the ways in which we make ideas accessible to learners
- International perspectives – looking at our practices in relation to practices elsewhere

The *Teaching in Secondary Schools* series brings together collections of articles by highly experienced educators that focus on the issues surrounding the teaching of National Curriculum subjects. They are invaluable resources for those studying to become teachers, and for newly qualified teachers and more experienced practitioners, particularly those mentoring students and NQTs. The companion volume to this book is *Aspects of Teaching Secondary Mathematics: Perspectives on practice*.

Linda Haggarty is a Lecturer in Education at The Open University and has responsibility for the Open University *flexible* PGCE, Mathematics course.

Set book for the Open University *flexible* PGCE, Mathematics course EXM880.

Teaching Mathematics in Secondary Schools

A reader

Edited by Linda Haggarty

London and New York

First published 2002
by RoutledgeFalmer
11 New Fetter Lane, London EC4P 4EE

Simultaneously published in the USA and Canada
by RoutledgeFalmer
29 West 35th Street, New York, NY 10001

RoutledgeFalmer is an imprint of the Taylor & Francis Group

Typeset in Goudy by Bookcraft Ltd, Stroud, Gloucestershire
Printed and bound in Great Britain by Biddles Ltd, Guildford and King's Lynn

British Library Cataloguing in Publication Data
A catalogue record for this book is available from the British Library

Library of Congress Cataloging in Publication Data
Haggarty, Linda
    Teaching mathematics in secondary schools: a reader / Linda Haggarty
        p. cm
    Includes bibliographical references and index.
    1. Mathematics – Study and teaching (Secondary)   I. Title

QA11 .H24 2001
510'.71'2–dc21   2001034987

ISBN 0–415–26068–X (hbk)
ISBN 0–415–26069–8 (pbk)

Contents

Illustrations

Figures

Tables

Abbreviations

ATM   Association of Teachers of Mathematics
DES   Department of Education and Science
DfEE   Department for Education and Employment (now Department for Education and Skills)
CSE   Certificate of Secondary Education
FIMS   First International Mathematics Study
GCE   General Certificate of Education
GCSE   General Certificate of Secondary Education
HMI   Her Majesty's Inspector
ICT   Information and Communications Technology
IEA   International Association for the Evaluation of Educational Achievement
NC   National Curriculum
NCC   National Curriculum Council
NCTM   National Council of Teachers of Mathematics
QCA   Qualifications and Curriculum Authority
SAT   Standard Assessment Test
SIMS   Second International Mathematics Study
SMP   School Mathematics Project
SoA   Statement of Attainment
TIMSS   Third International Mathematics and Science Study
TTA   Teacher Training Agency

Sources

Where a chapter in this book is based on or is a reprint or revision of material previously published elsewhere, details are given below, with grateful acknowledgements to the original publishers. In some cases chapter titles have been changed from the original; in such cases the original chapter title is given below.

Chapter 2 This is an edited version of a chapter originally published in Hoyles, C. Morgan, C. and Woodhouse, G. (eds) (1999) *Rethinking the Mathematics Curriculum*, RoutledgeFalmer, London.

Chapter 3 This is an edited version of a paper originally published as 'New Numeracies for a Digital Culture [1]' in *For the Learning of Mathematics* 18(2), FLM Publishing Association, Kingston, Ontario, Canada (1998).

Chapter 4 This is an edited version of a paper originally published as 'Arbitrary and Necessary Part 1: A Way of Viewing the Mathematics Curriculum' in *For the Learning of Mathematics* 19(3), FLM Publishing Association, Kingston, Ontario, Canada (1999).

Chapter 6 This is an edited version of a paper originally published in *For the Learning of Mathematics* 20(1), FLM Publishing Association, Kingston, Ontario, Canada (1999).

Chapter 7 This is an edited version of a paper originally published as 'Open and Closed Mathematics: Student Experiences and Understandings' in the *Journal for Research in Mathematics Education* 29(1), National Council of Teachers of Mathematics, San Diego (1998).

Chapter 9 This is an edited version of a chapter originally published in Hoyles, C, Morgan, C. and Woodhouse, G. (eds) (1999) *Rethinking the Mathematics Curriculum*, RoutledgeFalmer, London.

Chapter 10 This chapter uses ideas from material originally published in 'Integrating Computers' in Micromath 13(1), Association of Teachers of Mathematics, Derby and Dynamic Geometry, NCET, Coventry. The latter is available from http://vtc.ngfl.gov.uk/resource/cits/maths/dynamic/index.html.

Chapter 15   This is an edited version of a chapter originally published in Nickson, M. (2000) *Teaching and Learning Mathematics: A Teacher's Guide to Recent Research and its Application*, Cassell, London. Where a chapter in this book is based on or is a reprint or revision of material previously published elsewhere, details are given below, with grateful acknowledgements to the original publishers.

Foreword

The nature and form of initial teacher education and training are issues that lie at the heart of the teaching profession. They are inextricably linked to the standing and identity that society attributes to teachers and are seen as being one of the main planks in the push to raise standards in schools and to improve the quality of education in them. The initial teacher education curriculum therefore requires careful definition. How can it best contribute to the development of the range of skills, knowledge and understanding that makes up the complex, multi-faceted, multi-skilled and people-centred process of teaching?

There are, of course, external, government-defined requirements for initial teacher training courses. These specify, amongst other things, the length of time a student spends in school, the subject knowledge requirements beginning teachers are expected to demonstrate or the ICT skills that are needed. These requirements, however, do not in themselves constitute the initial training curriculum. They are only one of the many, if sometimes competing, components that make up the broad spectrum of a teacher's professional knowledge that underpin initial teacher education courses.

Certainly today's teachers need to be highly skilled in literacy, numeracy and ICT, in classroom methods and management. In addition, however, they also need to be well grounded in the critical dialogue of teaching. They need to be encouraged to be creative and innovative and to appreciate that teaching is a complex and problematic activity. This is a view of teaching that is shared with partner schools within the Open University Training Schools Network. As such it has informed the planning and development of the Open University's initial teacher training programme and the *flexible* PGCE.

All of the *flexible* PGCE courses have a series of connected and complementary readers. The *Teaching in Secondary Schools* series pulls together a range of new thinking about teaching and learning in particular subjects. Key debates and differing perspectives are presented, and evidence from research and practice is explored, inviting the reader to question the accepted orthodoxy, suggesting ways of enriching the present curriculum and offering new thoughts on classroom learning. These readers are accompanied by the series *Perspectives on practice*. Here, the focus is on the application of these developments to educational/subject policy and the classroom, and on the illustration of teaching skills, knowledge and understanding in a variety of school contexts. Both series include newly commissioned work.

This series from RoutledgeFalmer, in supporting the Open University's *flexible* PGCE, also includes two key texts that explore the wider educational background. These companion publications, *Teaching, Learning and the Curriculum in Secondary Schools: A reader* and *Aspects of Teaching and Learning in Secondary Schools: Perspectives on practice*, explore a contemporary view of developments in secondary education with the aim of providing analysis and insights for those participating in initial teacher training education courses.

Hilary Bourdillon – Director ITT Strategy
Steven Hutchinson – Director ITT Secondary
The Open University
September 2001

Introduction

Mathematics teaching is both exciting and intellectually challenging. It is exciting to be involved with young people's learning of the subject, particularly when that learning has taken place as a result, partly, of our own efforts. It is also intellectually challenging because there are so many complex decisions to be made, not only in advance of each lesson but also during each lesson.

Mathematics teachers have an important responsibility as they try to inspire learners with the power and elegance of mathematics at the same time as they help them to become successful mathematicians (as measured in a much narrower sense in national tests and examinations). Indeed, attending to both of these simultaneously is in itself a demanding task for any teacher.

Intellectually challenging tasks are unlikely to be accomplished successfully through decision-making based simply on common-sense, naive ideas. Rather, teachers need to be educated about the powerful ideas already available in relation to mathematics and the teaching and learning of mathematics. Providing a richer, informed set of ideas about each of these helps teachers to extend the boundaries within which they make their decisions. It also allows teachers to make choices – and be aware of the nature, purpose and likely consequences of those choices – as they teach and as they reflect on their teaching.

This book is concerned with examining some of the big ideas associated with the teaching and learning of mathematics. It is aimed particularly at those who are learning to become mathematics teachers and at those experienced mathematics teachers who are interested in further developing their thinking and practice.

It is divided into seven sections to help the reader structure their own reading and thinking as they go along. However, there are overlaps between ideas and sections so that many chapters may inform thinking for other sections as well as for those in which they are placed.

Section 1 is concerned with teacher learning and the chapter by Linda Haggarty is addressed directly to those who are learning and developing as mathematics teachers. It is relatively unusual to acknowledge the learning needs of the readers of a book – yet if we take seriously the importance of helping to make powerful ideas accessible to those readers, it must also be important to examine some of the issues that influence those readers as they engage with the text and the ideas in that text. The chapter is an important one as it aims to help readers reflect on the learning opportunities which are being offered to them and the ways in which they act as mediators of those learning opportunities.

Section 2 is concerned with mathematics itself. Student teachers often arrive on teacher education courses with an implicit assumption that they 'know' what mathematics is – after all, haven't they been doing 'it' for many years? Yet being a mathematics teacher requires more than an implicit view of mathematics, which may or may not be available for conscious inspection and which may or may not hold up to public scrutiny. Being a thoughtful and informed mathematics teacher requires an awareness of a rich vision of mathematics and the ways in which school mathematics fits inside this vision and might develop within it. Johnston Anderson (Chapter 2) takes an historical perspective on mathematics and developments within mathematics; many themes introduced in his chapter are taken up by Richard Noss (Chapter 3), who looks to the future to identify issues that are likely to be of central concern to mathematics teachers. Dave Hewitt's chapter (Chapter 4) is in this section, although it could equally have been placed with chapters on learning or on teaching mathematics. His ideas are particularly thought-provoking in that he looks at the nature of school mathematics and essentially challenges the reader to distinguish between the 'arbitrary' and the 'necessary'.

Section 3 is concerned with learning mathematics. Naive views about learning mathematics abound: yet a teacher soon discovers that helping pupils to learn – even just one pupil – is not that easy. There have been many attempts to understand and explain how learners learn, each with implications for the role of the teacher. Examples include associationism (associated with 'drill and practice'), behaviourism (still in evidence in many classrooms and associated with teachers trying to find effective ways of 'handing over' knowledge), and constructivism (currently at the centre of much exciting thinking in mathematics education and being refined into new understandings). Barbara Jaworski (Chapter 5) takes ideas from constructivism and examines ways of understanding learning from a radical constructivist standpoint and from a social constructivist standpoint. These powerful ideas are presented in such a way that the reader is able to learn about current debates as well as understand the different 'lenses' through which learning can be understood. Mary Barnes (Chapter 6) explores moments of learner insight in mathematics lessons, calling these 'magical' moments, and from her research is able to identify classroom learning opportunities which can be offered by teachers where such insights seem able to take place. Jo Boaler (Chapter 7) has carried out important and influential research from the close study of two schools, each using a different approach in their mathematics teaching. She presents findings suggesting that learning, including that measured by national tests, is influenced by the teaching approach adopted. Her results, surprising to many, help us to question the appropriateness of teaching approaches still encouraged in many of our schools.

Section 4 is primarily concerned with the teaching of mathematics. It is important for mathematics teachers to see what kinds of actions in the classroom can lead to useful learning. Whilst the companion volume to this (*Aspects of Teaching Secondary Mathematics*) is concerned with particular pedagogical strategies, the chapters here present important visions from influential writers in the field. Ole

Skovsmose (Chapter 8) presents a framework within which we can better understand the choices available in our teaching and, through the identification of powerful examples, helps us to consider our own teaching in relation to his 'landscape' of possibilities. Gillian Hatch (Chapter 9) draws on ideas about learning which challenge much existing practice and she identifies important issues which need to be addressed if we are to 'maximise energy' in our classrooms. The importance of ICT in the teaching and learning of mathematics is beyond dispute, yet it is clear that it does not always lead to useful learning. Ronnie Goldstein (Chapter 10) reflects on this as he identifies the kinds of activities using ICT which lead to worthwhile learning outcomes in mathematics.

Section 5 is concerned with assessment in mathematics. Thinking about assessment is increasingly dominated by concerns associated with issues such as SATs, league tables and accountability of teachers, departments and schools. Yet learners, both informally and formally, assess their learning; and teachers assess what learning has taken place as well as assessing the effectiveness of their actions. Thus it is important that we develop a wide view of assessment issues to help our thinking and actions in the classroom, not least because those actions have significant effects on learners and their learning. The three chapters in this section look at quite distinct areas: Anne Watson (Chapter 11) writes a thoughtful chapter reflecting on what we mean by understanding and identifies for teachers the issues which need to be considered when making judgements about learners' understanding; Kenneth Ruthven (Chapter 12) explores assessment at a number of levels and indicates important ways in which the quality of pupil learning in mathematics can be enhanced (or not) through assessment; and Barry Cooper (Chapter 13), by examining questions from national tests, and from his extensive research, is able to identify ways in which the use of 'real' mathematics disadvantages some learners.

Section 6 is concerned with challenging teachers' traditional practices and responsibilities in the mathematics classroom. Peter Gates (Chapter 14) explores areas where learners are disadvantaged in mathematics because of ways in which mathematics is defined. He also examines how embedded structures and practices in classrooms favour powerful groups in society. Marilyn Nickson (Chapter 15) starts from the theoretical perspective of a growing acceptance of mathematics as social in its origins and its applications and considers what it means therefore to learn it and teach it, arguing that we need to take account of the social aspects of the teaching and learning of mathematics and the critical aspects of mathematics in its applications. Importantly, whether our concern is with social justice or with helping pupils 'come to know' mathematics (or both), the conclusions reached by each writer are remarkably similar.

Section 7, the final section in the book, takes an international perspective within which we can locate our own mathematics education practices, and subjects taken-for-granted assumptions to serious scrutiny. Birgit Pepin (Chapter 16) identifies issues from her extensive research on mathematics teaching in England, France and Germany which help us to understand not only why things are as they are in England but challenges us to widen our thinking about other possibilities for practice. In the final chapter (Chapter 17) Geoffrey Howson offers ideas from research in international comparative studies. As well as identifying some important issues that mathematics teachers in this country need to consider, he also offers a lively critique of issues raised through international comparisons of achievement in mathematics.

Learning and developing as a mathematics teacher requires more than 'training' in a diverse set of skills or techniques. Learning and developing as a mathematics teacher requires engagement in, and reflection on, powerful ideas in mathematics education. Through engagement and reflection, mathematics teachers can locate themselves and their endeavours in an intellectually stimulating and challenging setting which recognises (as teachers recognise themselves) that learning and teaching are demanding activities which deserve the best efforts of informed, educated and thoughtful professionals. This book represents a stimulus for thinking and intelligent action.

I would like to thank all the contributors to this book who, without exception, are as keen as I am to make powerful ideas available and accessible to everyone in the mathematics education community. I would also like to thank Sue Dutton, whose guidance, help, support and friendship helped to make this book a reality.

Linda Haggarty

Section 1

Student teacher learning

1 Learning and developing as a mathematics teacher

Linda Haggarty

Why can't we just tell you how to teach?

Imagine yourself in this situation …

> … It's Tuesday morning and it's raining …
>
> … you're about to teach mathematics to a lower band Year 8 class …
>
> … it's lesson 4 – just before lunch and just after PE …
>
> … you're starting a new topic on index notation, leading on later to index laws for multiplication and division …
>
> … you know what the previous teacher has taught the class already, but you don't know which pupils know – or even remember – the prerequisites for this lesson …
>
> … there are textbooks and practical equipment available, and there are two computers in the room …
>
> … Dan has just returned to school after being away for several weeks …
>
> … the back table of girls seem completely switched off from work at the moment …

Of course, it is possible to give many more details about this particular situation.

You might be interested to know more about the pupils. For example, you might like to know that very many of the pupils had no breakfast before they arrived, that Dan has been worried about the work he has missed whilst he was in hospital;,that some of the girls are finding mathematics 'boring', that a pupil who you may not even have noticed has problems at home which makes concentration in school difficult.

You might like to know how they work with their usual teacher. For example, it may be important to know that she usually likes pupils to work together in small groups, deciding for themselves which activities to do and for how long. But this could have been different. Maybe the teacher preferred the class to work predominantly through exercises in the textbook at the pace she set.

You might like to know that pupils have been using index notation for units in area and volume (when reminded) and that they will soon be moving on to using index notation in algebra.

The point of all this is to demonstrate that classrooms are complex places. Every lesson has its own story to go with it and the stories are different every time. Every classroom is full of individuals with their own concerns and motivations, their own learning experiences, their own thoughts about mathematics, mathematics lessons and school. Experienced teachers are often able to recognise types of situations and can use already practised and established routines to manage the complexity of scenarios like this. Relatively inexperienced teachers are less likely to be able to do this because they have too few experiences on which to draw. It is simply not easy to make sensible decisions about what might be done with the Year 8 class described above unless there is already a bank of experiences of what kinds of things have been tried in what circumstances, why, and with what effect.

So what can you as a student teacher do? Well first, it is very unlikely – and almost certainly unhelpful – for you to have to face this complexity early on in your learning. Indeed, it is very likely that you will switch to 'survival' mode just to get through an experience of this kind. In other words, the challenge becomes one of 'getting through' to the end of the lesson and managing the pupils so that no serious disruption occurs: concerns for learning and learners simply are not (and probably could not be) attended to.

But could anyone else tell a student teacher what to do in the situation described above? An experienced mathematics teacher will be able to say what *they* would do in the circumstances, but they will know there are other things that might work equally well. In addition, their advice is likely to be different from that given by the mathematics teacher down the corridor or the mathematics teacher in another school. So, even amongst experienced teachers, there is no consensus on what is 'right' in a particular situation. Rather, even though they may use a relatively limited range of strategies themselves, they will be aware that there are many more available that might also be appropriate. And while developing a bank of suggestions from a range of teachers is a useful strategy for learning about new possibilities, there is still the problem that what 'works' for one teacher does not always 'work' for another: even at the level of classroom management, an experienced teacher's observed strategy of smiling at the class until they quieten down is unlikely to be successful for a student teacher if simply copied!

Practical advice, therefore, is useful and important but unlikely to provide definitive answers that 'work' in similar situations or with different teachers. In addition, there are likely to be too few opportunities to provide the amount of detail required in which to embed that practical advice so that it can be used by the beginner. Theoretical advice is also useful and important since it may be (but is not always) grounded in serious and disciplined research and scholarship. Some of it can therefore describe generalised situations and offer useful ideas about sorts of actions that lead to particular kinds of outcomes in certain situations. Whether or not the outcomes can be replicated by you with the Year 8 class above is not something, however, which other people's research can ever attend to: the ideas from research –

and theories offered by others – offer generalised possibilities for exploration rather than answers about what to do in particular circumstances.

As an example, Askew and Wiliam (1995), in their review of research in mathematics education, report that:

> Learning is more effective when common misconceptions are addressed, exposed and discussed in teaching. We have to accept that pupils will make some generalisations that are not correct and many of these misconceptions remain hidden unless the teacher makes specific efforts to uncover them.
>
> (p. 12)

Now this is clearly an important finding from research yet, when the details in their comments are read, it is clear that very many of our textbooks and teaching materials do not adopt recommended teaching strategies. In addition, the research does not tell us exactly how to achieve this with the particular Year 8 class. So simply putting it into practice will need time, thought and care – and its success is likely to be influenced by very much more than the original claim.

It seems, therefore, that practical advice is useful because it can provide contextual ideas relating to the immediate situation: a great deal can be learnt from the usual teacher of the Year 8 class about the context described briefly above and about possibilities for future actions based on their own knowledge of the situation. Theoretical ideas are also useful because they extend the range of possibilities for action, although once again, such ideas can rarely be offered as likely to be successful in all situations nor can they provide answers about what to do in the set of complexities of a particular group of learners in a particular set of circumstances.

Although both theory and context can influence the range of possibilities available to a teacher, both practical and theoretical advice may well be influenced by particular sets of values or beliefs. And everyone has particular beliefs about teaching, learning, mathematics, education, and so on, whether or not they are implicitly or explicitly held. These beliefs form the basis of each person's choice of action or attitudes towards self and others. For example, Cooney (1984) suggests that teachers make decisions about students and the curriculum in a rational way according to the conceptions they hold and that their, often implicit, theories of teaching and learning influence their classroom acts. These conceptions have a powerful impact on teaching through the selections of content and emphasis, teaching style, and modes of learning (Ernest, 1989).

It is possible, for example, to hold the belief that for pupils to learn, mathematics teachers need to explain bite-size pieces of mathematics to pupils who then work through practice exercises at length until questions become familiar and the answers routine. On the other hand it is possible to believe that, in order for pupils to learn, mathematics teachers need to find a variety of challenging experiences to offer them allowing those pupils to construct meanings for themselves. Even with this example, it is clear that even the simplest advice can then be influenced by those contrasting beliefs. The types of questions asked of those pupils, for example, may be relatively closed – in order to elicit the extent to which what was in the teacher's head is now in the pupils' – or relatively open and exploratory – in order to probe the nature of the understanding constructed in the learner's mind.

It is similarly possible to hold the belief that the role of the mathematics teacher is to help prepare pupils for engagement as active citizens in a democratic society. It is equally possible to hold the belief that the mathematics teacher – and the mathematics teacher alone – is responsible for managing the learning and the learning activities in the classroom. Advice from each of those teachers might range from encouraging pupils to ask and answer their own questions and then take an active part in assessing their own learning, to ensuring as the teacher that all pupils answer the particular questions set and that the classroom remains as quiet and calm as possible.

What is important about these examples is that they open up the likelihood that when advice is given it is almost certainly going to be influenced by a particular set of beliefs, and that these beliefs may or may not be made explicit. This is true of advice offered not only by individuals but also by researchers and Government. To accept advice, therefore, without considering the possible underlying beliefs informing it is clearly foolish. What is needed is a much more deliberate testing of that advice in terms not only of its success and manageability but also of the extent to which it fits with one's own beliefs.

So how can anyone be told how to teach? The argument presented here is that it is impossible. The contexts in which teachers work are so complex ,the range of possibilities for action so wide, the beliefs underlying that advice so diverse, that simply telling someone is at best misleading and at worst likely to inhibit that learning significantly.

Finally, even if it *were* as simple as telling someone how to teach, it appears that the strategy is doomed to failure anyway because learner teachers themselves have their own very strongly held beliefs about mathematics teaching and how it should be 'done'. This is explored in the next section.

What gets in the way of learning to teach?

Some important ideas relating to student teacher learning concern the importance of students' previously acquired images of teaching during what Lortie (1975) calls a student teacher's 'apprenticeship of observation', so that your own experiences as a pupil in classrooms provides images of how you see yourself as a teacher. This is an important idea and one worth further thought.

As a pupil in school, it is very likely that you spent at least 500 hours in secondary mathematics classrooms – and thousands of hours in school altogether. During that time as a pupil, some lessons will have been perceived as 'good' and others 'bad', some teachers as 'good' and others 'bad'. The characteristics of good and bad lessons can probably be identified and descriptions given of the kinds of things which happen in good lessons (the sort you want to teach) and bad lessons (the sort you're not going to teach). From those memories, it may also be possible to describe your ideal teacher – the kind of teacher you want to be like. Maybe you have one in mind, or maybe it is a mixture of characteristics from different teachers. (You will almost certainly have memories of at least one teacher you do not want to be like.) Now the good teacher will probably have been well organised, interested in the subject and able to make it interesting for you, be interested in you as a person, had few if any management problems, was fair and firm when necessary, but also friendly, and so on. Indeed, they probably made teaching look relatively easy and effortless. Now, of course, at one level it is good to have such positive memories of teachers and it may well account for significant numbers of people wanting to teach themselves. At another level it causes problems for later learning.

It seems, for example, that the images carried through from experiences in school are both powerful in terms of shaping student teachers' agendas and also resistant to change (e.g. Calderhead, 1988). In addition, these agendas for learning are influenced by images created from observation of teachers rather than understanding of their actions, so that student teachers are in danger of thinking about teaching as telling (because that may be all you actually saw the teacher *do* overtly) and learning as memorising (because as a learner, that was an occasion when 'learning' was a conscious act) (Calderhead, 1991).

So a particular problem for teacher educators is how to persuade you that teaching and learning are complex activities, and that teaching which addresses the needs of learners is an intellectually demanding task. In addition, if you see teaching as relatively easy, there is the added problem of helping you to understand that issues not even on your agenda as things that need to be learnt about actually need to be addressed. Furthermore, unless some sort of cognitive dissonance occurs – a recognition of a need to know on your part – then much of what takes place during your teacher education course will seem (and remain) irrelevant (Haggarty, 1995). A consequence of this is that not only will many theoretical ideas be dismissed as apparently unimportant, or inconsistent with ideas already formed, but also the practical advice offered by teachers who are not considered to be sufficiently like your ideal teacher will also be ignored (Haggarty, 1997).

Further, much of what can be learnt from observation of experienced teachers, certainly at an early stage, is also in danger of being ignored because the teacher observed does not fit your idiosyncratic image of a good teacher, or the practices observed do not fit those used by teachers you perceived in the past to be good, or the complexity of what is observed is not appreciated because it simply is not recognised for what it is: an enactment of a complex, demanding and often conflicting set of teacher intentions.

Thus, it has been argued that student teachers in general are far from being 'empty vessels' as learners but have richly connected and idiosyncratic ideas about mathematics, mathematics teaching and mathematics learning which are informed by theory (ideas developed from hours of observation), context (your own perspective and needs as a learner), and values (possibly not consciously examined but likely to be influenced by perceived motives behind observations of teachers).

It must be emphasised at this point, however, that this research evidence is generalised and is unlikely to apply in equal measures to every learner teacher. Nevertheless, so much of it has been replicated in so many studies that it may be wise not to dismiss it too readily.

So how can you best learn to become a Mathematics teacher?

The argument so far has been that it is impossible to tell someone how to teach: theory, or theoretical ideas, can never provide answers in complex settings like classrooms; contextual constraints make particular demands which in turn mean that even the most prescriptive of theoretical advice can only be drawn upon and never directly utilised. Each person's particular belief systems underlying their actions means that even practical advice offered needs to be subjected to scrutiny before it is tested, never mind accepted.

In addition, student teachers themselves almost certainly have strongly held beliefs about mathematics, mathematics teaching and good mathematics teachers, so that even if it was possible to give 'answers', they are unlikely to be accepted unless they fit existing understandings of the teaching situation.

An alternative strategy, and one which fits within a constructivist paradigm of learning, is that those engaged in teacher education – wherever it is located – offer learning experiences that allow you to challenge existing conceptions of teaching and learning and modify them in the light of experience. Ideally, these experiences are offered when it is perceived you are ready to learn about them, although in practice, and within the demands of teacher education courses, there is limited time to wait for this to happen. Then, there also needs to be attention to creating a readiness for learning – a cognitive dissonance – which helps you to understand the need to learn about the issue, whilst at the same time taking care not to seriously overwhelm you. This requires a recognition that just like mathematics learners in classrooms, beginning mathematics teachers are also individual learners with their own concerns, strengths, agendas, and so on. Helping each one to learn as an individual becomes at least as complex as helping learners in classrooms.

Elliott and Calderhead (1994) present a two-dimensional model of mentoring and argue that growth requires that mentors – those involved in helping student teachers learn – need to provide both support and challenge.

They argue that in the quadrant where challenge and support are both low the *status quo* is likely to be maintained but when challenge is increased without comparative changes in support there is likely to be no growth. In this case the student teacher is likely to withdraw physically from the development programme or, at best, resort to using previously formed ideas. In other words, there will be little increase in problem-solving characteristics and the student will sternly defend practice in terms of images from the past. They go on to argue that there is evidence to suggest that challenge is a necessary component for professional growth to occur.

Getting this balance right is demanding for mentors since it is likely to be different for different students, and in different situations throughout the year. In addition, the cognitive dissonance caused when challenge is high can also be uncomfortable. It can seem safer for everyone if support remains high and challenge low! Nevertheless, high challenge and high support seem to be an important combination for useful learning – and it is in the interests of you as a learner to ensure that this is achieved.

High

C
H
A   Novice grows through
L   development of
L   new knowledge and
E   images
N
G
E

Novice withdraws
from the mentoring
relationship with no
growth possible

Low   High

SUPPORT

Novice is not encouraged   Novice becomes
to consider or reflect   confirmed in
on knowledge and   pre-existing
images   images of
                                  teaching

Low

In offering these learning opportunities, the student teacher becomes a problem-solver, testing ideas offered from both theoretical and practical perspectives, exploring those ideas in their own and others' contexts, and developing their own theories and practical know-how about teaching and learning in the mathematics classroom. In turn, those developing ideas need to be subject themselves to scrutiny by testing them against theoretical ideas (for example, are the developing ideas consistent with what is already known about teaching and learning mathematics?); by testing them against practical constraints (for example, what other possibilities were available and manageable given the particular context in which the lesson took place?) and by testing them against shared and personal beliefs (are the developing ideas consistent with those of natural justice; are they consistent with personal beliefs about the role of the mathematics teacher; what does this imply about the ideas I had at the beginning of the course?).

You then have available a variety of material and human resources from which to draw in order to move forwards. Each of these sources has its strengths and weaknesses, and each is likely to offer a different perspective on issues. It is not surprising, then, when many student teachers in mathematics find this frustrating: they may never have been asked to work in this way before. Mathematics for many was certain, with 'right' ways of doing things. And here is a situation where, despite the rhetoric from recent Governments which has implied that virtually anyone can be 'trained' to teach mathematics, uncertainty is not only inevitable but is seized upon as an opportunity to learn even more!

But there are also potential pitfalls in this learning. Research tells us that it is not always easy for you to elicit from teachers all that they know about teaching (Hagger, 1997). We also know that the inevitable uncertainty mentioned above can often lead to quite significant tensions between the theory offered by sources outside school and practice within a school. There are issues associated with the student/mentor relationship which is often hindered by the need for 'politeness' (Haggarty, 1995) and this links with the need for the student to be accepted into the teaching culture (Lacey, 1977). It is worth examining each of these in turn.

Thinking back to the scenario of the Year 8 class outlined at the beginning of the chapter, it is clear that *any* student teacher can learn a great deal from the more experienced teacher who usually teaches the class. Indeed, for the student teacher to think otherwise would be breathtakingly arrogant. But immediately there are two potential difficulties: the usual teacher may not be used to talking about what they do and why with a particular class – after all, teaching tends to be a pretty isolated experience and much that is learnt by teachers is internalised but rarely articulated. The other difficulty is that the student teacher may either fail to recognise that anything very special has happened in terms of managing the complexity of the teaching and learning situation, or may be in danger of thinking that there were better ways of doing it anyway (having compared what they saw with their memories of their 'good' teacher), thus adopting a judgemental and critical tone in any ensuing conversation.

However, it appears that you can access experienced teacher's tacit or 'craft knowledge' embedded in their practice if you adopt an open and non-judgemental stance in which, after observing the teacher teaching the class, you focus on the particular lesson observed and ask:

- what the teacher thought was good about the lesson (talking about what was judged to be less successful is clearly likely to result in a defensive stance from the teacher);
- what the teacher did to make this come about;
- why the teacher chose to do what they did to make this come about.

(Brown and McIntyre, 1993; Hagger, 1997)

The 'politeness' issue is another potential pitfall for both student teacher and mentor. Teacher education courses tend to be organised so that you are placed in schools chosen by others (and they may be quite different from the one you expect to teach in after the course) and working alongside mentors and other teachers in a school that has probably had no direct say in your acceptance on the course. You are completely dependent on the help and support of the teachers in the mathematics department, who are also likely to have a large responsibility for assessment and the writing of your reference. Because you will spend a significant amount of time in the department, members of the department will want you to fit in and behave like they do as quickly as possible: they want you to be enculturated into very many if not all of their practices, whatever they happen to be. Equally, it is clearly in your interests to be accepted as one of the department, and here we are set up for the tensions that will almost inevitably arise.

First, you will be becoming increasingly familiar with a range of theories about mathematics, teaching and learning. You are likely to be excited about some of those ideas, unfamiliar as many may be, and will want to try them out or at least observe and discuss them in your placement school. But the reality in very many mathematics departments is quite different from that described in books and journals, and even departments where innovative practice can be observed are rarely putting (the full range of) theory directly into practice. Second, you may actually find yourself critical of the department's practice, simply because the practices are unfamiliar and therefore not understood or because teachers do not behave in ways consistent with your image of 'good' teachers. So what do you do? There may be a theory–practice dilemma, with you at one extreme rejecting the ideas offered by theory and accepting the department's practice in an unquestioning way. At the other extreme you may find yourself being critical of the department because it does not enact theory. There may also be a dilemma about what can be questioned and how, with you making it clear at one extreme that there is little to be learnt from experienced teachers and at the other that whatever you feel, there is a need to be seen to accept the practice in the department (Haggarty, 1995).

Lacey (1977), in his study of the socialisation of student teachers into school, argues that student teachers adopt one of the strategies of internalised adjustment (in which, in this case, you comply with practices in the department and accept them as the best solution), strategic compliance (in which you go along with the practices and retain private reservations) and strategic redefinition (in which you change the department in which you are placed). It is perhaps not surprising that student teachers in general tend to follow the route of strategic compliance. However, it has to be said that it is nevertheless helpful, even when this strategy is adopted, to find someone who can be trusted in the department to share concerns with since it is only through exploration of those ideas that learning can move forward and developing theories become subject to scrutiny.

Moving from competence to enquiry

The ideas presented in this chapter demonstrate that learning to teach is a demanding process, with the beginning mathematics teacher being encouraged to test ideas and develop personal theories whilst charting their way through a range of complex social interactions. This argument is based on two main propositions: neither theory nor practice can provide answers about how to teach, and student teachers are individuals who are not likely to learn solely through being told what to do.

Clearly, though, whilst it is important to educate you as a student teacher to become a thoughtful and enquiring professional, there is also a need to ensure that you reach an acceptable level of competence in the classroom. Quite simply, at the end of any teacher education course everyone has to be confident that you can do a reasonable enough job in helping pupils to learn mathematics. Currently, this competence is measured by the achievement of imposed standards (DfEE, 1998, annex A). Whether or not such standards are an appropriate or desirable way of measuring competence is beyond the scope of this chapter. What is clear, though, is that the standards focus attention on their achievement, sometimes at the expense of thoughtful reflection on issues raised by them. For example, standard B4e (and there are over 80 statements of this kind) states that ' ... those to be awarded qualified teacher status must, when assessed, demonstrate that they ... ensure coverage of the ... National Curriculum programmes of study'. This example was chosen because, at one level, it is self-evident that teachers must be able to teach the statutory curriculum. Attention of student teachers and teacher educators is therefore focused on the inclusion of the relevant National Curriculum statement in every lesson plan. But further consideration of the statement leads to much which should be questioned, not least the interesting use of the word 'coverage' and its implied link with learning. Or what about the notion that the National Curriculum defines mathematics and all that takes place in the mathematics classroom? Are we to assume that (at least when assessment takes place) no other mathematics can be touched on?

Thus, there is a tension in trying to strike a balance between meeting the training needs imposed by Government (and it seems to be no accident that the requirements are for courses of Initial Teacher *Training* rather than Initial Teacher *Education*) and the wider educational goals to be achieved if you are to become a thoughtful and reflective professional. However the balance is struck, your main preoccupation is achieving competence and it is likely that professional development at this stage is focused on achieving that end. Once it has been achieved, however, there are opportunities to engage in enquiry since you are now in a position, with competence agreed and assured, to examine your teaching objectively and openly in relation to your own aspirations as an educator.

Reflection has been a central idea in the teaching literature since the early 1980s and provides a useful way into thinking about becoming an enquiring teacher. Schon (1983) writes that:

> It is when professionals reflect on the understanding which has been implicit in their actions, and criticise, restructure and reapply that understanding, that they begin to create knowledge which is of value to them in informing action.

The idea here of a deliberate act of restructuring is echoed by Kemmis (1985):

> Reflection is 'meta-thinking' (thinking about thinking) in which we consider the relationship between our thoughts and action in a particular context ... we do not pause to reflect in a vacuum. We pause to reflect because some issue arises which demands that we stop and take stock or consider before we act. We do so because the situation we are in requires consideration: how we act in it is a matter of some significance.

An enquiring teacher is a developing professional who is concerned with 'meta-thinking' about their own practice in order to improve that practice. As a student teacher working towards competence it could be said that through the processes of testing ideas and developing robust personal theories you are beginning to behave as a reflective practitioner. Once competence has been achieved, however, you are able to take some control of your personal development as a mathematics teacher. It is at this stage that it is possible to begin to identify those aspects of teaching that have *personal* significance (not significance because someone else has said so, or because it is demanded in externally imposed standards) and require consideration. It is at this point that it is possible to begin to create knowledge which is of personal value.

The ideas that follow in this section are equally applicable to beginning teachers in their induction year or experienced teachers continuing to develop their practice. However, the arguments are presented now because once student teacher competence has been achieved it is perfectly possible to move into the phase of beginning teacher as enquirer during the teacher preparation year. Of course, it also allows the mentor–student relationship to be maintained albeit with a change for the mentor from supporter of learning and assessor to one simply of supporter of learning.

Suppose the issue for personal consideration is that …

> … you do not feel you have appropriately differentiated material to use with a Year 7 class … or …

> … you feel you are still relying too heavily on didactic teaching approaches … or …

> … despite what you have been told, you still think there's room for improvement in your management of your Year 10 class!

The list is endless! It can include issues relating to mathematics, teaching, learning, … whatever. But after competence and before the Induction period provides an excellent opportunity to draw on available expertise and resources. There is time to observe, be observed, develop materials, read – and think.

Looking back at the first example above: '… you do not feel you have appropriately differentiated material to use with a Year 7 class …', what might you do next?

First, ask questions and gather information. In this example, your questions and data gathering might include:

Possible questions	Possible data-gathering strategies
How do experienced teachers differentiate in their lessons?	discussion and observation
What does differentiation mean and what tactics seem helpful?	reading and discussion
What materials are available to you which usefully differentiate?	search libraries / websites / department resources
What differentiation are you already achieving?	ask someone to observe, collect information, discuss

Next, the development of a plan:

> From the information gathered, what can you try with the class which takes into account theory, context and personal values. Discussion with another teacher might help here.

Next put it into practice:

> Try out your strategy – ask someone to observe and look out for particular events which will provide evidence of success or failure.

... and reflect on what has taken place:

> Stand back and consider what can be learnt from your plan and its implementation – again discussion might help here.

And as you complete this reflective cycle, you can then begin to think about what you have learnt and how it influences what might be addressed next.

What this strategy assumes is that there is at least one collaborator who will support the enquirer, although with determination it is possible (just) to do this kind of enquiry alone. It seems that reflective capacities in beginning teachers are more likely to be developed and sustained within departments which themselves are questioning and reflective. Indeed I suggest that:

- reflection is most likely to take place for any teacher within a climate in which they feel satisfied with most aspects of their performance (otherwise, the task of trying to improve elements of it can seem daunting);
- teachers seem to be helped to reflect when they have opportunities to talk about their practice to others (since this allows for conscious inspection of thinking);
- teachers seem to be helped to reflect when they see those around them modelling reflective behaviour (so it helps to be working in a reflective department and school);
- reflection is most likely to take place within a climate in which it is acceptable to identify elements of practice that you want to improve (otherwise, you will become – and will have to become – satisfied with the mediocre);
- reflection is most likely to be a positive experience when the issue to be worked on has been identified by you (otherwise, you may be neither convinced of its importance nor committed to its improvement).

However, it is important not to leave it there because the novice-enquiring teachers may find themselves working in mathematics departments that do not provide support for this kind of reflective endeavour. There are of course other networks of support, whether they are to be found elsewhere in the school or in local centres. In either case, since there is a growing and financially supported network of teacher researchers, it is unlikely that the situation is impossible for many in that position. BSRLM[1] provides opportunities for teachers to discuss and present school-based research projects.

But growth in teaching is multidimensional and Zimpher and Howey (1987) suggest that beginning teachers can be supported as they develop along four types of competence: technical, clinical, personal and critical competence. The domain of technical competence relates to the kinds of skills assessed in the Standards documents (DfEE, 1998), with utilitarian outcomes designed to satisfy calls for proficiency. The others are concerned with personal enquiry and reflection: clinical competence involves practical reasoning and problem-solving (of the sort described earlier on in the chapter); personal competence involves a developing understanding of self from multiple perspectives (linked closely with the awareness and examination of personal values and their enactment, or not, in the classroom) and critical competence (linked to asking 'big' questions about, say, the purposes of education, the place of mathematics in the curriculum, the wider responsibilities of mathematics teachers, the ways in which mathematics is taught, and issues relating to pupils and their learning). Whilst it is clear that within the DfEE Circular 5/99: *The Induction Period for Newly Qualified Teachers* it is *possible* that each of these competencies can be addressed, it is by no means certain that they will go very much beyond attention to technical competence (and its assessment). Nevertheless, it is important to recognise what has been put in place for the beginning and developing teacher, even though it seems that teachers themselves will still need to take responsibility for developing beyond technical competence and towards thoughtful, personal enquiry and reflection.

Concluding remarks

Learning to teach is a complex activity. It is also stimulating and intellectually challenging. An examination of the research literature suggests that it is not only possible to find ways of doing this which take account of student teacher needs, but that this also results in moving beyond striving for competence towards a view of teachers as developing and reflective professionals who can acquire habits of learning about teaching enabling them to research their own practice as teachers.

Mathematics teachers need more than technical competence to find solutions to the challenges around them!

Note

1   British Society for Research into Learning Mathematics, http://www.warwick.ac.uk/BSRLM

References

Askew, M. and Wiliam, D. (1995) 'Recent research in mathematics education 5–16', *Ofsted Reviews of Research*, London: HMSO.

Brown, S. and McIntyre, D. (1993) *Making Sense of Teaching*, Buckingham: Open University Press.

Calderhead, J. (ed.) (1988) *Teachers' Professional Learning*, Lewes: Falmer Press.

Calderhead, J. (1991) 'The nature and growth of knowledge in student teaching', *Teaching and Teacher Education* 7(5/6): 531–5.

Cooney, T.J. (1984) 'The contribution of theory to mathematics teacher education', in H.G. Steiner (ed.) *Theory of Mathematics Education* (TME), Bielefeld, Germany: Universität Bielefeld/IDM.

DfEE (1998) *Teaching: high status, high standards. Requirements for courses of initial teacher training.*

Elliott, B. and Calderhead, J. (1994) 'Mentoring for teacher development: possibilities and caveats', in D. McIntyre, H. Hagger and M. Wilkin (eds) *Mentoring: perspectives on school-based teacher education*, London: Kogan Page.

Ernest, P. (1989) 'The knowledge, beliefs and attitudes of the mathematics teacher: a model', *Journal of Education for Teaching* 15(1): 13–33.

Haggarty, L. (1995) *New Ideas for Teacher Education: a mathematics framework*, London: Cassell.

Haggarty, L. (1997) 'Readiness among student teachers for learning about classroom management issues', in D. McIntyre (ed.) *Teacher Education Research in a New Context. The Oxford Internship Scheme*, London: Paul Chapman.

Hagger, H. (1997) 'Enabling student teachers to gain access to the professional craft knowledge of experienced teachers', in D. McIntyre (ed.) *Teacher Education Research in a New Context. The Oxford Internship Scheme*, London: Paul Chapman.

Kemmis, S. (1985) 'Action research and the politics of reflection', in D. Boud, R. Keogh and D. Walker (eds) *Reflection: turning experience into learning*, London: Kogan Page.

Lacey, C. (1977) *The Socialisation of Teachers*, London: Methuen.

Lortie, D. C. (1975) *School Teacher: a sociological study*, Chicago, IL: University of Chicago Press.

Schon, D. A. (1983) *The Reflective Practitioner: how professionals think in action*, London: Temple Smith.

Zimpher, N.L. and Howey, K.R. (1987) 'Adapting supervisory practices to different orientations of teaching competence', *Journal of Curriculum and Supervision* 2(2): 101–27.

Section 2

Mathematics

2 Being mathematically educated in the twenty-first century
What should it mean?

Johnston Anderson

Introduction

The history of the development of mathematics indicates that, until recently, mathematics was a subject studied and practised by an elite few. In nineteenth-century Britain, 'grammar' and 'public' (which, in the quaint English cultural tradition, actually means *private*) schools catered for only a small minority of children; the mathematics that was taught in their classes was either of a pure type, such as the study of geometry, or topics that 'would be useful to a nation of inventors and engineers'. For the majority of young people, anything other than the most basic education was regarded as a waste of resources. A protracted battle was fought in Parliament on the issue of compulsory schooling, on both political and financial grounds. William Cobbett, speaking in the House of Commons in 1833 argued against any kind of national education because he would not countenance a tax for the purpose of 'promoting education' although he claimed not to be opposed in principle to the poor being educated. He also argued that such a development 'would create a new and most terrific control in the hands of Government'. Eventually the Education Act of 1870 introduced compulsory education for the first time, although, as we shall see, the standards to be achieved in mathematics were limited. Over the next hundred years, other Education Acts have followed, culminating in 1988 with the introduction, for the first time, of a National Curriculum in England and Wales (though other countries had long gone down this road).

Part of the rationale behind this was a realisation, first articulated in the 1960s and 1970s, that it was in the UK's economic interests to have an educated, skilled workforce and that too many school pupils were leaving school, both earlier and less well-qualified, than their continental counterparts. Soon came the further realisation of a similar threat posed by the emerging economies of the Far East. In this chapter, we review some aspects of mathematics and mathematics teaching, as they have developed in the twentieth century. With this perspective, we may then speculate as to what might constitute the answer to the question posed in the title.

Mathematics in the twentieth century

In 1900, David Hilbert gave a seminal address to the International Congress of Mathematicians in Paris. In it, he discussed twenty-three unsolved problems that he forecast would occupy the attention of mathematicians in the twentieth century. Mathematics, both pure and applied, had accomplished much by 1900; however, the formalisation of analysis under the influence of Weierstrass and abstract algebra in the shape of group theory and determinants were less than 50 years old, the works of Cantor and Dedekind, and Felix Klein's 'Erlanger Program', even more recent.

Whole new areas of mathematics have sprung up in this last century: mathematical statistics (already mentioned), discrete mathematics and its applications, graph theory (even though its roots may have been in the nineteenth century), quantum mechanics, chaos and game theory represent just some of the more novel ones; but geometry and analysis have advanced, almost out of all recognition, in the last hundred years, fusing and separating, enriching and being enriched by their applications to disciplines such as mathematical physics. The foundations of mathematics have been shaken, by Gödel and others; we now know that there are propositions that are undecidable and that there are problems whose solutions are, from a practical point of view, unreachable. It is claimed that there are more mathematicians actively working today than the sum total of all mathematicians throughout recorded history (though how one validates that claim might be an interesting exercise!). To Hilbert's agenda has been added a vast compendium of new challenges. The frontiers of mathematical research are today more remote from the average educated person than they have ever been. To make major contributions to half a dozen different areas of mathematics, as some (Euler, Gauss, Cauchy, Poincaré) have done in the past, looks increasingly remote. It was Hilbert himself, quoted by Hermann Weyl (1944), who said:

> The question is forced upon us whether mathematics is to face what other sciences have long ago experienced, namely to fall apart into subdivisions whose representatives are hardly able to understand each other and whose connections, for this reason, will become ever looser. I neither believe nor wish this to happen; the science of mathematics as I see it is an indivisible whole, an organism whose ability to survive rests on the connections between the parts.

The story of professional mathematics in the twentieth century has confounded this hope; what then are the implications for those teaching and learning the subject? In order to try to answer this, we look at how the content and style of what has been included in school mathematics has changed.

Some aspects of Mathematics in schools

Following the introduction of compulsory schooling, 'standards of instruction to allow a school to be certified as efficient' were published in 1876:

- 50 per cent of those above 7 years will be individually examined (in reading, writing and arithmetic). One half of the children examined ought to pass in two subjects. One half of the children so passing ought to pass in arithmetic.

- 7–8 years: Form (from dictation) figures up to 20. Name at sight figures up to 20. Add and subtract figures up to 10, orally and from examples on the blackboard.
- 8–10 years: Simple addition and subtraction of numbers of not more than four figures. Multiplication tables to 6.
- 10+ years: The four simple rules to short division (inclusive).

In view of current concerns and pronouncements on standards in schools, it is perhaps salutary to note the following comments from HMI and others over the last century or so (McIntosh, 1977):

In arithmetic ... worse results than ever before have been attained – partly attributable, no doubt, to my having framed my sums so as to require rather more intelligence ... but the failures are almost invariably traceable to radically imperfect teaching.

(Farm, Stafford and Derby, 1876)

The accuracy of the work in Standards I and II are all that can be desired, and in many cases marvellous; at the same time, the oral test shows that the children are working in the dark. In these standards, at least, far too much time is given to the mechanical part of the subject. The result of this unintelligent teaching shows itself in the inability of the upper standards to solve very simple problems.

(1895)

62 per cent of Standard V [i.e. typically 12-years-old or over] could take 1 from 10 000 correctly.

(1910)

There is a prevailing opinion that London children are slower and less accurate in computation than they were ten years ago. I have searched for evidence in support ... but failed to find it. But even if there has been a loss in accuracy, there has been a great gain in intelligence and intelligence is an equipment incomparably more valuable than facility in calculation.

(Board of Education, 1912)

Instruction in many primary schools continues to bewilder children because it outruns their experience.

(Plowden, 1966)

In general, ... the results show that teachers of first-year secondary children should not, except in the case of very bright children, take their understanding of multiplication and division for granted.

(Brown, 1977)

There was much confusion in other reports (e.g. Hadow, 1931) about the relative merits of learning principles and being actively involved as opposed to acquiring 'facts' and memorising rules. So the current debate on the claimed shortcomings of alternative approaches to learning mathematics is nothing new. But it is also of interest to review the content of mathematics examinations taken by pupils around the age of sixteen, who attended grammar schools.

'Elementary Mathematics', from the year 1933, contained ten questions. The rubric stated that 'Logarithms, Slide-Rule, or Algebra, may be used in any question'. The composition of the paper can be roughly broken down as follows:

- three questions on 'pure' geometry
- two questions on practical arithmetic (conversion of units, ratio)
- one question each on scale drawing, [piecewise-linear] graphs, trigonometry, algebraic manipulation, and number and proof.

Typical of the geometry questions is:

> Give a construction for drawing two tangents to a circle from an external point, and prove that the tangents so obtained are equal in length.

> Prove that if the sides of a parallelogram touch a circle, then the four sides of the parallelogram are equal.

Sixty years later, the effects of the virtual disappearance of Euclidean geometry from the curriculum of many British schools can be seen from the evidence that, of a class of 50 third-year mathematics undergraduates in 1995, less than a quarter could complete the first part and the majority made little progress with the latter part, introducing all sorts of extraneous, unnecessary, and often unhelpful, construction lines in their diagrams.

While the word 'prove' is consistently used in the geometry questions, a different word occurs in another question:

> Show that the sum of a number of four digits and the number formed by reversing the digits is always divisible by 11.

> The greatest and least of four consecutive numbers are multiplied together; so also are the middle pair. Show that the difference of the two products is always 2.

Clearly, the ability to translate the information given into an appropriate general algebraic form (for example in the first of these, getting to the expression $1001(a + d) + 110(b + c)$) is a key process being tested. One suspects that verifying the result in a small number of cases would not have gained many marks.

In 1949, 16 years later, 'Elementary Mathematics II' now had 12 questions, of which four were compulsory and at most five others were to be attempted (in two hours). They were:

- three questions on 'pure' geometry (one compulsory)
- two questions on practical arithmetic (one compulsory)
- three questions involving accurate drawing and measurement (one compulsory)
- three questions on algebra (one compulsory, on the factor theorem)
- one question on graph-drawing ($y = x^2$ and $2y = x + 4$).

As in 1933, apart from the geometry, there is little in the paper that involves *proof*. The word occurs in question 8:

It is given that

$$x = 1 + \frac{p}{(p - q)} \quad and \quad y = 2 - \frac{3q}{(p + q)}$$

Prove that

$$\frac{x}{y} = \frac{(p + q)}{(p - q)}$$

$$\frac{3}{x} + \frac{1}{y} = 2$$

But the question is simply one of algebraic manipulation (and of a fairly trivial kind).

The mathematics being taught to these pupils could be regarded as the comfortable outcome of an unwritten conspiracy between the grammar schools and the universities, to preserve the supply of professional mathematicians and not to worry too much about any other national needs.

The 1960s saw the beginnings of a new wave of mathematical change in schools. The Schools Mathematics Project (SMP) was just under way. The main thrust in the construction of the syllabus was that it was primarily for those *who would do no mathematics beyond O level*, while at the same time being also suitable for those who would wish to take it further. The 1964 rationale for the proposed syllabus (Schools Mathematics Project, 1971) stated:

> for this reason, any reform of GCE syllabuses, in our opinion, must begin in the lower school and it would not be sound policy to attempt to initiate the first changes at A level.

Thirty years on, we have seen a whole raft of reports and initiatives, some implemented, some rejected: N and F levels (Institute of Mathematics and its Applications, 1978; Schools Council, 1980); Cockcroft, 1982; and the National Curriculum, 1988 (revised several times since).

However, there are other stated aims in the SMP report with which one feels there would be considerable consensus:

- to make school mathematics more exciting and enjoyable;
- to impart a knowledge of the nature of mathematics and its uses in the modern world;
- to encourage more pupils to pursue further the study of mathematics;
- to bridge the gulf between university and school mathematics (in both content and outlook);
- to reflect the changes brought about by increased automation and the introduction of computers.

In the light of some of the strictures made in the report of the London Mathematical Society (1995), on the lack of algebraic and manipulative facility among contemporary incoming undergraduates, it is interesting to read that, in their syllabus:

> we have constantly tried to shift the emphasis towards mathematical ideas and away from manipulative techniques.

While it is conceded that facility in manipulation is indeed required by those who would aspire to be mathematicians (and physicists, and engineers), more controversial is their view that:

> it is [our] opinion that the acquisition of techniques is best left until the post-O level stage; then, technique will come more rapidly, because the need for it will be more apparent. It will also free the pupil who stops at O level from much *unnecessary* learning.

The new SMP O level, and similar initiatives in Scotland with the almost simultaneous introduction of the Scottish Mathematics Group's Modern Mathematics for Schools (MMS) brought a change in focus, not only in the way mathematics should be taught, but also in the content. The widening of access to more and more pupils, coupled with a successive raising of the School Leaving age (the age at which pupils were no longer required to attend compulsorily) meant that curriculums had to cater for a far wider range of abilities. Although there was to be an increased emphasis on algebraic structure ('conveying the nature of algebraic concepts rather than [merely] imparting a body of knowledge'), definitions and axioms would 'grow out of concrete illustrations', (a theme later taken up by Skemp, 1986) while *proof* was to be accorded a significant role. The nature of geometry would change: though conceding the merits of formal deductive geometry for a minority, for the majority of pupils it 'offers little training in logical reasoning' and simply forces them into 'memorising theorems and proofs of no particular worth'. Instead, transformation geometry, with its links to matrices, was introduced, and more attention was devoted to three-dimensional geometry and the construction of polyhedra. Also making an appearance were topics such as inequalities, treated both graphically and algebraically, elementary statistics and probability, estimation and degrees of accuracy.

Table 2.1 Numbers of entries at GCE Advanced level (A level) in England and Wales in four options of mathematics, by year and sex

		Maths	*Further Maths*	*Pure Maths*	*Applied Maths*
1984		42 854	6 286	8 744	6 948
	M	34 699	4 729	5 787	5 090
	F	13 555	1 557	2 957	1 858
1987		43 746	5 567	6 180	7 669
	M	30 829	4 171	3 911	5 431
	F	12 917	1 396	2 269	2 238
1992		54 889	4 180	3 176*	1 271*
	M	35 249	3 096	2 021	982
	F	19 640	1 084	1 155	289

Note: *partly attributable to a change in definition

A typical SMP paper of the time (Paper II, 1971) comprised:

- four questions on geometry
- two questions on graphs
- one question each on inequalities, probability, composition of functions, and number.

The change in style can be seen in the following geometry question. The question is not only contextualised but also concerned with measure and calculation rather than with proof.

> An isolated hill standing on a plain has the shape of a perfect circular cone. A and B are points at the foot of the cone, A being due North and B due South of the summit. The distance from A to B over the summit is 600 m while the direct distance through the hill is 540 m. Sketch the shape you would cut out to make a cardboard model of the hill (showing all necessary measurements).
>
> There is a path over the slope of the hill, following the shortest route from A to B. Show this path in your sketch and find its length. Find also the shortest distance from the summit of the hill to the highest point on the path.

The 1980s and 1990s have been characterised by a number of significant changes (some already alluded to), in the style and the content of school mathematics, at both GCSE (the integrated successor to the distinct qualifications of O level and CSE) and A level. There has been a marked shift away from 'Double Maths' at A level, as shown in Table 2.1.

Table 2.2   Numbers of entries at GCE Advanced level (A level) in the four principal named
options of mathematics (single subject), 1992, by sex

Maths	M	14 669	66.5%
	F	7 378	33.5%
Pure and Applied	M	9 606	71.0%
	F	3 938	29.0%
Pure-with-Mechanics	M	3 859	76.3%
	F	1 198	23.7%
Pure-with-Statistics	M	7 115	50.0%
	F	7 126	50.0%

By 1992, there was apparent an equally significant shift towards syllabuses such as *Pure-Mathematics-with-Statistics* and away from *Pure-Mathematics-with-Mechanics*, notably among female candidates.

The proportion of female candidates taking mathematics at A level, over all combinations, had risen steadily from 28.4 per cent in 1984 to 33.6 per cent in 1992, but the composition of different single-subject entries showed considerable variation. For example, the figures for 1992 for the four principal named qualifications were as in Table 2.2.

In addition, in the A level examinations of 1992, there were 73 different examinations (as distinct from papers) available which led to a qualification that included 'mathematics' in the title; there were also two separate statistics examinations as well as numerous ones in computing. Since then, the introduction of 'modular' A levels has further dented, for sixth-form students, Hilbert's hope of an indivisible discipline. The new agreed Common Core represents about half the material in the syllabus for the single subject 'Mathematics'. The inference seems to be that, in the twenty-first century, one mathematically-educated person (in the UK) is likely to know something quite different from another mathematically-educated person.

The restructuring of school mathematics in England may have contributed to other side effects. In international comparisons, England (and Scotland) appear to fare badly; but such comparisons frequently exclude topics such as statistics and data-handling, and credit for good performance (e.g. in problem-solving, in which England recently came second, behind South Korea) is often grudging. Personal experience of teaching undergraduates from the Far East shows them to have good technical competence, high motivation to absorb (and regurgitate) new knowledge, but relatively poor ability to adapt this knowledge to novel situations and to tackle non-standard or open-ended problems.

It should be noted, however, that other countries also suffer anxiety about the state of their mathematical education. The Japanese see a crisis in mathematics, and the natural sciences, in their schools (Fujita *et al.*, 1996). They too call for an increase in the time allocated to mathematics at high school (particularly the formative Junior High School level) and for a widespread 'mathematical literacy' for all pupils, because of the increasing impact of mathematics in the social sciences and humanities, implemented through a 'flexible and enjoyable' curriculum which progresses systematically from elementary school through to college level, and which develops the cognitive processes central to the study of mathematics. They also note that the lowering of entrance qualifications (in mathematics) for colleges and universities has created a vicious circle in which, because less of a premium is placed on mathematics, less time gets spent on the subject at high school, resulting in a further erosion of mathematical skills.

Technology

One of the most significant developments in the last twenty years has been the widespread availability of cheap, but powerful, calculators and computers. The UK has perhaps, in its schools, embraced the calculator culture more enthusiastically than many countries. Most A level examining boards in mathematics now recommend that the student/pupil has access to a *scientific* or *graphical* calculator both during the course and in at least some of the examinations. Calculators are now available that are capable of handling complex numbers, inverting matrices (up to 6×6), finding eigenvalues and eigenvectors, as well as many advanced statistical functions. Algebra packages such as *Maple*, *Mathematica* and *Derive* are commonplace in personal computers in university departments; the last is also incorporated into the *Texas TI–92* calculator. It is therefore disappointing that the use of IT in mathematics teaching in school is claimed to be as little as once per term on average (Taverner, 1996). However, more significant than the use of computers as a tool to overcome drudgery is the opportunity they offer to develop mathematics as an *experimental* subject, though the point is well made (Tepper Haino, 1995) that while there is a place for experimentation and conjecture, and while these may take place with or without the assistance of a computer, part of the essence of mathematics is the central role of rigorous proof. Technology-based developments in teaching, which include both computer-aided-learning packages as well as inter-active and dynamic teaching materials (such as dynamic geometry software, and see also Chapter 10 in this book), have the capability to transform the way pupils understand and learn mathematics. The richness and variety of the visual presentation of mathematical knowledge through these media, in contrast to the somewhat one-dimensional world of the textbook will open new horizons for pupils of all abilities, but particularly for those who find verbally-presented data more difficult to comprehend. The increasing availability of CD-ROM materials will make access to all sorts of information potentially universal.

How therefore can we best equip the average school-leavers of the future, in order that they can make use of this mathematical information, to be able to participate in a process of life-long learning and adapt to ever-changing demands for new skills? In the final section, I look at some implications for mathematics within the political and social structure of this country and try to offer some tentative suggestions.

Mathematical education in the twenty-first century

As we have seen, the growth of mathematics, both as a subject in its own right and in its fields of application, has been accelerating throughout the twentieth century. Most of this has been undertaken, and is understood, by only a tiny minority. The majority of the population is unaware of the impact of mathematics, through its interaction with developing technology, on people's everyday lives. Unfortunately, in the popular conception, 'mathematics' is synonymous with 'number' and various forms of computation. Freudenthal, as usual, has something germane to say (1973). Commenting that *mathematics* is now often used to describe what is really *arithmetic*, he adds:

> Soon 'mathematics' will be taught in the lower grades of the schools of quite a few countries by people who do not even know what mathematics is.

The lack of a sense of what mathematics can and cannot achieve means that political policy-makers, who may take advice on all manner of issues from civil servants using mathematical models, often lack any means of judging whether those models are appropriate, or indeed of what questions they should be asking. This situation arises in part because mathematics is perceived, not just as difficult, but as remote, opaque in its language and symbolism and 'lacking a human face'. It is no accident that, among a range of books purporting to explain the new subject of chaos, one of the most popular was that by James Gleick (1988) – not because he explained the mathematics of chaos particularly well (there are many which do a better job) but because he turned it into a story of human endeavour, in which the reader could relate to real people. The history of mathematics and its symbiosis with the development of advanced societies is a missing dimension in its teaching, at all levels.

What, then, should be taught, and to whom? A major problem is to cater for the needs of the minority who will eventually become professional mathematicians (or who will, at least, practise mathematics in some form) and at the same time equip the generally-educated citizen and tax-payer with both the mathematical skills they will need and an appreciation of the role, place and power of mathematics as a discipline in its own right. Freudenthal (1973) reminds us that:

> A mathematician should never forget that mathematics is too important to frame its instruction to suit more or less the needs of future mathematicians.

There are many laudable sets of principles upon which an instructional programme might be constructed. For example, the Mathematical Association Teaching Committee suggested:

- the acquisition of basic skills and knowledge necessary for everyday life;
- the acquisition of further skills pertinent to particular careers;
- the development of the ability to think and reason logically ... including spatial thinking;

- an appreciation of the idea of a mathematical model (and therefore of the role mathematics can play in a wide variety of situations);
- mathematics as queen and servant – as a tool in mankind's control of its environment and as an intellectual activity ...;
- mathematics as a social activity, in its conduct, its existence and its applications, with concurrent emphasis on communication skills – verbal, graphical and written;
- mathematics as a language;
- an appreciation of the problem-solving powers of mathematics through personal experience of investigation and open-ended problems.

(Mathematical Association, 1976)

If such a set of aims as these is to be implemented, then there are some tricky political issues that need to be addressed before one can get down to such relative trivialities as deciding what the content of appropriate mathematical syllabuses should consist of. Two such issues are: the supply of *teachers* capable of delivering this mathematics, and the amount of *time* that should be devoted to mathematics (in the widest sense) within the curriculum at different stages.

Geoffrey Howson (1996), in a recent article, surveys the educational scene in mathematics over the last century and concludes that the most important and crucial lesson to be learned from history is the central position of the teacher. He points out that 75 per cent of all mathematics graduates in 1938 entered the (school) teaching profession, compared with less than 10 per cent fifty years later, and makes the assertion that 'the probability of a bright 11–16-year-old having a (mathematics) teacher who can comprehend and meet his or her needs would seem markedly less today than thirty years ago'. The mathematically-educated person of the next century will likewise require the instruction and intellectual leadership of good teachers of mathematics.

Mathematics is now compulsory for all pupils up to the age of sixteen. If we are serious about providing both basic skills (with sufficient practice for fluency) as well as building the platform that will encourage the further study of the subject (to whatever level), then mathematics will need to be assigned more time within the school curriculum. It is perhaps worthy of note that in the Pacific Rim economies of Japan, Korea, Taiwan and Hong Kong, the time devoted to mathematics in the school curriculum is considerably more than in the UK and probably many other Western countries. Not only, for example, do Taiwan schools teach for 222 days a year, compared with 190 in England but, more strikingly, the typical pupil will spend around 15 hours a week on mathematics (including classes, homework and extra 'cramming'), which is probably three times as much as a typical pupil in Britain (Lin and Tsao (1999) have discussed a downside to this, in terms of a wider cultural education). However, an increase in the time allocated to mathematics, either within the standard school day or as part of a general expectation of pupils, will not happen unless the mathematical community can make out a sufficiently persuasive case for the unique importance of learning and appreciating mathematics that will either (a) persuade other subject areas to concede some of their time allocation (not very likely) or (b) convince political agencies that the school day or year needs to be extended to cope with these demands (perhaps marginally more plausible, since other subject areas might see some self-interest in supporting such a move).

Post-16, the situation is more complex. There is, I believe, a rational argument to be made that some mathematics ought to be a compulsory part of a Baccalaureate-style education (while those intending to become mathematics specialists at universities might follow a 'Mathematics Baccalaureate', which could be different, in depth and quantity). The hard part, again, is deciding the content of this compulsory 'Mathematics for the majority'.

In trying to define what being 'mathematically educated' might mean, perhaps one should distinguish between mathematics as a discipline in its own right and part of our cultural tradition (akin to Music, Literature and the Arts) and mathematics as a necessary tool for coping with and understanding the complex world in which we live. The mathematically-educated person should certainly have encountered both facets.

Under the first heading, I would hope that the mathematically-educated person will have an appreciation of principles in mathematics (such as the purpose of abstraction, of generalisation, the role of proof), an understanding of why the tools work and which tools are appropriate in given circumstances, and especially an awareness of interconnections within mathematics. One would like to see the mathematically-educated person being exposed to an account of the major concerns of contemporary mathematics (a current instance would be some of the things in Ian Stewart's book *From Here to Infinity* (1996)), as well as learning about the historical impact of the subject in the development of the modern world and its symbiotic relationship with the growth of science and technology, and the industrial consequences of these two.

Under the second heading, it would be nice to aspire to a state where the mathematically-educated person would have an appreciation of such things (beyond standard numeracy and geometry) as probability and risk, and what statistical analysis can tell one. Is it unreasonable to hope that this person could work out for themselves why their chance of winning £10 in the National Lottery is about 57 to 1, and could interpret the parameters μ and σ in the normal distribution and so realise that μ specifies the 'centre' of the curve, while σ determines whether the 'bell' is tall and narrow, or short and wide, and interpret this in context?

There are questions about computability and its limitations (what can and can't be solved by computers); chaotic and deterministic behaviour; the idea and some of the methods of mathematical proof, as opposed to empirical theory; generality (including infinite processes); isomorphism (recognising the same structure in superficially different situations); invariance (the preservation of some aspect, notwithstanding other changes).

Conclusion

It has been my aim to draw attention to the fact that there are many constituents to be addressed when debating mathematics for the new millennium: pupils who will need some basic mathematics as part of their 'life-skills', employers who may require not only mathematical techniques and knowledge but also transferable skills such as the ability to reason logically and to be organised and systematic, policy-makers and decision-makers (for example, in Government) who need to be able to weigh up both qualitative and quantitative evidence, not to mention parents, teachers and mathematics professionals.

The accelerating pace of change that has been apparent throughout the twentieth century shows no sign of slowing. This applies not only to the technological changes which have transformed life in the 'First World', with rapid travel and communications making the transfer of technology much more widely and quickly accessible, but also to the development of subjects such as mathematics. Driven by all kinds of demands, from innovative industries to arms developments and hi-tech projects such as the space race, mathematicians are pushing forward the boundaries of their subject to the extent that no individual can be totally knowledgeable about more than a part. A striking feature of this is the 'mathematisation' of subjects which, twenty or so years ago, would have been generally thought of as having little scope for such treatment: biology, medicine and the life sciences are examples. This creates its own dilemma for its professional practitioners: on the one hand, the subject is expanding beyond the capability of the ordinary person to understand and appreciate – on the other, this remoteness is an obstacle to persuading the ordinary person that mathematics at a more elementary level is a worthwhile activity for them to become engaged in. But, as the world in which we live becomes even more complex, its problems more difficult and challenging to solve, the more important it is to strive for the means of comprehending those problems.

The continuing health of mathematics as a subject depends not only on recruiting students for advanced study, but also of creating a wider understanding of why mathematics should be financially supported. This in turn requires changing the perception of mathematics as a difficult, arcane and minority pursuit to one in which the acquisition of mathematical skills, understanding and knowledge are valued, and its exactness and rationality provide a counter against numerology and spurious beliefs. In promoting the view that no one in the twenty-first century can claim to be educated unless they are, *inter alia*, mathematically educated, perhaps the last word should be left to Brown and Porter (1995):

> There is a general lack of appreciation of what mathematicians have accomplished, and the importance of mathematics. Some of this has come about through mathematicians themselves failing to defend and explain their subject in a global sense to their students, to the public and to government and industry. It is possible for a student to get a good degree in mathematics without any awareness that research is going on in the subject.

> Another danger is the growing reliance on computers as a black box to give the answer, without understanding the processes involved, or of the concepts which are intended to be manipulated ... .

We need in society a real understanding of the work of mathematicians, and of the way mathematics has played a role in the society in which we live. It is our responsibility to the subject we love to find ways of developing this understanding.

The goal is to achieve as wide a mathematically-educated populace as is possible. If the mathematical community can't or won't do it, then no one else will: it is in our own hands.

References

Brown, R. and Porter, T. (1995) 'The methodology of mathematics', *Mathematical Gazette* 485: 321–34.

Cockcroft, W.H. (1982) *Mathematics Counts*, London: HMSO.

Freudenthal, H. (1973) *Mathematics an Educational Task*, Dordrecht, The Netherlands: Reidel.

Fujita, H., *et al.* (1996) 'Mathematics education at risk', *Mathematical Gazette* 488: 352–5.

Gleick, J. (1988) *Chaos*, London: Heinemann.

Hadow Report (1931) *The Primary School*, London: HMSO.

Howson, A.G. (1996) 'Looking back – and looking forward', *Mathematical Gazette* 487: 129–36.

Institute of Mathematics and its Applications (1978) *The N and F Proposals in Relation to Mathematics: proceedings of symposium*, London: Institute of Mathematics and its Applications.

LMS/IMA/RSS (1995) *Tackling the Mathematics Problem*, London: London Mathematical Society/ Institute of Mathematics and its Applications/Royal Statistical Society.

Lin, F-L, and Tsao, L-C. (1999) 'Exam maths re-examined', in C. Hoyles, C. Morgan and G. Woodhouse (eds) *Rethinking the Mathematics Curriculum*, London: Falmer.

McIntosh, A. (1977) 'When will they ever learn?' *Forum*, 19(3).

Mathematical Association (1976) *Why, What and How?*, Leicester: Mathematical Association.

National Curriculum (1988) *Mathematics for ages 5 to 16*, National Curriculum Council, Mathematics Working Group, DES.

Schools Council (1980) *Examinations at 18+: report on the N and F debate*, Schools Council Working Paper, 66, London: Methuen Educational.

Schools Mathematics Project (1971) *The First Ten Years*, Southampton: The Schools Mathematics Project.

Skemp, R.R. (1986) *The Psychology of Learning Mathematics*, London: Penguin.

Stewart, I. (1996) *From Here to Infinity*, Oxford: Oxford University Press.

Taverner, S. (1996) 'Comparing boards in A level mathematics', *Mathematical Gazette* 488: 362–6.

Tepper Haino, D. (1995) 'Experiment and conjecture are not enough', *American Mathematical Monthly* 102(2): 102–12.

Weyl, H. (1944) *Obituary Notices of Fellows* 4(13), London: Royal Society.

3 Mathematics in the digital technology age

Richard Noss

The culture of utility in Mathematics education

1982 was the year which saw the publication in Britain of the Cockcroft report, emerging from a Government committee which had been given a simple yet compelling brief:

> To consider the teaching of mathematics in primary and secondary schools in England and Wales, with particular regard to the mathematics required in further and higher education, employment and adult life generally, and to make recommendations.
>
> (DES, 1982, p. ix)

The report also attempted a redefinition of the word 'numeracy', a term first coined in the Crowther Report of 1959, which defined it as:

> an understanding of the scientific approach to the study of phenomena – observation, hypothesis, experiment, verification […] the need in the modern world to think quantitatively, to realise how far our problems are problems of degree even when they appear as problems of kind.
>
> (Ministry of Education, 1959, p. 270)

By 1982, the word had lost much of the richness with which it had been invested two decades earlier. Cockcroft noted that most of those submitting evidence to the committee had used the word in the narrow sense of the ability to perform basic arithmetic operations, and he tried to broaden the idea a little by arguing not only for an 'at-homeness' with numbers, but for:

> some appreciation and understanding of information which is presented in mathematical terms, for instance in graphs, charts or tables.
>
> (DES, 1982, p. 11)

This is essentially the view of numeracy which, some 15 years later, has been used as a working definition in the *Framework for Numeracy*, a document of the

National Project for Literacy and Numeracy set up by the outgoing Conservative Government in 1996, and continued under the present administration. In their formulation, there is similarly an attempt to broaden the concept of numeracy beyond merely knowing about numbers and operations, to include the need to 'make sense of numerical problems' (Straker, 1997, p. 4). Nonetheless, in this new formulation, as clearly as in its predecessor of 1982, much of the original depth of the idea of 'numeracy' has been discarded in favour of a relatively narrow, number-based conception.

The trend looks set to continue: the recent UK Government White Paper *Excellence in Schools* bases its campaign for literacy and numeracy by noting that:

> the first task of the education service is to ensure that every child is taught to read, write and *add up*.
>
> (DfEE, 1997, p. 9 – emphasis added)

It may be that the drawing of ever narrower boundaries around 'numeracy' has been entirely justified, and that there is no cause to sound the educational alarm. Nevertheless, there has been little serious discussion of what constitutes numeracy within the educational community. What, if anything, has been lost by the gradual erosion of broader mathematical connections in favour of basic number skills? What effects have there been on our perception of mathematical attainment as a result, and whom has it affected? More generally, what is the theoretical and practical rationale that has driven this narrowing of the idea of numeracy, and what are its potential effects for the mathematical knowledge of the citizens of the next millennium?

It is unusual for a Government report to contain an explicit formulation of its theoretical antecedents, and Cockcroft is no exception. But there is, nonetheless, an implicit theoretical framework underpinning its vision of mathematics, and the kinds of cultural assumptions that frame it. It is the culture of *utility*. Mathematics should be taught to the extent that it is useful 'in the workplace, and in adult life'.

If that is so, there are a number of obvious questions. Useful to whom? For what purposes? Equally, if the definition of utility is based on what is 'seen' in workplace practices, it is legitimate to enquire how these may have changed, and in what direction. We should wonder to what extent mathematics in practice is, in any case, 'visible' in the sense that its presence or absence is unproblematically evident.

Charged with looking to see how mathematics is used in the workplace, Cockcroft did just that. The committee took evidence from a variety of sources and has much that remains interesting to say about the range of mathematics required for diverse occupations: *operatives* (' ... whose jobs do not appear to require any formal application of mathematics'), *craftsmen* ('He [*sic*] may also need to ... estimate or calculate areas and volumes of non-rectilinear shapes ... '), *engineering technicians* ('variable, but roughly at the level of grade 3 CSE'), *clerks* ('most of whom are female [...] predominantly arithmetic'), *retail workers* ('only a limited range of arithmetical skills'), *hotel and catering* ('concerned with calculations involving money, with weighing and measuring') and *nurses* ('concerned with measurement and recording, often in graphical form').

The report noted that workplace practices seldom demand standard arithmetic operations such as $\frac{2}{5}+\frac{3}{7}$ (para. 75, p. 22), and it failed to locate much need for algebra (para. 77, p. 22), let alone ideas such as proof, modelling and mathematical rigour. Accordingly, it allocates these kinds of mathematical notions little if any role in the curriculum, a reasonable conclusion based on the assumption that mathematics at work is defined by the presence of numerical or algebraic calculation, and on the utilitarian framework of the report as a whole. This framework is pressed to its logical conclusion: 'those who do not travel by bus or train probably have no need to consult timetables' (p. 2), and those who do not eat in restaurants have 'no need to calculate a service charge'. Summing up, the report puts it succinctly:

> We believe that it is possible to summarise a very large part of the mathematical needs of employment as a feeling for measurement.
>
> (p. 24)

In the last twenty years, the structure of the labour market has changed radically: demographic patterns, working practices and required skills have been transformed in complex ways. It is still true that many people appear to use practically no mathematics in their working and adult life generally. Yet the situation is not nearly so simple as it seems. For example, by carefully studying what kinds of problems people actually solve in a variety of workplaces, Harris (1991) has shown that there exists a rich source of mathematical activities that people exhibit in their working lives, even though these are flatly denied by those involved. Similarly, Wolf (1984) has amply illustrated that individuals are most reluctant to admit that they use mathematics in work, even when a mathematically-attuned observer can point to various practices that would count as mathematical. Quite simply, mathematics is not always visible: it lies beneath the surface of practices and cultures.

Here is a first paradox. If we, like Cockcroft and his successors, look at the surface of arithmetical activities in adults' working lives, we are bound to find only traces and shadows of mathematics, and we may conclude that the mathematical needs of adult life are both insignificant in quantity and trivial in quality. Once it is accepted that people tend to use little mathematics in work, the utilitarian imperative necessarily redraws the boundaries of the mathematical in equally restricted terms. As the mathematics in working practices become less visible, so the mathematical knowledge of the school curriculum becomes less applicable. The utilitarian perspective gives rise to a recursive cycle, in which what is taught at school becomes less and less relevant to working practices, as working practices show less and less evidence of making use of what is taught at school.

Here is a second paradox. Educationalists have been right to locate lack of mathematical confidence and alienation on the part of the many. But in attempting to alleviate this problem, we have risked divorcing school mathematics from its broader roots in science and technology and, ultimately, cast a fundamental question mark over its place in the curriculum. In trying to connect mathematics with what is learnable, we have disconnected school mathematics from what is genuinely useful.

So the culture of utility has left us with two paradoxical situations: the first arising from the assumption that mathematical knowledge is visible (and broadly static) within the cultures of work; the second from the apparent impossibility of broadening the appeal of mathematics without progressively restricting its content to simple calculation.

I close this section with a final comment on Cockcroft. It concerns one of the very few references to the role of computers, a subject about which I shall have much more to say in the remainder of this chapter.

> Relatively few school leavers are likely to work directly with a computer. Their work will usually be at clerical or operator level dealing with the input and output of data, though some leavers with A level [18+] qualifications obtain posts as junior programmers. The preparation of data for input to a computer entails the strict discipline of presenting data accurately in the required format; the handling of computer output often involves extracting data from tables which contain more information or more figures than are needed at that moment. These tasks demand little in the way of mathematical expertise apart from the need to feel 'at home' with the handling of numerical information. In some cases it is also necessary to be able to carry out straightforward arithmetical calculations which may involve the use of decimals and percentages.
>
> (DES, 1982, para 144, p. 40)

It is chastening to reflect that the first sentence was written only about twenty years ago. Less obviously, I think this paragraph sums up the difficulties bedevilling the culture of utility. In casting the computer in the role of thinker, it assigns to the worker only a marginal role in interpreting numerical information, and assumes that the interpretation of computer output will hardly ever involve understanding what the computer has done to the input. In a pre-computer epoch, where useful mathematics was equated with calculation, the advent of new technologies served only to reinforce the view that working practices would inevitably be 'de-mathematised'. The educational corollaries of this argument flow smoothly from the culture of utility; and it is these, and the assumptions on which they are based, to which I now turn.

A parable

I open the door of the glistening bank and advance to the red and grey vinyl-covered desk marked ENQUIRIES. I smile at the red and grey-uniformed clerk, whose badge neatly proclaims her first name and she smiles at the computer screen, which is neatly angled so as not quite to separate us. I start to enquire, but it seems that nothing can be done until the computer has been gratified. I hand over my passbook and she enters 13 alphanumeric characters expertly.

Now Chris knows my name, where I live, how much money I have, how much I owe; now the computer will talk to her and she will talk to me.

I begin my first request. 'Bear with me,' Chris interjects. She walks over to a desk marked ACCOUNTS where Tammy is on the phone. Chris waits until the call is finished, and asks her something I cannot hear. When she returns, both Chris and the computer are happy with the answer. I ask a second question. This, it turns out, necessitates a call to one of the help-lines, whose codes are pre-programmed onto the multi-buttoned telephone in front of her. 'Bear with me,' she says. After a short call, Chris knows the answer, tells me, smiles and punches some keys on the computer.

My third and fourth enquiries generate a second call (to a different help-line) and a visit to the supervisor, apparently because my request falls outside the limit that Chris is allowed to handle unsupervised. The supervisor – whose uniform is several shades darker than Chris's, and who sports both her first and family names on her badge – looks at me, at my cheque, then back to me and, without speaking, nods. Chris places the passbook on a printer attached to the computer, and the machine punches information onto the book (by some miracle, it knows where to start typing on the page).

I am sent to queue for a teller, each of whom sits in a line behind a glass panel with their own computer. Their uniforms are like Chris's, but unlike her, the tellers are sedentary – they are tied to their machines. They chat to each other, crack jokes while their printers print, help each other with troublesome computers.

'The computer won't let me do that,' my teller says, smiling.

'Why not?' I ask.

'Bear with me,' she says, and calls the supervisor who comes to talk to me through the glass.

'We can't do that,' explains the supervisor.

'Why not?' I ask.

'It's the computer,' she explains again, 'it won't let us … look.'

She types the numbers on the keyboard: they disappear as she types 'Enter'. She is right: the computer won't let her. The computer doesn't explain why. The supervisor doesn't ask. Neither does the teller. Neither do I.

Cultures of the workplace

Technology has transformed work, and Chris's role is as an appendage to technology, deskilled, alienated. But Chris is using mathematics to an unprecedented degree; it is hidden in the chips of her computer terminal, in the underlying models that have been programmed into them. For Chris, this mathematics is completely invisible: she has, it seems, no need to understand, to disinter the relationships and structures from beneath the surface of her practice.

Chris (and her customers) are trapped within a Fordist nightmare, a modern variant of the automobile magnate's system of controlled and authoritarian production which was so chillingly captured in Chaplin's film *Modern Times*. Central to Ford's vision, and that of Frederick Taylor, his ideological counterpart, is the idea that effective management of the labour process demands the separation of conception from execution, the removal of human intellect from the working process, and the fragmentation and gradual removal of skills and craft knowledge. The tendency to try to routinise and deskill is ubiquitous, even for those who program the machines in which knowledge is invested. As Straesser *et al.* (1991) point out, the more Taylorised a working practice, the less mathematics its practitioners require.

Not all occupations, of course, have been deskilled in this way. Yet if ever there were a straightforward relationship between understanding a mathematical tool and using it in application, technology has made that relation problematic. If it used to be the case, for example, that engineering workers could make use of their simultaneous equations in the turning of gears, that engineers could use their slide-rules as points of discussion and tools for appreciation of their materials, that bank clerks could put to good use their drilling in commercial arithmetic, and that draughtsmen and -women were able unproblematically to exploit their Euclidean geometry in the service of their drawings, it is true no longer. And it is this tendency, the deskilling of the labour process, which – if not providing a *rationale* for the deskilling of the mathematics curriculum – gave rise to a culture in the UK which allowed it to occur.

Now, as a mathematician, I would be happy to rest my case for the inclusion of mathematics as a school subject on aesthetic and cultural grounds alone. But I know that, in the post-Thatcherite era, that would not be enough. In any case, it is important to know whether the aesthetic and utilitarian are antithetical, and more important still, whether the gap between them is widening or narrowing. It is to this end that I, together with my colleagues Celia Hoyles and Stefano Pozzi, have recently been studying how different groups of employees – clerical and technical workers in an investment bank, paediatric nurses and airline pilots – make use of mathematics in their professional practices.

I will illustrate this work by sketching two episodes. The first concerns Peter, in charge of support and maintenance of computer equipment in a major European investment bank. His operating budget was some one or two million pounds a year, and one of his tasks was to assess the relative merits of buying or leasing computer equipment based on its 'present value' – how much it would be worth now given knowledge of its value some time in the future. To do this, he entered various parameters on a spreadsheet model with which he had been provided. Peter explained, 'I press the button marked *present value* and see what it says.' We asked Peter what *present value* did, how it worked, how it had been programmed. He didn't know. He did, he told us, have an infallible procedure which he invariably followed: 'I look at the answer. If it says what I think we should do, I use the number to justify my decision. If not, I ignore it, or put in figures which will support my hunch.'

The second episode concerns a pair of nurses in a paediatric ward. The ward is,

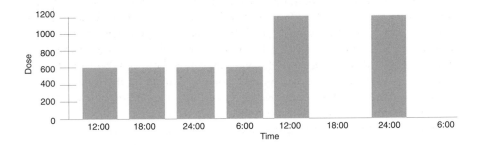

Figure 3.1 Wanda's strategy, in which the double dose is given straight away

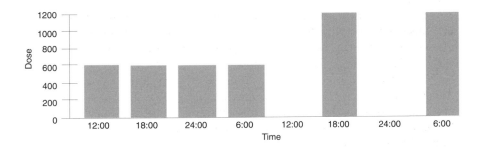

Figure 3.2 Betty's strategy, in which the double dose is delayed for six hours

like Peter's bank, technology rich, containing a vast array of electronic apparatus for measuring patients' conditions and for administering a range of therapies. Wanda and Betty are looking after a renal transplant patient who has been prescribed *vancomycin*, an antibiotic. This had been prescribed at regular intervals – 600 mg every six hours for 24 hours. Then, as sometimes happens, the doctor had prescribed a change of frequency: from four times a day ('QDS' in nursing jargon) to twice a day ('BD'). The new dose was 1200 mg and it was to be administered every 12 hours. We encountered Wanda and Betty at midday, as they were discussing when to give the first 12-hourly dose: the last six-hourly dose had been given at 6 a.m. that morning. The problem was this: should the first double dose be given now (Wanda's strategy) or should it be postponed until 6 p.m. (Betty's preference)? The two strategies are represented diagrammatically in Figures 3.1 and 3.2.

The discussion that ensued was wide-ranging. Changing drug times is relatively common, as drug administration needs to fit with the effective use of nurses' times. But in this case, there were clinical considerations. Wanda was worried that if the level of drug in the blood fell too low it would cease to be therapeutic. On the other hand, Betty was well aware that too high a level of *vancomycin* is known to produce deafness. Clearly the model of drug-level employed can be a matter of life and death.

When the decision had been made, we asked other nurses what they thought. Cathy agreed with Wanda, but for a different reason: she argued that the QDS and BD doses should be thought of as separate regimes, and that the 1200 mg doses should be started right away as the low doses had been 'completed'. Amy advocated delaying the dose, so that the 'maximum daily dose' was not exceeded in *any* 24-hour period. Francis proposed a delay: she was concerned that renal patients 'clear' drugs more slowly than normal ones, and that a midday dosage might produce a dangerously high level of drug in the body.

The details of these different positions are not important. What is fascinating is that each was underpinned by a more or less explicit *model* of drug level. All five nurses mentioned that the problem could be solved empirically, by checking the drug level with a blood test. But such tests are not always taken (for various reasons, including the need not to disturb the patient unnecessarily) and sometimes the only course of action left open is to try to take a decision on the basis of a conceptual model of drug level over time. These models were surprisingly diverse, and their complexity was given expression by the nurses' language which involved mathematical terms like 'peaks' and 'gradients' – at some level, they were thinking about graphical representations of the patient's drug concentration over time.

I want to draw attention to two issues that emerge from these episodes. First, they describe how people try to make sense out of complex situations by building models, or, if they do not have access to the raw material of model-building, by circumventing them as Peter did. Peter could not open up his model, he could not make sense of it or fine-tune it to his purposes: so he was left in the position merely of accepting or ignoring the computer's output as best he could. To gain access to underlying models, to make them *visible*, is to focus on the quantities that matter, and on the relationships among them. But in order to think at that level, one needs two further elements: tools that bring the model to life (like graphs, variables and parameters) and the means to express its structure (like numerical, algebraic or geometrical tools).

The second issue concerns the complexity of interaction between professional and mathematical considerations. We saw how professional expertise and intuitions were mobilised in powerful ways to make sense of the situations. Clearly the problem would not be resolved by building more intelligence into the technology, leaving still less room for intuition. But neither would Peter or the nurses want to be in situations without computational support, without some ways of processing the mass of information at their disposal. Decision-making seems most likely to benefit from models that can be fine-tuned by individuals and groups, situations in which professional knowledge and intuition can be webbed together with mathematical understanding and computational support.

At the fringes of industrial and commercial practices, this lesson is being learned. In certain kinds of occupations, particularly those in which technology plays an important part, it is no longer the case that the human employer can be seen as merely an adjunct of the computer system. On the contrary, even judged on the criterion of efficiency alone, more and more people are having to make sense of the models that underpin the systems they use. In the words of a recent document on social exclusion, published by IBM:

> Demand is rapidly shifting in favour of people with skills and against those without them.
>
> (IBM, 1996, p. 4)

This trend is not a new one. Since the 1980s, certain sections of industry have been arguing that there are disadvantages to firms that maintain Fordist or Taylorist strategies of dividing tasks and divorcing responsibility from job execution, that there is, as Mathews (1989) puts it, a post-Fordist option. As banking is one area in which I have done some research, it is instructive to look more closely at the roles that technology is playing there, as well as throwing a little more light on Chris's plight:

> most banks have proceeded down the Taylorist road, equating on-line access with deskilling, and assuming that counter staff would need less and less training as the terminal took over more and more of their functions. However, this deskilling approach […] is now coming up against the same sort of limits […] Banks are finding that their entire financial networks are becoming vulnerable to input errors perpetrated by unskilled counter operators.
>
> (Mathews, 1989, p. 62)

Put simply, the problem is *not* that the counter operators are unable to do arithmetic: that is one aspect that the computer systems can do admirably. It is that they have no understanding of what it is they are doing, what the computers do with their inputs, and how they might make sense of the output the computer gives them. Their problem is not that they cannot calculate, not that they cannot 'add up', but that they have no *model* of the system. Even more crucially, they have no sense of what it means to construct such a model. And in some contexts, the educational implications are far-reaching.

There are signs around the edges of the system that the personal and social needs of individuals can sometimes converge: there is evidence that job satisfaction and personal empowerment are not necessarily antithetical to the efficiency of large-scale systems. More surprising still, it is the computer which points to this possibility: the evidence is that it *is* possible for computer systems to treat human beings as partners rather than inconveniently expensive appendages. The sense of loss, of alienation from computer systems that leave no room for human intervention, can sometimes be simultaneously alienating for individuals, and inefficient for the purposes for which they were designed. The key issue here is that judgement and calculation are often conceived as opposed, and in such cases, the outcome for the individual (and the system) is always negative. The divorce between experiential, tacit knowledge and intellectual, 'scientific' knowledge is made more intense; it results in individuals losing their sense of intimacy with the tools of their practice.

The effects of designing out human beings from computer systems can have much greater than mere personal consequences: they threaten the very existence of life itself. In the report into the nuclear accident at Three Mile Island, the President's commission stated:

> Operator trainees were not provided with a fundamental, comprehensive understanding of their reactor plant design and operation which would enable them to recognise the significance of a set of circumstances not explicitly predicted by the operation procedures and which would lead them to place the plant in a safe condition. Essentially, operators learned how various pieces of equipment worked, how plant operating and safety systems worked, and how to apply preconceived, stepwise procedures to various abnormal and emergency situations. In other words, they were dependent on 'the manual'. They were not taught or expected to know how or why a specific nuclear power plant would respond to different types of failures and lacked the basic understanding necessary to deal safely with what was, in fact, a relatively minor failure when it occurred.
>
> (Raizen, 1994, p. 91)

There is no question that the dominant philosophy of commerce and industry is still to 'vest intelligence and control in technical systems, and treat workers like donkeys' (Mathews, 1989, p. 184). But there is a tension in the professional air, a gradual acknowledgement that the deskilling design strategy is robbing computerised systems of their potential, both individual and social. I have no idea whether Western economic systems will choose the post-Fordist future for the productive process. That is not my concern here. My interest is to understand how some signposts in the world of work are pointing towards new, post-Fordist futures for learning.

Increasingly, not only scientists and social scientists, but technicians, clerks and health workers will need to understand basic principles, they will need to sort out what has gone wrong, what mathematical knowledge has been buried invisibly beneath the surface of their computers, and how to dig it out. As the demands of workplace practices point beyond mere pattern recognition, and beyond that which can be grasped by any one individual – however well-educated. Solutions to problems will need to draw on precisely the kind of 'mathematisation' that is embodied in computational models. People will need to represent to themselves what has happened, particularly whenever the activities in which they are involved become in some way non-routine. (See Suchman (1987) for a fascinating analysis of these issues in the context of photocopier design.) Our own work with nurses and bankers indicates that the need to represent models occurs in non-routine situations, and that a workplace mathematics far broader than basic numeracy is required when decisions become contested or problematic (Pozzi *et al.*, 1997).

Representations are crucial to non-routine practice, and representations need a language, a set of intellectual tools that can reliably represent what is happening. At the same time, our research testifies to a communicative role for representations. For example, the 'rocket scientists' who build the complex models on which a bank's operations rely, are increasingly unable to talk to those who use them. They have no language in common, no shared set of representational tools with which to understand each others' problems and practices. Building systems for others with whom you are unable to communicate, and whose problems you are unable to grasp, seems bound to end in disaster.

The essence of professional practice is difference and diversity: the efficiency of routine lies in the specificity of its language and conventions. But the essence of mathematics lies in its sameness: in the search for common structures, invariants and equivalencies. If the foreign exchange department cannot communicate with the options department, this does not matter until someone (but who?) gains a sufficiently broad view to spot common errors, or possible inefficiencies. If nurses from paediatric and geriatric wards cannot understand each others' charts, it will not matter until a nurse moves wards and a breakdown in routine occurs. There are horizontal and vertical failures of communication, and mathematical expression is one way in which they can be overcome.

My argument to this point is that there are possibilities in technology-based working practices that suggest an increasing need to make underlying structures visible to those who work within them. These, in turn, will involve people in the need to express themselves mathematically, to gain ways to think about the geometry and algebra of situations. We will need to think carefully about how to make mathematics visible in ways that are at once accessible and intellectually honest – ways which do not rob mathematics of its essence, and which do not open still further the gaps between the mathematics of school and the mathematics of work, science and technology.

It will not be easy to tap the emerging cultures of the workplace to transform schools. There is no wave of post-Fordism to ride, and little hope of any spontaneous transformation of the working lives of Chris and her counterparts in the near future. Neither, it must be said, are there any signs in the UK that Government or its advisors understand the need to consider what kinds of new mathematical knowledge are required, rather than simply more 'effective' ways to transmit old knowledge.

If we are to address the problem, it will need imaginative and creative thinking, and it will involve collaboration between mathematicians, mathematics educators, employees and employers, as well as others involved in learning and teaching. It will involve choosing the high-skill option for education, against the tide that runs in favour of the deskilled future for work. The computer, the epitome of deskilled and dehumanised social relations in so many contexts, may be part of the problem. Yet in my third and final section, I turn to outline why, surprisingly perhaps, I believe that the computer may also prove to be part of the solution.

New cultures of expression

In the workplace, the computer presence is two-edged. On the one hand, it is a potential instrument for deskilling and isolation, and on the other, a putative instrument of intellectual liberation and collaboration, perhaps lending to an unprecedented degree a human element to the working process. What determines this choice? A complete answer would involve the realm of sociology and politics, for technology is not neutral, and the uses to which it is put and the social forces that shape it are complex. But whatever the explanation, there is no question that *design* is a fundamental issue: computer cultures do not just happen, they are constructed. Underlying that design are epistemological principles, congealed knowledge built into structures and intended applications. It is these principles, as much as the social and political context of their use, which determine choices among the relationships human beings develop with computers.

These choices confront us in education too. Computers have only been present in any substantial numbers in classrooms for less than two decades, but the choices have been present since their introduction. They are, in essence, choices about knowledge, about skilling or deskilling, closure or openness, calculation or modelling – just as they are in the workplace. And, as in the workplace, they structure the relationships individuals will need to have with the principles underlying their design. Does it suffice for students to be consumers of programs, to learn to punch in answers or vary parameters in models that have been built by software developers? Or will they need to gain insight into how the programs are built, what it means to build a mathematical model, how the construction of algorithms provides a rich source of metaphors and knowledge on which to develop mathematical understandings? Will students merely need to know how to run other people's programs, or will they need to reconstruct them for themselves in order to read and interpret the output creatively?

The former, Fordist, future for computers in mathematical learning has recently re-emerged in the form of Integrated Learning Systems, or ILS. The principles underlying the system's design date back to the principles of programmed learning, briefly attempted and abandoned as a failure in the 1960s, and are based on an unreconstructed behaviourist psychology. But my concern, as I have said, is epistemological. The assumption is that mathematical knowledge is strictly hierarchically ordered: that pieces of mathematical knowledge can always be broken down into smaller pieces.

I would not deny for a moment that students need, as part of their mathematical learning, to acquire the routine skills of calculation, the facts of numbers. On the contrary, I *want* them to learn them so that they can forget about them. The point is that while it is important to understand the little bits and pieces of numerical facts, such knowledge is only a very small part of what mathematics is about, and what it is for.

Mathematics itself is in a state of change. Boundaries between pure and applied mathematics are shifting, and the computer has entered firmly into the mathematical arena where once it was shunned. Fierce debates rage on the computer's role, its place in the sanctity of mathematical proof, its position as an exploratory tool, its contested role in turning parts of mathematics into experimental, rather than only theoretical, domains. Geometry, once the epitome of the abstract and formal, is becoming, in part, an experimental science under the influence of powerful computational systems that allow the manipulation and investigation of geometric structures in insightful ways.

To say that this redefinition of mathematical boundaries is a result of the computer's presence is to avoid engaging with its most important facet. This is its ability to offer alternative means to express mathematical relationships, novel kinds of symbolism, and innovative ways to manipulate mathematical objects: in short, the emergence of new mathematical cultures. The computer points to new ways to say mathematical things, as well as new mathematical things to say.

It is hard to understand a mathematical idea until you have used it, until you have seen its connection with other mathematical ideas, and possible applications. And so, as I have said, there is a tendency in educational circles to postpone rigour in the name of intuition, to delay formality as it seems to stand in the way of appropriation, and to hesitate on the road to abstraction, in favour of the practical and concrete. This dichotomising of concrete and abstract has recently come under sustained criticism (see, for example, Noss and Hoyles, 1996; Wilensky, 1991).

On the other hand, it is hard to use a mathematical idea until you have understood it: at the very least, you need to be able to express it in some formal way, appreciate why it works, how it works. Hence the paradox, and the downward spiral we have come to see as inevitable, in which less and less mathematics is taught to more and more children. Manipulating the variables instantiated in boxes or procedures on the screen is a kind of algebra. It may not quite be algebra in its accepted sense, but it opens up the possibilities of new cultures of mathematical expression that can allow students to think about abstraction and generalisation in powerful ways. Here is the essential difference that the technology brings: the seeds of the abstract are sown by actions with the concrete.

Using the computer in carefully designed ways, it is possible simultaneously to use and come to understand; to build and use or, to put it more succinctly, to build *in* use. In short, I contend that the computer offers us a means to build numeracies in which learnability and knowledge are not antagonistic. (Many of these ideas are elaborated in Noss and Hoyles (1996).)

We do not have to make a choice between knowledge and pedagogy. But we will surely be led down this road if we concentrate our attention on teaching methods rather than what is to be taught. It will lead us back to educational cultures that proffer Frederick Taylor's system of scientific management reincarnated in the UK classroom as Key Stage tests, Ofsted school inspections and ILS monitoring. It will return us to the logic of Fordism, in which schools and teachers will be encouraged to teach fragmented and isolated numerical skills, instead of assisting in the task of redefining the boundaries of what needs to be understood as a mathematical whole.

We need new pedagogies to teach old knowledge in accessible ways, but we need to consider how technologies can help us build new curriculums as well. The limitations of old technologies have hung around the necks of mathematics classrooms for two thousand years, shaping what it was possible to teach, what it was possible to learn. Thanks to the barely-tapped potential of new technologies, all of us engaged in the educational enterprise have an opportunity to recapture the spirit of

Crowther in our understanding of numeracies, to devise a breadth to the concept that compares equally with the notion of literacy. We can exploit technologies to develop new learning cultures, ones that challenge our notions of schools and classrooms, and support rather than supplant the professionalism of teachers. And we can construct new kinds of mathematical knowledge for children and adults to learn, new intellectual tools designed to make visible the mathematics lying beneath our social and working lives. We can build new numeracies.

Acknowledgements

I would like to acknowledge the debt I owe to Celia Hoyles for her support and encouragement during the preparation of the lecture on which this paper is based. Thanks also to my erstwhile colleagues Lulu Healy and Steve Pozzi.

References

DES (1982) *Mathematics Counts*, London: HMSO.

DfEE (1997) *Excellence in Schools*, London: HMSO.

Harris, M. (1991) 'The maths in work project', in M. Harris (ed.) *Schools, Mathematics and Work*, Brighton: Falmer.

IBM (1996) *Social Exclusion, Technology and the Learning Society*.

Mathews, J. (1989) *Tools for Change: new technology and the democratisation of work*, Sydney: Pluto Press.

Noss, R., and Hoyles, C. (1996) *Windows on Mathematical Meanings: learning cultures and computers*, Dordrecht, The Netherlands: Kluwer.

Pozzi, S., Noss, R. and Hoyles, C. (1997) 'Tools in Practice, Mathematics in Use', paper submitted to Educational Studies in Mathematics.

Raizen, S. (1994) 'Learning and work: the research base', in L. McFarland and M. Vickers (eds) *Vocational Education and Training for Youth*, Paris: OECD.

Straesser, R., Barr, G., Evans, J. and Wolf, A. (1991) 'Skills versus understanding', in M. Harris (ed.) *Schools, Mathematics and Work*, London: Falmer Press: 158–68.

Straker, A. (1997) 'Framework for numeracy: years 1 to 6', London: National Project for Numeracy and Literacy.

Suchman, L.A. (1987) *Plans and Situated Actions: the problem of human-machine communication*, Cambridge: Cambridge University Press.

Wilensky, U. (1991) 'Abstract mediations on the concrete and concrete implications for mathematics education', in I. Harel and S. Papert (eds) *Constructionism*, Norwood, NJ: Ablex Publishing Corporation: 193–204.

Wolf, A. (1984) *Practical Mathematics at Work: learning through YTS*, Sheffield: Manpower Services Commission.

4   Arbitrary and necessary

A way of viewing the mathematics curriculum

Dave Hewitt

I start with a conjecture and a task:

If I'm having to remember ... then I'm not working on mathematics.

Task 4.1

Katie was about four years old when her mother, Barbara, mentioned New York whilst talking to someone else.

Katie:　　Where is New York?
Barbara:　In the United States.
Katie:　　Why?

Decide how you would answer Katie's question before reading on.

When I heard this conversation I was struck by the simplicity of the question and the difficulty I felt in deciding how to provide an 'answer'. Barbara did give a response, which in some ways reflected what I felt – *because it just is*. An alternative answer to Barbara's could be to say it was when people were in the United States that they decided to name their town *New* York after the town *York* which some of them had known. New York, as far as Katie was concerned, could be anywhere. There would be no reason for her to know that it had to be in the United States, because it does not have to be, it just so happens that it is. Katie could only find out where New York is by being informed by someone who already knows, or gathering the information from some other source – be it a book, television, map or whatever.

It is similar for me if I am asked someone's name, someone whom I have never met or heard of before. If they are within my sight, I can look at them and wonder what their name is, seeing whether I can guess it. If I do guess, I have to wait to see whether it is confirmed or not. To know someone's name, I have to be told, and even then I am in a position of having to trust that the person telling me is not lying to me. Even when I do have that trust, learning a person's name will require work from me to remember it and to associate it with that particular person. Such things are in the realm of memory. If I am going to know someone's name, then I will need to be informed of what it is, and I will need to memorise it if I am going to be in a position to know it again at a later time.

I can make up my own name for this person; however, I will have difficulty in referring to this person when communicating with other people, since we do not share the same referent. So making up my own name may have some interest to me but it will be of little use when communicating with others. So, I am back to needing to be informed of this person's name and memorising it for later use.

I considered what a mathematical equivalent might be of the Katie anecdote, and offer the following:

Task 4.2

Student: How many sides has a square?
Teacher: Four.
Student: Why?

Again, consider how you would respond before reading on.

The only reason why a square has four sides is that a decision was made a long time ago to call four-sided shapes with particular properties *squares*. There is nothing about these shapes that means that they have to be called squares – indeed in other languages, the same shapes are given different names. Looking at the shapes carefully is not going to help a student know what the name of the shapes is, just as looking at the person does not reveal what their name is. All names, within mathematics or elsewhere, are things that students need to be informed about, and a teacher's role is to inform students of such things.

Once a student is informed, there is more work the student still needs to do. They have to memorise the word and associate that word with shapes with those particular properties. It is typical of the realm of memory that not only has a word, for example, to be memorised but that word also has to be associated with the right things. Many times students successfully remember a word but may not have made the appropriate association. For example, a student may not call Figure 4.1 a square

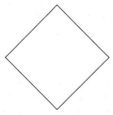

Figure 4.1 A square?

since the properties they associate with *square* do not include sides that are not horizontal or vertical.

Even the names that are rule based, such as *octagon*, *heptagon* and *hexagon* which are generated from particular roots, do not lead a student to know for sure that a five-sided polygon will be called *pentagon* as the example of *square* shows, since a four-sided polygon is not called a *tetragon*. Since names are socially and culturally agreed, then someone within that culture will have to inform a novice as to whether their – quite sensible – guesses of *pentagon* and *tetragon* are indeed the names accepted within that culture, and so deemed to be 'correct'.

Arbitrary

Names and labels can feel arbitrary for students, in the sense that there does not appear to be any reason why something has to be called by that particular name. Indeed there is no reason why something has to be given a particular name. Ginsburg (1977) gave a transcript of a conversation with a second-grader, Kathy:

I: Why do you write a 13 like that, a 1 followed by a 3?
K: 'Cause there's one ten, right? So you just put 1. I don't know why it's made like that. They could put ten 1s and a 3. So you see 13 is like ten and a three, but the way we write it, it would be 103 so they just put 1 for one ten and 3 for the extra three that it adds on to the ten.

(p. 116)

Kathy shows an awareness that the symbolic way in which numbers are written is a choice and does not have to be the way that it is. She even offers an alternative. Names (I include labels and symbols under this heading for convenience of writing) are about choices that have been accepted within a particular community. If a student wishes to become part of the same community, then the student needs to *accept* that name, rather than *question* it.

I describe something as *arbitrary* if someone could only come to know it to be true by being informed of it by some external means – whether by a teacher, a book, the Internet, etc. If something is arbitrary, then it is arbitrary for all learners, and needs to be memorised to be known. Gattegno (1987) said:

… there is knowledge that is distinguished sharply from awareness – the knowledge solely entrusted to one's memory, such as the label for such an object or a telephone number, items which are arbitrary. Without someone else, that knowledge would not exist for us.

(p. 55)

It is not only labels, symbols or names that are arbitrary. The mathematics curriculum is full of conventions which are based on choices that have been made some time in the past. For anyone learning those conventions today, they may seem arbitrary decisions. For example, why is the *x*-coordinate written first and the y-coordinate second? This is only a convention, and there is no reason why x must be first. As a consequence, a student might say that they will write the y first then! The issue of students wanting to do things their way and not accepting a cultural convention can be a tension point for a teacher since there is no reason a teacher can offer for why this convention must be so. Some phrases are offered, such as *walk along the hall and then up the stairs* or *x comes before y in the alphabet*. However, these are stories invented by teachers mainly as memory aids rather than justifications. The truth is that there is no reason why x must come first.

I recall a time I was playing snooker with my five year old nephew, Robert, on a small snooker table and had just potted the yellow. I was next to the green and was snookered on the brown. Robert said that the brown was next. I said that the green was next. He insisted the brown. There was no reason I could offer to justify the green being next, there was nothing in the colours which meant that green must come after yellow, and this was a convention that Robert was not going to accept, particularly since it was to his advantage not to! Getting students to accept and adopt the names and conventions is not always easy.

The fact that 360 was chosen as the number of units in a whole turn had as much to do with the people who were making such a decision, and what they were aware of at the time, as for any other reason. The Babylonians had a number system based on 60 and were looking at the ratio of the perimeter of a regular hexagon with the circumference of a circle. Knowing that the perimeter of a regular hexagon is six times the radius of the circumscribed circle, apparently led to the circle being divided into 6 × 60 (that is 360) degrees. If such a decision were to be made today, in our metric system of measurements, perhaps 100 would have seemed just as natural. For a pupil in a classroom, who lives in today's world, 360 is by no means an obvious choice. A student cannot look closely at a whole turn, analyse it and come to the conclusion that a whole turn *must* be split up into 360 units (Figure 4.2).

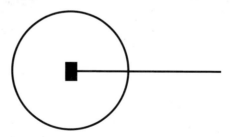

Figure 4.2   Teacher: As can be observed from this diagram, a whole turn must be divided up into 360

As Clausen (1991) commented:

> ... I have long felt that our use of degrees to measure amounts of turn (angles) is very arbitrary. There is no way that a child (or adult) can *intuit* that there are

360 degrees in a whole turn. This is totally arbitrary, formal, true-because-Teacher-says-so knowledge.

(p. 16, her emphasis)

A teacher has to inform a learner about how many degrees there are in a whole turn. One attempt to make it feel less arbitrary is to bring a historical perspective into the classroom. Students may learn some history from this approach but they will not be developing mathematically through memorising the arbitrary. As Pimm (1995) commented:

> The way of thinking embodied in the simple phrase 'it is or it is not' is profoundly mathematical.
>
> (p. 187)

However, *it could be* is not so profoundly mathematical! And the arbitrary is full of *could be*. In contrast to the arbitrary nature of degrees, Clausen (1991) goes on to say:

> On the other hand, the idea of half-turns, quarter-turns, two-thirds turns, and so on, has a real, valid meaning in itself. If I turn right round, so that I am facing the way I was to start with, then I know that I have done a whole turn. There is nothing new to learn – no arbitrary number, like 37, for Teacher to tell me. And I can work out for myself what half-turns, quarter-turns and so on mean, using my own experience of turning half-way round, or a quarter round, or whatever. Fractions of a turn have an intuitive validity which the concept of degrees lacks.
>
> (p. 16)

Here Clausen highlights the 'it is or it is not' nature of fractions of turns which can be known without being imparted by a teacher.

Necessary

There are aspects of the mathematics curriculum where students do not need to be informed. These are things that students can work out for themselves and know to be correct. They are parts of the mathematics curriculum that are not social conventions but are properties that can be worked out from what someone already knows. As Clausen (ibid.) pointed out, there are properties about the act of turning that I can know for myself. For example, if I turn a quarter-turn and then a quarter-turn again, I have made a half-turn. It is possible to find out about other fractions of a whole turn without having to be informed. So, the mathematical content that is on a curriculum can be divided up into those things which are arbitrary and those things which are necessary.

All students will need to be informed of the arbitrary. However, the necessary is dependent upon the awareness students already have. For example, it is necessary that the required side of the triangle in Figure 4.3 is $\frac{\sqrt{3}}{2}$. However, not every student will be in a position to be aware of this. So although this is necessary, it does not imply that all students have the awareness to be able to work this out, only that *someone* is able to work this out without the need to be informed of it.

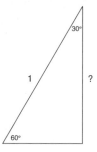

Figure 4.3   What is the length of the side?

Those things that are necessary can be worked out, it is only a matter of whether particular students have the awareness required to do so. If not, then maybe it is not the best choice of topic to be taught at that moment in time. For example, I did not choose to teach integration of trigonometric functions to the majority of 11-year-olds I taught. If a student does have the required awareness for something, then I suggest the teacher's role is not to inform the student but to introduce activities that help students to use their awareness in coming to know what is necessary. What is necessary is in the realm of awareness, whereas the arbitrary is in the realm of memory (Figure 4.4).

Arbitrary	*All* students *need* to be informed of the arbitrary by someone else	*Realm of memory*
Necessary	*Some* students *can* become aware of what is necessary without being informed of it by someone else	*Realm of awareness*

Figure 4.4   Arbitrary and necessary

Viewing the curriculum

I asked my student teachers to write down a list of those things in the mathematics curriculum that cannot be worked out (might be so), and those things that can be worked out (must be so). They came up with the list in Figure 4.5.

Cannot be worked out (*might* be so)	Can be worked out (*must* be so)
Names of shapes	Interior angles of regular polygons
Definitions of ...	$V = IR \longrightarrow I = \dfrac{V}{R}$
Measuring bearings from north	Solution of a linear equation
x- and y- coordinates	What happens to numbers if multiplied by another number <1 or >1
How heavy is a kg?	Rough estimates of measurements
How long is a metre?	2×3
Terminology – e.g. names of theorems, such as 'factor' theorem	Finding factors of $a^3 + b^3$
Word/label	Finding angles or lengths in triangle problems, for example based upon this triangle:
	Property of primeness
	Symmetry
Summarised as words, symbols, notation and conventions	Summarised as properties and relationships

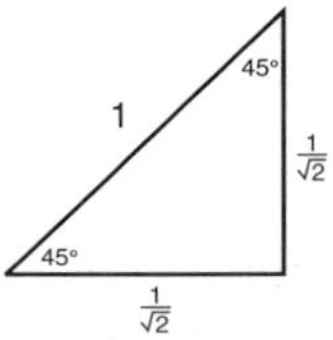

Figure 4.5 A way to divide the curriculum

Such division of the mathematics curriculum into arbitrary and necessary is based upon the philosophical roots of contingent and necessary. Kripke (1996) said that:

> If [something] is true, might it have been otherwise? ... If the answer is 'no', then this fact about the world is a necessary one. If the answer is 'yes', then this fact about the world is a contingent one.
>
> (p. 36)

It is true that the x-coordinate is written before the y-coordinate. However, it might have been otherwise, a different decision could have been made with the y-coordinate coming first. This is possible and the mathematics that would be based on such a convention would be just as consistent. So the fact that the x-coordinate does come first is a contingent truth. Nozick (1984) proposed that:

> Let us state the principle of sufficient reason as: every truth has an explanation. For every truth p there is some truth q which stands in the explanatory

relation E to p … When any other truth holds without an explanation it is an arbitrary brute fact.

(p. 140–1)

There is no explanation why the x-coordinate must come first, so this is an arbitrary fact, and indeed so is much of the rest of the mathematics curriculum on coordinates. Many chapters in textbooks are concerned with students knowing

---

Task 4.3

Before reading on, can you think of something within the curriculum on coordinates which is necessary and not arbitrary?

---

how to draw and label axes, how to write down coordinates, knowing that the x-coordinate comes before the y, knowing the coordinate of a given point, and knowing how to mark a point given a coordinate. These are all arbitrary and I suggest that mathematics does not lie with the arbitrary but is found in what is necessary.

I am concerned that little time is spent on what is necessary and so much time is spent on memorising and practising conventions. Mathematics is concerned with properties – and properties can be worked out or found out. This implies that many of the chapters on coordinates are not concerned with mathematics. What mathematics does lie within the heading of coordinates? There is the awareness that a position cannot be described without starting from somewhere. An origin is required. This is not something a teacher needs to inform a student about, students can become aware of this through a suitably constructed activity. Some form of base vectors (not necessarily at right angles) or their equivalents (such as angles in the case of polar coordinates) are also necessary, although, of course, they need not be known by that name. These are some aspects of where mathematics lies within the topic of coordinates, rather than with the practising of conventions. I am not saying that the acceptance and adoption of conventions is not important within mathematics classrooms, but that it needs to be realised that this is not where mathematics lies. So I am left wondering about the amount of classroom time given over to the arbitrary compared with where the mathematics lies.

Approaches to teaching and their consequences

How might a teacher work on a given topic with a class given this division of the curriculum into arbitrary and necessary? For example, when carrying out an activity involving throwing two six-sided dice a number of times and finding which total occurred most, one student, Sam, said to the teacher that he did not know the mathematical name given to the score which occurs most often. The teacher replied to Sam that he was there in a previous lesson when this was mentioned and that he should think about it. I wondered what there was to 'think about'. The name – *mode* – will either be remembered or not, and Sam is indicating that he does not remember. There is nothing here that can be worked out. The only options for him are to remember (which he didn't), or to be informed. Inviting students to 'think about it' is appropriate for what is necessary, not for what is arbitrary. Since the name was not memorised on this occasion, an issue for the teacher was how students could be helped to memorise. For the arbitrary, a teacher's role is to assist memory. For what is necessary, a teacher does not need to inform students, since what is necessary can be worked out and a teacher's role is with the realm of awareness rather than memory. For example, the 'fact' that the internal angles of a triangle (in Euclidean geometry) add up to half a full turn is something which students can become aware of themselves. The role for the teacher is to provide an activity to help students to educate their own awareness of the angles inside a triangle. So, the teacher's role is to educate their students' awareness, rather than give them something to memorise (see Figure 4.6).

	Student	Teacher	Mode of teaching
Arbitrary	*All* students *need* to be informed of the arbitrary by someone else	A teacher *needs* to inform students of the arbitrary	*Assisting memory*
Necessary	*Some* students *can* become aware of what is necessary without being informed of it by someone else	A teacher does *not need* to inform students of what is necessary	*Educating awareness*

Figure 4.6 Modes of teaching

If a teacher decides to inform students of some mathematics content that is necessary, then they are treating it as if it is arbitrary, as if it is something that needs to be told. For example, if a teacher stated that the angles inside a triangle add up to half a full turn rather than offering an activity for students to become aware of this, then students are left having to accept what the teacher says as true. In this case, it becomes just another 'fact' to be memorised. I call this *received wisdom*.

It is possible for students to use their awareness to try to work out for themselves why this received wisdom is true. If a student succeeds then this becomes a necessary fact and rightfully returns to the realm of awareness. All too often, however, a student just accepts this received wisdom and treats it as something to be memorised or, indeed, forgotten.

In a lesson I observed, some 14–15-year-olds were working on solving simultaneous equations, and one male student was having difficulties with rearranging an equation. He had written:

$$x - y = 2$$
$$y = 2 - x$$

I asked him about the '–' sign in front of the y and his response was to rewrite the second equation as:

$$y = 2 + x$$

I said that I felt he had done the correct thing when taking away the x but that there was still a '–' sign in front of the y. I wrote a '–' in front of the y in the original second equation:

$$-y = 2 - x$$

He then changed both the negative signs to positive signs saying *two negatives make a positive*:

$$+y = 2 + x$$

This is one example of a student remembering some received wisdom – *two negatives make a positive* – but not remembering the situations in which this received wisdom is appropriate. Rather than basing his actions on a mathematical awareness of inverse, his actions are informed by a memory of something to 'do' when there are two negatives. Transformations of equations are concerned with what is necessary and a teacher providing such a phrase turns such awareness into received wisdom which a student may then try to memorise. The problem with memory is that it gives the opportunity to forget. In this case, the phrase is remembered, but the associated situation it relates to (which is relatively complex) is forgotten.

Received wisdom may be accompanied with an explanation of why something is true. A teacher may explain why the angles in a triangle add up to half a full turn. The fact that a teacher gives an explanation does not mean that students have the awareness necessary to understand this explanation, or will do the required work to be in a position where they too know why this must be the case. A careful explanation may increase the possibility that some students will be able to use the awareness they have in order to come to realise why this 'fact' is true. Other students may not have the awareness, or not choose to use the awareness they have to get themselves in such a position. For these students, the fact that the interior angles of a triangle add up to half a full turn remains received wisdom and in the realm of memory, despite the teacher's efforts.

Poincaré (undated) considered the following scenario:

> In the same way our pupils imagine that they know it when they begin to study mathematics seriously. If, without any other preparation, I come and say to them: 'No, you do not know it; you do not understand what you imagine you understand; I must demonstrate to you what appears to you evident,' and if, in the demonstration, I rely on premises that seem to them less evident than the conclusion, what will the wretched pupils think? They will think that the science of mathematics is nothing but an arbitrary aggregation of useless subtleties; or they will lose their taste for it; or else they will look upon it as an amusing game.
>
> (p. 128)

A teacher's explanation is often based upon the teacher's awareness, and so may use things that students do not find *evident* – things which are not in the students'

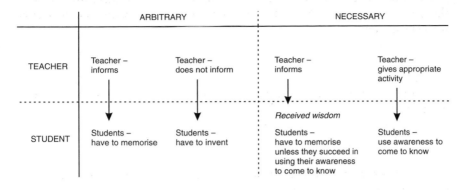

Figure 4.7   A summary of teacher choices and student consequent way of working

awareness – and so the explanation will not be one that will help those students to educate their own awareness. As Poincaré points out, for many students mathematics can become *an arbitrary aggregation of useless subtleties* or just a game with symbols (although I doubt it is often considered *amusing*).

Figure 4.7 gives a summary of the choices available to a teacher with the arbitrary and necessary, and the consequent result in terms of the way in which students have to work.

Givens – assumed properties

When using awareness to find out that something is necessary, there may be certain information provided other than arbitrary names and conventions. For example, in Figure 4.8, the task might be to find the area and perimeter of the rectangle. The area and perimeter are necessary since they can be worked out, but only because there have been properties already given, such as the angles or the length of the sides of the rectangle. These properties I describe as *Givens*.

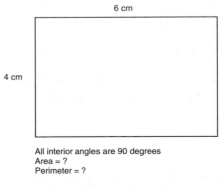

All interior angles are 90 degrees
Area = ?
Perimeter = ?

Figure 4.8   A traditional question

Thus, what is necessary comes as a consequence of certain accepted givens. If insufficient properties were given to determine the area then they could be created – with either a number chosen or a label assigned. For example, the following statement about area:

area $= L \times B$

can only be articulated with the assigning of the unknowns L and B. It should be noted here that there is a combination of arbitrary labels (the labels L and B) and the properties which they are labelling – the actual lengths of the sides of the rectangle. It is the former which are arbitrary, and the latter which are the givens. The arbitrary labels are adopted, and the given properties accepted and worked with in order to find what is necessary.

Givens can become known to a student in three ways:

- a student can 'receive' them, such as verbally from a teacher or through written text (as with Figure 4.8);
- a student can observe them through their senses, such as seeing that one side of a rectangle is longer than another, or feeling that the corner of a room is more than 90 degrees;
- a student can create their own givens, such as allocating the property of the length of a side a rectangle to be L, or inventing an equation to try to solve.

Givens are required in order that other things become necessary. However, the givens in Figure 4.8, such as the length of the sides of the rectangle, are themselves properties which might have been necessary if the area and perimeter had been given in the first place (see Figure 4.9).

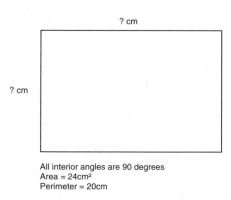

? cm

? cm

All interior angles are 90 degrees
Area = 24cm²
Perimeter = 20cm

Figure 4.9 An alternative question

If some properties are given but not sufficient to determine the lengths, such as in Figure 4.10, then this does not stop some things being worked out from the facts that are given. For example, I can say that the smallest the perimeter can be

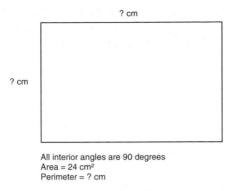

? cm

? cm

All interior angles are 90 degrees
Area = 24 cm²
Perimeter = ? cm

Figure 4.10   What can be known for sure now?

is $4 \times \sqrt{24}$ cm. Perimeter remains a part of the mathematics curriculum that is about properties and I can use my awareness to derive new certainties within this area of the curriculum based on related givens.

Although givens are properties, they lie in the realm of memory, since these are assumed facts rather than derived certainties. As such they cannot be worked out and so need to be memorised if they are to be available in the future (without being informed of them again). So, although perimeter is an aspect of the curriculum that is necessary, a given particular perimeter such as in Figure 4.9, is one that I will have to memorise. So, the properties given within particular mathematical questions have to be memorised, whilst other related properties can be derived through awareness from these memorised givens.

Generates – generating new possibilities

Although the arbitrary requires memory in order to be retained, awareness can still be used with the arbitrary. This can be done in two ways. Firstly, an awareness concerning properties can be applied to a convention and secondly, awareness can be used with conventions to generate new names or extend the use of those conventions, even beyond usual social usage. As an example of the former, if I adopt the convention that there are 360 degrees in a whole turn and that measurement of turn is based on a linear scale (both arbitrary), then I can use the awareness I have about linearity to say *if I halve this, then I halve that*. This leads me to be able to say definitely that there are 180 degrees in a half turn – a certainty worked out through awareness from the original adopted convention.

My use of the word 'certainty' here is based upon the premise *if I adopt this convention* then there is a property I can state about a half turn which is true (and I didn't need to be informed about it). Of course, if a different convention is adopted, then the property may no longer be true. Ayer (1962) gives an example within philosophy:

> For apart from the fact that they [a-priori propositions] can properly be said to be true, which linguistic rules cannot, they are distinguished also by being

necessary, whereas linguistic rules are arbitrary. At the same time, if they are necessary it is only because the relevant linguistic rules are presupposed. Thus, it is a contingent, empirical fact that the word 'earlier' is used in English to mean earlier, and it is an arbitrary, though convenient, rule of language that words that stand for temporal relations are to be used transitively; but, given this rule, the proposition that, if A is earlier than B and B is earlier than C, A is earlier than C becomes a necessary truth.

(p. 17)

The *if … then this must be so* scenario is at the basis of working mathematically to establish new certainties. The second way of using awareness with the arbitrary is based upon being creative with the conventions themselves: *if … then this could be so*. For example, let me consider number names. The names used for our numbers are arbitrary, as are the conventions of how these names are used. *One, two, three, hundred, thousand*, etc., are arbitrary as they could equally well be *un, deux, trois, cent, mille*, etc. The convention in English is that 21 is said with the higher value digit first – *twenty-one* – whilst in German it is said with the lower value digit first – *einundzwanzig*. So the way in which the words are combined is also arbitrary. Yet, having adopted the names and conventions in English, I can use my awareness to generate new number names. For example:

Say the number below out loud

4280581

I claim that you have never said this number before in your life or heard it being said. As a consequence you cannot have memorised how to say it. The ability to generate new number names from adopted conventions is in the realm of awareness. Yet these are not necessary, since they are still only names. So I describe such things as *generates*. These have been generated from names and conventions using awareness. Issues of 'right' or 'wrong' are not appropriate since alternatives are always possible, it is only a matter of whether alternatives are accepted within a certain culture. What was accepted in the past, such as *billion* meaning 1 000 000 000 000 in the UK, can become changed over time, as indeed *billion* is used now to mean 1 000 000 000 in the UK.

As well as awareness being applied to conventions to produce names for numbers never said before, some conventions can be explored to extremities that are not usually carried out within a culture. For example, a child saying the following number names: *one hundred, two hundred, three hundred, …* may continue and say: *eight hundred, nine hundred, ten hundred, eleven hundred, …* There is nothing 'wrong' with this and indeed I have heard such usage on the television and radio (as well as it being common in terms of naming centuries). However, this can be explored further: *two hundred and forty-seven hundred* for 24 700; or *twenty-three point four tenths* for 2.34. These are not heard on the radio, and yet they only explore an accepted convention further than is usual.

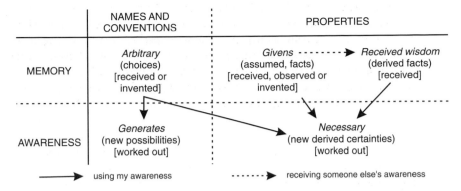

Figure 4.11   An overview

Pedagogically this exploration has its uses, as it is helpful to be flexible about ways of viewing numbers.

Conventions can also be extended, for example the notation for two-dimensional coordinates can be extended to three, four and more dimensions, and so offer a way to work with otherwise conceptually complex scenarios. Conventions can also be combined, such as writing ½(3, 4) to represent (1½, 2). These are ways in which someone can use their awareness to generate new possibilities within the world of conventions. Not all of them will be accepted within the mathematics community, but they are examples of using awareness within this area. The ability to generate such possibilities reduces the otherwise overwhelming demand on memory. Borges (1985) created a character, Funes, who never forgot anything and used to create a new name for every number. Thankfully for us, the demands on memory are less taxing through the use of our ability to generate names for numbers from relatively few words.

Summary

An overview of the dynamics discussed in this article is contained in Figure 4.11. Viewing the mathematics curriculum in terms of those things that can be worked out by someone (necessary) and those things that everyone needs to be informed about (arbitrary), can clarify the roles both teacher and students have within the complexities of teaching and learning. The arbitrary is concerned with names and conventions and students have no choice but to memorise the arbitrary, and a teacher will have to inform them of what is arbitrary. I have indicated this in Figure 4.11 as the student having 'received' the arbitrary. The only other option is for the teacher to refuse to inform students and leave them to invent something instead. This is perfectly possible and can be desirable at times, however, it does not change the fact that students will still need to be informed sometime in the future if they are to be included within a mathematics community that communicates through adopted conventions.

As Mandler (1989) pointed out:

> The good theory can well say with Humpty Dumpty: 'When I use a word, it means just what I choose it to mean – neither more nor less.' However, the history of the social sciences is strewn with abandoned concepts and terms that have failed to heed a corollary that Humpty Dumpty never told us about: Once you choose a word to mean something (exactly), then you have to start convincing other people to use it that same way; otherwise, monologues will never be replaced by dialogue and consensus.
>
> (p. 237)

Students are unlikely to convince the mathematics community to change the names and conventions already established, even if they had the platform to attempt to do this. So it is the student who, perhaps unfairly, needs to accept and adapt in order to communicate with the mathematics community.

The necessary is about properties and one possibility is for students to 'receive' properties through a teacher informing them just as for the arbitrary. However, this turns the necessary into received wisdom and students may well treat this as something else to be memorised. Indeed, they will have no other choice unless they are able or willing to do the work necessary to become aware of the necessity of this received wisdom. Some students may be able to do this work, in which case the received wisdom will become a derived certainty and be known through awareness rather than memory.

Another choice for a teacher is to provide an activity that will make properties accessible through awareness. An appropriate activity will help these properties to be more accessibly known through awareness than if the teacher informed students of them and left the students to their own devices to work out why they must be so.

A teacher taking a stance of deliberately not informing students of anything except the arbitrary is aware that developing as a mathematician is about educating awareness rather than collecting memories. Furthermore, this stance clarifies for the students the way of working which is appropriate for any particular aspect of the curriculum – the arbitrary has to be memorised, but what is necessary is about educating awareness.

If I'm having to remember … then I'm not working on mathematics.

References

Ayer, A.J. (1962) *Language, Truth and Logic*, London: Victor Gollancz Ltd.

Borges, J.L. (1985) 'Funes, the memorious', in A. Kerrigan (ed. and trans.) *Fictions*, London: John Calder: 97–105.

Clausen, T. (1991) 'Turning logo', in *Micromath* 7(1): 16.

Gattegno, C. (1987) *The Science of Education. Part 1 – theoretical considerations*, New York: Educational Solutions.

Ginsburg, H. (1977) *Children's Arithmetic. The learning process*, New York: D. Van Nostrand Company.

Kripke, S. (1996) *Naming and Necessity*, Oxford: Blackwell.

Mandler, G. (1989) 'Affect and learning: reflections and prospects', in D.B. McLeod and V.M. Adams (eds) *Affect and Mathematical Problem Solving. A new perspective*, New York: Springer-Verlag: 237–44.

Nozick, R. (1984) *Philosophical Explanations*, Oxford: Clarendon Press.

Pimm, D. (1995) *Symbols and Meaning in School Mathematics*, London: Routledge.

Poincaré, H. (undated) *Science and Method*, trans. F. Maitland, London: Thomas Nelson and Sons.

Section 3

Learning Mathematics

5 Social constructivism in mathematics learning and teaching

Barbara Jaworski

This chapter is about a way of viewing knowledge and learning known as constructivism. We shall be looking particularly at what is loosely termed 'social constructivism', although there are many versions of this, and differing interpretations. The chapter will weave theoretical ideas with practical situations from a real classroom, in order to start to address the issues in applying constructivism to aspects of mathematics learning and teaching.

The 'social' as a basis of knowledge and learning

As you read this chapter you will engage in a social process, through which your knowledge and understanding will be challenged and grow. I call it a social process because it involves social actions and social artefacts. This text is a social and historic artefact. It has developed through social (inter)actions of a variety of people at a variety of occasions in time and space. As the writer, I bring to it considerable experience of learning and teaching, some of which I am going to draw on here in relating theory to schools and classrooms in which I have been present. I draw on theoretical perspectives that I have encountered in a number of forms, some of these the writing of others. The others in turn have drawn on their own experiences and their own readings and their conversations with others. In making sense of what you read, you will draw on your own experiences, perhaps those of your own learning in school or beyond, your interactions with other people and your reading from other texts. You may talk about what you read with your colleagues or friends and, through such talk, your own perceptions are likely to be modified and enhanced.

The picture I have painted here is based on a social constructivist perspective. I will come to what I mean by 'constructivism' shortly, but I should like to start by offering you an anecdote from my recent experience. I intend to use this anecdote to get at what I mean by social constructivism.

My anecdote of Farooq[1]

My work takes me quite often to Pakistan where I work with teachers in a variety of ways, sometimes in schools and classrooms. This anecdote reports an experience I had in a small community school in the north of Pakistan where a teacher-educator, Rubina, was working with some teachers and young students. The experience was an important one for me as a mathematics teacher and educator, but also as a person who is still learning a great deal about mathematics learning and teaching through the social interactions in which I take part.

The anecdote is presented as I wrote it, soon after the event.

Midmorning, I depart for the Community Action primary school, where Rubina is working. We enter and pass a number of small classrooms to reach a room with almost no furniture, the concrete floor spread with blankets on which are sitting 20 or more small children (aged about four). Rubina and another teacher (a volunteer as I discover) are sitting with them. There is a variety of home-made materials around, and the walls show evidence of students' work. I learn later that the children are in three groups, English, Mathematics and Urdu.[2] There is a fourth group of children who are not supposed to be there (no fees have been paid); however, teachers do not want to turn them away.[3]

Rubina is working with the maths group and I sit with them on the floor. Talk is mainly in Urdu (or one of the local languages – I cannot be sure). I observe Rubina's work for a while. She is working with children on number, using circular cut-outs on each of which is a printed number. A boy near to me, Farooq, does not seem to be participating. I reach out for a number disc, and hold it up for him to see. It reads 13. He says, 'Thirteen,' speaking in English. I smile and say, 'Shabash!' (good!). I pick up other numbers up to 20, and he reads then all correctly in English. A lot of *shabash*! I then reach for a plastic jar (home-made from a water bottle) of small stones. Counting, '1, 2, 3 ... ,' I place stones around the thirteen disc, until I reach thirteen. I then invite Farooq (in sign language) to count with me. He does, up to 13. I remove the stones and start again, inviting him to count this time by himself. He does, as I place the stones: '1, 2, 3, ... 13.' I then gather the stones together and give them to him, indicating that he should do it himself. He does, placing stones and counting for each stone, '1, 2, 3, ... 12, 13, 14, 15, 16.' He stops at 16. This is all he can fit around the circle. I laugh inwardly, and I'm excited by the insights this gives into where his attention is. With a lot of *shabash*, we start again, together. I stop us at 13, and emphasise holding the disc 'thirteen', then point to the stones and say, 'Thirteen.' He looks at me and says, 'Thirteen!' What is he thinking?

I reach for some other discs, and show him 5. He says, 'Five.' We go through the above stages with the stones, counting together. When I place the stones I stop at 5. When he places the stones, he continues until the circle is full. As a teacher, what do I do? I could abandon this process, arguing that Farooq is not yet ready to link the number of stones with the written figure (to start to understand cardinality). However, I continue systematically with special cases: the discs for 6, 7 and 8. Farooq seems quite willing to go along with me. Up to 7, the outcomes are the same as for 13 and 5. We both count, but when I place the stones I stop at the number given. When Farooq places them he continues until the space around the disc is full. At 8, I am beginning to give up hope, desperately trying to think of other approaches. Then, amazingly, Farooq counts out the stones himself, and stops at 8! I feel thrilled, but recognise that I still know very little about his thinking. Of course language has been a barrier but, nevertheless, I feel this has been an important episode. Unfortunately, Rubina indicated that it was time to move on, so no further work with Farooq was possible. There was also no time to discuss this with Rubina.

The episode is indicative of many issues that arise for teachers considering children's mathematical development, in this case that of just one child, but more widely of a community of children within the complexity of needs in this school and this area and beyond.

Why is this anecdote significant?

I have drawn on an experience from Pakistan because its lack of familiarity for me, and possibly for you, can be instructive. I am much less likely to take factors for granted than might be the case in my own culture. I am not used to working with small children in poorly resourced environments. I am only just starting to appreciate the nature of society in this region, the social and cultural aspects of everyday life, expectations and values, for example. And I know only a few words of the local language so my understanding of what is said, and my communication through language is very limited. However, despite all of this, I interacted with Farooq, and I learned a lot in the process of our interaction.

Farooq could recognise certain numbers in written form and could say them in English. I was not sure what this recognition involved. He could read the number, but how much did he know about it as a number? I discovered he could count, also in English. But he seemed not to be able to do what I wanted him to, which was to link the number he was reading on the disc with the number of stones placed around it.

Why did I think it was important to be able to do this? Well, my own mathematical knowledge of numerals, numbers, order and counting suggests to me that such linkage is important to an understanding of ordinality and cardinality, two key concepts in the construction of number systems.[4] As a teacher of mathematics, I want to find ways of enabling students to gain access to such concepts. To do this, I have to work within the social environment in which I find myself, and in accordance with my own sociocultural limitations. These may not be as obvious to me as the environment I am trying to make sense of.

For example, it seemed 'natural' to me that the number of stones around the disc would match the number on the disc. I was therefore surprised when Farooq counted stones beyond this number. It seemed to me, after observing this action a number of times, that it was more important to him to fill the space around the disc with stones. Presumably we were both working from some position of sense-making. Mine was based in my own logico-mathematical culture of being a mathematics teacher and educator in an English educational setting. In what was Farooq's based? I know too little to speculate. However, it is a characteristic of Pakistani society that children respect their elders, and especially teachers, doing what they are asked, and not questioning. Farooq's behaviour, sitting quietly, patiently and politely, responding to my actions, was typical of that expected in this society. English children might not have been so patient or attentive.

After some time, Farooq was able to count out the number of stones to match the number on the disc. Does this mean he had in any sense 'learned' this from our interactions? Or had he finally realised what it was that this strange person was doing? And perhaps her constant use of the word *shabash* indicated what he had to do to please her. In the end he did just that – she was delighted. But who had learned and what had been learned? I would hesitate to say anything at all about Farooq's concept of cardinality. I can say a lot about what *I* learned, and some of it is evident in my words above.

I am now ready to say something about constructivism, and to relate this to the anecdote and my analysis of it.

Constructivism

Constructivism is a theoretical perspective concerning how people 'come to know'. Hence it is about *knowledge* and *learning*; in this paper we shall be thinking about *mathematics* and the *learning of mathematics*. This perspective can be seen in a number of ways depending on whose work the theory is based.

One branch of constructivism is rooted in the work of Piaget, who was concerned about children's development of cognitive processes and the structuring of cognition.[5] According to Piagetian theory, we learn by forming mental structures or *schemata* to represent our perceptions of what we experience in the world around us. New experiences result in new schemata, or in the reinforcement or modification of existing schemata. Piaget suggested two processes of mental (re)structuring: *assimilation*, the process of fitting new knowledge into existing schemata and *accommodation*, the process of adapting schemata to fit new perceptions that challenge existing structures (see, for example, Piaget, 1950; Piaget and Inhelder, 1966). Piaget was interested in child development, and believed that development precedes learning. Development was seen to be a natural process through interactions with physical and social worlds, and learning was seen to be derivative of the developmental process.

Deriving from Piaget's work, Ernst von Glasersfeld, and colleagues in the United States, developed a theoretical perspective known as *radical constructivism* (see for example, Cobb and Steffe, 1983; von Glasersfeld, 1987, 1990). Briefly, this suggests that knowledge is not something that people take in from outside themselves, but rather something they construct themselves as a result of their experiences, physical and social, in the world around them; also, if knowledge exists externally to ourselves, we cannot know it, as we can only know what we ourselves experience. 'Coming to know' is an adaptive process (von Glasersfeld, 1987): that is, our cognitive structures adapt according to new experiences. Cognition is about testing out our current understandings against new experience and fitting these together in ways that make sense to us currently. Such ideas sit very firmly in the realm of psychology.[6]

Radical constructivism has been widely criticised for its perceived failure to give due attention or importance to processes of communication and to social interaction more generally. As I have expressed it above, it may seem to be a theory focused almost entirely on the individual constructing personal knowledge. Yet, communication is fundamental to such construction. Individuals rarely exist outside of society. Interactions within society can challenge sense-making. If conversation with another person seems to suggest they have a very different way of seeing something, then we are likely to argue our case, perhaps to re-examine what we think ourselves, perhaps ultimately to change that view. Either way, we think more explicitly about the issues involved, and our knowledge becomes clearer to us. Thus the process of communication is important in offering challenges to conceptions and resulting in accommodation, to use Piaget's term.

What I have said so far is very brief, and I have ignored many important issues. I shall come to some of these shortly when we look at an alternative to the Piagetian perspective. For the moment, let us come back to the anecdote.

Analysis of the anecdote from a (radical) constructivist perspective

The anecdote concerned two people, Farooq and myself, interacting within a school environment. Farooq was a student in a classroom, expected to behave like a student in a classroom. I was an adult and teacher-figure, to whom he was obliged to attend. Both of us were in a learning situation. Farooq was learning mathematics (among other things). I was learning (among other things) about Farooq's learning of mathematics.

In order to teach mathematics well, we need to know something about the learning of the students we are teaching. This enables us to respond more effectively and offer appropriate questions and opportunities. My engagement in the task of teaching Farooq was incidental, not planned or deliberate. Rubina's attention was on other students, and Farooq seemed to be just sitting. When I held up the first disc that came to my reach, and Farooq read the number, I learned something: that he could read the number. I conjectured that he 'knew' the number, but I had to find out if this was actually true. I was going, personally, through a sense-making process, trying to learn about Farooq's concept of number. I could not ask him questions, so I had to find out through other actions.

So, for me, my teaching was a sense-making process. I did not have clearly defined actions or activities. I drew on what I already knew – about mathematics,

about Farooq, and about teaching, and set out to learn more through our interactions. However, I did not explain this to myself in terms of my own learning, but
rather in terms of Farooq's learning. I wanted Farooq to learn.

I can speak less easily about Farooq's learning, because I had no access to his
thoughts. I learned that he could count, because I saw and heard him do it – my
evidence. After a time, I conjectured that he could not link the written 13 with a
collection of 13 stones, but I did not have enough evidence to support this conjecture.
For example, his attention might have been with fitting as many stones as possible
around the disc. He may have been wondering why I left a gap, and seeing it as his
job to complete the activity, filling the gap. Either way, how could I get him to show
me that he could connect the two forms of 13, or to learn to connect them?[7] My
activity was directed at this question: the careful counting, stopping at 13, the
emphasising of 13, pointing to the stones, pointing to the disc. My teaching acts
were addressed at enabling Farooq's cognitive structuring to formulate this mathematical concept. I could not *give* him the concept. He had somehow to construct it
himself. I might be seen to provide experiences through which assimilation and
accommodation could take place.

Yet, as I speak in this fashion, I seem to suggest that there *is* a concept. Indeed it
is possible to talk about *giving* the concept. Where is this concept? Where does it
exist? Does it exist externally to my understanding of it? If knowledge is a result of
human construction, and humans cannot know any knowledge outside of themselves, how can a concept be independent of the person constructing it?

Well, I'm sure we would all agree that there are concepts such as cardinality of
numbers that are in some sense 'in the public domain'. If I talk to other people who
know mathematics, they are likely to 'know what I mean' by cardinality. But, how
can they know what I mean since they have no access to what is in my head? This
leads me to a concept that is sometimes called *intersubjectivity*. We each have a subjective sense of what we know and understand. Intersubjectivity occurs when it
appears that we agree, or share that understanding. So how do we come to an
*inter*subjective understanding of cardinality?

This takes me back to constructivism, and the social processes involved.

Social constructivism

Let us stay with cardinality as a concept, an item of mathematical knowledge that
we would expect any mathematically literate person to know. In the history of
mathematics, cardinality evolved or emerged in mathematical thought (see the
remarks of Leo Rogers[4]). Its emergence can be seen in terms of its construction
through the thinking and activity of individual mathematicians, discussing ideas,
refining ideas, writing about ideas for others to share, consider and question. Discussing, refining, sharing, considering and questioning are acts undertaken by
human beings, either individually or together, often in a process of reciprocality.
Hence they are social acts. Individual thinking and social thinking alternate and
interweave.

Compare the historical process with a current day classroom activity of working as a group on a mathematical problem. Individual thought moves in and out of the group as an individual speaks, listens, thinks – often some or all of these at the same time – and in the process constructs something that fits with previous conceptions or challenges them. However, as the people in the group interact, talk with and across each other, challenge, argue, disagree, ask questions, offer explanations, it can be as if knowledge grows within the group; as if knowledge is located somewhere in the group space, rather than in the heads of individuals. For any member of the group, what they know as a result of all of this interaction is as much a product of the interaction, as it is an act of individual construction. We might see, atomistically, the individual making sense of aspects of group dialogue, and assimilating and accommodating in response. Or we might see a more holistic scene, in which the joint engaging with questions and ideas, results in a growth of common knowledge.

The concept of cardinality has come through ages of group space. It is represented in the age-old writings of mathematicians and educators with which others can engage or interact. Through such interaction, these others can start to make sense of cardinality. Thus intersubjectivity in cardinality grows and cardinality enters into the body of (social) knowledge that is mathematics. As an educated mathematics teacher, I have a good sense of cardinality, and I can make this judgement with confidence because I have read about it, talked with others about it, and engaged with it myself. As a teacher, I want to provide opportunity for my students to access this social concept of cardinality and make sense of it for themselves. This is a social constructive process.

Social constructivism is often linked to the work of Vygotsky and his colleagues in Russia. It was Vygotsky's view that learning is fundamentally a social process, and that individual construction is derivative of social construction: 'Human learning presupposes a special social nature and a process by which children grow into the intellectual life of those around them,' (Vygotsky, 1978, p. 88). The following words are widely quoted:

> Any function of the child's social development appears twice or on two planes. First it appears on the social plane and then on the psychological plane. First it appears between people as an interpsychological category and then within the child as an intrapsychological category.
>
> (Vygotsky, 1981, p. 63)

This suggests that we learn from being a part of and interacting within a social environment, and that individual construction of knowledge is derivative of its social construction. This is to presume that there are two separate parts to the construction of knowledge. These can be labelled as individual and social construction. Important questions for social constructivism involve *how* social knowledge becomes internalised by the individual, and indeed what is the nature of social knowledge. Radical constructivists would put aside the notions of social knowledge as separate from individual knowledge, seeing all growth of knowledge in terms of individual construction relative to social interaction, and the corresponding intersubjectivity that allows people to understand each other.

It seems worth, however, making the distinction between two ways of seeing intersubjectivity, both hinted at above. The first sees individuals interacting and, through making sense of the words and actions of others, constructing their own perspective of what is being done and said. Social interaction allows alternative views to be addressed. The individual works on the meanings involved, construing them in an idiosyncratic way that develops as people express and reinforce their ideas. Sense-making can be an active process in which the individual is consciously working on ideas in order to develop an understanding compatible with wider experience. On the other hand, it might be more tacit as situations occur and, without conscious processing, the individual fits them into existing structures, perhaps to be recalled at some stage for further consideration.

The second way of seeing intersubjectivity is more fundamentally social. It sees knowledge as rooted in social structures and interactions, and inseparable from social, cultural and political forces in the community in which knowledge grows. It takes more account of environment, community and culture, overtly acknowledging these and not trying to separate individual cognition and intersubjectivity from these powerful forces on human thought.[8] I shall say more about such issues later in this chapter.

Analysis of the anecdote from a social constructivist perspective

Try to see what is going on from the point of view of Farooq, sitting on the floor, on a blanket in the classroom. He is surrounded by other small children and a few adults. There is activity around him. He is behaving as he is used to behaving in such a situation. He is participating in the activity of the classroom, albeit in a quiet, observant fashion. From this participation he is learning – how to sit on classroom floors, how to be part of the classroom group, what happens in classroom activities, what teachers say, what pupils say. When he responds to my questions it is from within his participation in this environment. The way he construes my actions is relative to his wider understandings in this setting and beyond, and his responses are part of the whole social context.

Gradually, he becomes familiar with what I am doing, and enters into it. He sees it relative to what he is familiar with, and his engagement is derivative of other social experiences in which he has participated. As he interacts with me and the materials, the particularities of this setting encourage a growth of understanding. It is through the two of us working together that our joint activity emerges. Eventually he seems to have made sense of my actions and to be replicating them himself. While we might have cast his 'coming to know' as a constructive act, it can also be seen as a socially enculturative act. His learning is derivative of the social interactions we have jointly experienced.

I have presented this other view deliberately to encourage you to contrast two seemingly different theoretical perspectives of the same practical situation, and to consider if they are compatible. Briefly we might consider them as the *constructive* versus the *enculturative*. In the first case, the learning is cast in terms of individual cognitive processes where the mental activity of the individual is actively fashioning the individual's knowledge, albeit influenced considerably by social interaction. In the second we see an enculturative process whereby the individual is gradually drawn into the social activity in which he is participating, with individual internalisation derivative of social participation.

Some people view these theories as incommensurable; that is they cannot both be tenable as they depend on quite different perceptions of knowledge. Others believe that theories are never adequate to explain the complexities of practice, and so alternative perspectives, even if strictly incompatible, serve as alternatively useful lenses into a situation, helping people to make sense of it.

However, I have not, as yet, addressed the teaching issues involved.

Vygotsky and Piaget on *teaching*

Vygotsky was born in the same year as Piaget (1896); he was in touch with Piaget's work and respected it. However, Vygotsky acknowledged an important difference between his perspective and that of Piaget. He wrote:

> Our disagreement with Piaget centres on one point only, but an important point. He assumes that development and instruction are entirely separate, incommensurable processes, that the function of instruction is merely to introduce adult ways of thinking, which conflict with the child's own and eventually supplant them. Studying child's thought apart from the influence of instruction, as Piaget did, excludes a very important source of change and bars the researcher from posing the question of the interaction of development and instruction peculiar to each age level. Our own approach focuses on this interaction.
>
> (Vygotsky, 1962, p. 116)

Piaget has written:

> Each time one prematurely teaches a child something he could have discovered himself, the child is kept from inventing it and consequently from understanding it completely.
>
> (Piaget, 1970, p. 715)

In the case of Farooq, this might suggest I had deprived him of inventing for himself the connections between 'thirteen' as a name for 13, and thirteen as the number of stones in one-to-one correspondence with the first thirteen positive integers. What are the implications of being so deprived? Is there an element of theory that suggests a child has to invent an idea for itself before understanding it? If so, how on earth are children going to encounter and construct, in a way that makes sense with wider social construction, all we want them to learn?[9]

Vygotsky wrote, in the quotation above, of the interaction of development and instruction. He offered a concept that acts as a sort of measure of the importance of the instruction. This is his Zone of Proximal Development, which he defines as:

> the distance between the actual developmental level as determined by independent problem-solving and the level of potential development as determined by problem-solving under adult guidance, or in collaboration with more capable peers.
>
> (Vygotsky, 1978, p. 86)

Coming back to Farooq again, one perspective is that our interaction enabled him to come to a perception of cardinality ahead of what might otherwise have occurred. His ability to perceive the relationship between the two manifestations of thirteen, as evidenced by what occurred, might be seen to suggest a potential to develop more rapidly with such interaction than without it. Of course I say this very tentatively as I spent too little time with Farooq really to make such judgments.

So what *is* constructivism?

It is hard to give you a definition of constructivism, as that would be to make an ontological statement that could be seen as incompatible with constructivist thought. I have tried to prepare the ground above through my use of the anecdote analysed from theoretical perspectives, albeit necessarily briefly. However, there are some things I can say, from my own perspective, and you will make your own interpretations that might be developed through discussion with others and in analysis of your own teaching situations.

Constructivism is a theory of 'coming to know'. This growth of knowledge occurs very fundamentally in social situations and with respect to social artefacts. It might be seen in two alternative ways, the first along the lines of Piagetian constructivism, the second of Vygotskian sociocultural theory. The first way involves the individual person as a cognising agent, making sense of the world around them, particularly their own social and cultural setting. As this individual interacts with their physical and social world, mental schemata are created through processes of assimilation and accommodation. Knowledge, for the individual, grows either explicitly or implicitly, relative to this cognitive processing. It is undeniable that the sociocultural world in which the individual is a part is a primary influence on cognition. The second way is to see any individual as a part of society or of social groupings interacting through their use of language and sociocultural tools. Any social grouping carries its own language, cultural forms and use of tools. Through participation in this society the individual is drawn into the culture, learns to speak in the way of the culture, and to behave as others do. This learning is derivative of cultural participation. It can be seen as an internalisation of cultural norms. Internalisation is seen to occur through language use.

At different times it may be useful to use one or other of these perspectives as they seem helpful in enabling us to make sense of learning and teaching situations. However, some scholars warn us that in doing so we may actually be encouraging contradictory positions on the status and meaning of knowledge, engaging with contradictory epistemologies. A fair critical analysis of these issues is beyond the scope of this chapter: however, briefly the issues are as follows. In the first position above, knowledge is a construction of the individual, and if there is any form of knowledge outside the individual it can only be known through individual experience. This makes it impossible to talk about 'truth', or the status of any item of knowledge, issues that are fundamental to epistemology. For this reason, Noddings (1990) has called constructivism 'post-epistemological'. Steffe argues that truth arises through intersubjectivity (see, for example, Steffe *et al.*, 2000). I have provided examples of such intersubjectivity and the issues it raises for knowledge construction in mathematics learning and teaching (Jaworski, 1994). In the second position, knowledge is a part of social fabric, that is, it does have existence independent of any individual, although all individuals are some part of the social fabric in which they interact, and they internalise knowledge as part of their interaction. Indeed the social fabric is constantly regenerated through language and interaction and it is in this way that knowledge grows. Intersubjectivity is common knowledge within a community. Truth is established within cultural intersubjectivity (see Lave, 1996; Lerman, 1996; Mercer, 1995). Jerome Bruner, in his address in Geneva in 1996 to celebrate the centenary of the birth of Piaget and Vygotsky, began with the words:

> What great good fortune for us, we students of human development, to have had two such giants, Jean Piaget and Lev Vygotsky inspiring our quest.

And he left us with the following thoughts:

> ... we are enormously fortunate to have had two such rich theoretical accounts as an inheritance from our mentors, even if they prove to be incommensurate. Just as depth perception requires a disparity between two views of a scene, so in human sciences the same must be true: depth demands disparity. So I conclude this excursion into the thoughts of these two great developmental psychologists with a salute to their profound difference.

Issues for mathematics learning and teaching in schools and classrooms in present-day societies

Relating to mathematics teaching and learning ...

One of the difficulties with mathematics as a subject is that mathematical concepts are not easily seen in the world around us. Mathematical ideas and skills are visible in everyday contexts in a wide variety of ways, but mathematical generality and abstraction are not. The power of mathematics lies in its nature to generalise and to express unambiguously in abstract forms. To grasp this power, students have not only to learn a variety of skills and their application, but also to relate mathematical ideas to each other and to the world around them, and to distinguish between the mathematical and the everyday. Research shows us that this is far from easy or straightforward. It is the task of a mathematics teacher to enable students to make, overall, a coherent sense of the subject: to develop skills and apply them in a wide range of contexts, and also to appreciate intrinsic mathematical forms and ways of expressing mathematics.

Where Farooq is concerned, a teacher needs to ensure he can count, that he can use numbers to order sets of objects, that he can recognise numbers as less than or greater than other numbers, and that he can see any number as a count of the objects in a set. He needs to be able to look at the written form of any number, e.g. 5, and be able to interpret it in any of these ways. He needs to be able to count to 5, both in terms of counting five everyday objects, and of counting in the abstract sequence, one, two, three, four, five; and he also needs to develop a general sense of *five-ness*. Thus he gains skills of using five but he sees also the *concept* of five as it relates to other numbers, and counts sets of objects.

For Farooq to gain such understanding, he needs opportunity to participate in activity through which he can encounter these mathematical ideas and come to know their meaning. This might be through activity in which he participates with the rest of his class, with a small group in the class, or with the teacher alone. In designing activities for all these settings the teacher will be creating a culture of mathematical learning in the classroom, providing opportunities for mathematical language to be used appropriately, for mathematical images to be developed and strengthened, and for students' mathematical understandings to become consistent with socially established understandings. The theories expressed above provide some starting points for thinking about how to satisfy such requirements and issues these raise for teachers (see, for example, Wood et al., 1993; Voigt, 1996; Jaworski, 1994).

Relating to the wider societal issues that affect schooling ...

Of course, none of this happens in a vacuum. The teacher had to deal with wider social contexts while providing suitable mathematical opportunity for learners. In the Pakistani classroom there was no furniture and few other resources. Activities had to be designed so that they could be done sitting on the floor. Homemade resources had to be made and used. Language used had to include all students, while working towards agreed common language use (either Urdu or English). Children whose parents could not afford fees, even very modest fees, had to be accommodated. The school was funded for only one teacher. Volunteer teachers had to be recruited and trained on the job, without pay. Buildings were inadequate and had to be adapted for use. Often lessons took place under a tree outside. The form of lessons and the nature of teaching were constrained by all these factors.

We might believe that the situation is much less problematic in a more socio-economically developed society, but this is not so. Wider social issues still prevail to influence what can be achieved: language issues, issues of race and social class, and differing needs of boys and girls. Social justice and issues of equity of provision raise serious questions for teachers in any system (see, for example, Chapter 14 by Peter Gates). The theoretical perspectives discussed above, focusing in a mainly psychological domain, might be seen not to take account of such issues that are largely sociological in nature. However, the design of classroom tasks to address mathematical concepts must take account of the social and cultural perceptions and expectations of students who are to engage with those tasks.

I shall highlight just one issue that has become evident in recent research. Theory has suggested that the use by teachers of everyday contexts in which to embed abstract mathematical ideas can be helpful to students in learning to cope with abstraction and make sense of the mathematics involved. Thus, questions and problems have been used that are set in real world (or pseudo real world) contexts in order to aid students' mathematical constructions. However, research now shows us that students from working-class backgrounds find it more difficult to see beyond the everyday context to the mathematics on which they are expected to focus, than are 'service-class' students. In practice, despite supposed contextual support, working-class students do less well (Cooper and Dunne, 2000; also Chapter 13 by Barry Cooper).

The challenge for theory

Constructivist theory, in whichever form, is useful in enabling us to think about knowledge and its growth, and ways in which learners come to know. It can be used, and research has used it, to describe and explain learning situations, particularly in the learning of mathematics. The growing awareness of learning and understanding and ways in which they can be encouraged and fostered is helpful in creating learning situations and monitoring learning. We are nevertheless alerted by theorists to dangers in our use of theories and our assumptions about application of theory.

However, the brief section on social issues, just above, alerts us to possibly more important considerations for learning and teaching than the compatibility or consistency of theories. In whatever ways we structure our approaches to learning and teaching, on whatever theoretical perspectives they are based, we cannot provide effective learning situations without addressing sociological issues, particularly those of equity and social justice.

It is currently a challenge for theorists, particularly constructivists, as to how theory addresses these huge social concerns. This could be one focus for the next decade of mathematics education research.

Acknowledgements

I should like to thank the Aga Khan University, Institute for Educational Development, Professional Development Centre North, in Gilgit, Pakistan, for enabling me to have the experiences reported in this article. In particular I should like to thank the Director, Gulzar Kanji, and Anila Kiani and the rest of the Professional Development Teacher team for their collaboration and the valuable discussions we had during my time at PDCN.

My thanks also go to Leo Rogers for a very helpful discussion on the history of mathematical concepts, and his contribution included here, and to John Jaworski for his insightful comments on the chapter as it developed.

Notes

1   The names used are pseudonyms.
2   Urdu is the national language of Pakistan.
3   Notice here an example of the wider social issues with which teachers have to work. No learning and teaching activity is independent of such issues. I return to wider social issues later on.
4   In personal communication, Leo Rogers, a historian of mathematics, has the following to say about ordinality and cardinality and my story of Farooq:

> Farooq's activities all seem to me to be to do with *ordinality*. He 'counts' the stones by placing them down in order, and associating the act of placing down with a verbal utterance (we like to call it a number word). Fundamentally, this is what I think (pure and simple) 'counting' is – the process of the association of a series of objects with a series of pointings and a series of noises. This is my interpretation of counting from various historical, archeological and anthropological sources.
>
> You could say that Farooq had learnt a ritual (that of 'naming' the stones and perhaps completing the circle) and he was showing you what he understood that he had to do in such a situation (respecting the teacher). You, on the other hand, were asking him to participate in another ritual; that of stopping at a certain point in the process. He was showing you what he could do, and you were showing him what you could do. At some stage in the process, he decided to play your game.
>
> The ability to recognise a sign '8' and say a word 'eight' is a learnt process of associating signs – written and verbal. This activity can be regarded as 'counting' the signs. I think *cardinality* emerges when we recognise that five pigs, five sheep, five baskets of wheat, etc. all have something in common – the fact that we can transfer the use of the sign '5' from the specific (qualitative) context to the general, (i.e. the very abstract idea that we can put them in one-to-one correspondence).

5   Knowledge: apprehension: knowing in the widest sense, including sensation, per- ception, etc. (Definition given in *Chambers English Dictionary*.)
6   Of psychology, *Chambers* says: 'Science of mind: study of mind and behaviour: attitudes, etc.'
7   In retrospect, I think I might have tried arranging the stones in a line. This would have obviated the necessity to complete the circle. However, at the time I didn't think of it, and hindsight is a wonderful thing – for a teacher it occurs very often! I need to try to learn from it for another time. Discussing the issue, as we are doing here, can help me to be more aware of the possibility.
8   These are hotly debated issues, and I am only skimming the surface here. See Confrey (1991, 1995), Lerman (1996) and Steffe (2000) for in-depth consideration of these issues.
9   See writing about teachers' tensions and dilemmas in Jaworski (1994, 1998).

References

Bruner, J. (1996) *Celebrating divergence: Piaget and Vygotsky*, keynote address delivered in Geneva on 15 September 1996, at a joint meeting of the *'Growing Mind Conference'* in honour of the centennial of Jean Piaget's birth and the *'Vygotsky-Piaget Conference'* of the 2nd Congress of Socio-Cultural Research.

Cobb, P. and Steffe, L.P. (1983) 'The constructivist researcher as teacher and model-builder', *Journal for Research in Mathematics Education* 14: 83–94.

Confrey, J. (1991) 'Steering a course between Vygotsky and Piaget', *Educational Researcher*, 20(2): 29–32.

Confrey, J. (1995) 'How compatible are radical constructivism, sociocultural approaches, and social constructivism?', in L.P. Steffe and J. Gale (eds) *Constructivism in Education*, Hove, UK: Lawrence Erlbaum Associates.

Cooper, B. and Dunne, M. (2000) *Assessing Children's Mathematical Knowledge: social class, sex and problem solving*, Buckingham: Open University Press.

Jaworski, B. (1994) *Investigating Mathematics Teaching: a constructivist enquiry*, London: Falmer Press.

Jaworski, B. (1998) 'Mathematics teacher research: process, practice and the development of teaching', *Journal of Mathematics Teacher Education*, 1(1): 3–31.

Lave, J. (1996) 'Teaching as learning, in practice', *Mind Culture and Activity* 3(3): 149–64.

Lave, J. and Wenger, E. (1991) *Situated Learning: legitimate peripheral participation*, Cambridge, MA: Cambridge University Press.

Lerman, S. (1996) 'Intersubjectivity in mathematics learning: a challenge to the radical constructivist paradigm', *Journal for Research in Mathematics Education*, 27(2), Reston, VA: National Council of Teachers of Mathematics.

Mercer, N. (1995) *The Guided Construction of Knowledge: talk amongst teachers and learners*, Clevedon: Multilingual Matters.

Noddings, N. (1990) 'Constructivism in mathematics teaching', in R.B Davis, C.A Maher and N. Noddings (eds) 'Constructivist views on the learning and teaching of mathematics', *Journal for Research in Mathematics Education*, Monograph, No. 4, Reston, VA: National Council of Teachers of Mathematics: 7–18.

Piaget, J. (1950) *The Psychology of Intelligence*, London: Routledge and Kegan Paul.

Piaget, J. (1970) 'Piaget's theory', in P.H. Mussen (ed.) *Carmichael's Manual of Child Psychology*, New York: Wiley.

Piaget, J. and Inhelder, B. (1966) *The Psychology of the Child*, London: Routledge and Kegan Paul.

Steffe, L.P. and Thompson, P.W. (2000) 'Interaction or intersubjectivity? A reply to Lerman', *Journal for Research in Mathematics Education* 31(2).

Voigt, J. (1996) 'Negotiation of mathematical meaning in classroom processes: social interaction and learning mathematics', in P. Steffe, P. Nesher, P. Cobb *et al.* (eds) *Theories of Mathematical Learning*, NJ: Lawrence Erlbaum.

von Glasersfeld, E. (1987) 'Learning as a constructive activity', in C. Janvier (ed.) *Problems of Representation in the Teaching and Learning of Mathematics*, NJ: Lawrence Erlbaum.

von Glasersfeld, E. (1990) 'An exposition of constructivism: why some like it radical', in R.B Davis, C.A Maher and N. Noddings (eds) 'Constructivist views on the learning and teaching of mathematics', *Journal for Research in Mathematics Education*, Monograph, No. 4, Reston, VA: National Council of Teachers of Mathematics.

Vygotsky, L.S. (1962) *Thought and Language*, Cambridge, MA: M.I.T. Press.

Vygotsky, L.S. (1978) *Mind in Society. The development of the higher psychological processes*, London: Harvard University Press.

Vygotsky, L.S. (1981) 'The genesis of higher mental functions', in J.V. Wertsch (ed.) *The Concept of Activity in Soviet Psychology*, Armonk: Sharpe.

Wood, T., Cobb, P., Yackel, E. and Dillon, D. (1993) (eds) 'Rethinking elementary school mathematics: insights and issues', *Journal for Research in Mathematics Education*, Monograph No. 6, Reston, VA: National Council of Teachers of Mathematics.

6 'Magical' moments in mathematics

Insights into the process of coming to know

Mary Barnes

Introduction

At the end of a mathematics lesson, Naidra, an eleventh-grade student, was asked to reflect on what he had learned and how this learning had come about. He talked about the advantages of working in a group and 'getting your ideas out into the open'. The following exchange then took place:

I: I wonder if there was any particularly significant moment during the lesson, anything particular that someone said, because we could play back a little bit of this to you on the video.

N: No, I really don't think anything magical happened today.

I: No? Do magical things sometimes happen in lessons?

N: Just, um, flashes of understanding can happen, and that's … it's great when it happens.

I: … Can you think of a time when that happened, a sudden flash of understanding?

N: Oh, it's happened a lot. It doesn't have to happen in a lesson. It's just, you suddenly understand something that you didn't follow, and lots of different things can spark that off. And when it happens, it's good.

I was delighted, if a little surprised, by the use of the word 'magical' in relation to mathematics lessons. The claim that 'It's great when it happens' suggested that these flashes of insight were highly motivating. This exchange aroused my curiosity and interest, and prompted me to investigate 'magical' moments – to seek to understand what they are and how they happen, to look for examples and to reflect on their impact on students' mathematics learning.

Describing 'magical' moments

References in the literature

That sudden flash of understanding, which Naidra described as magical, is often referred to in the literature as the 'Aha!' or 'Eureka!' experience. It has frequently been described by mathematicians writing about the creative process. Gauss spoke of 'a sudden flash of lightning' (Hadamard, 1945, p. 15). Hadamard (ibid.), drawing on the ideas of Poincaré, described stages in the creative process as preparation (a period of intensive conscious work on a problem), incubation (a period of rest or relaxation away from the problem) and illumination (when a solution suddenly becomes clear). Poincaré also linked mathematical insight with an appreciation of the aesthetics of mathematics. Polya spoke of:

> ... a sudden clarification that brings light, order, connection, and purpose to details which before appeared obscure, confused, scattered and elusive.
>
> (Polya, 1965, p. 54)

while Davis and Hersh referred to:

> ... the flash of insight, the breakthrough, the 'aha', symbolizes that something has been brought forth which is genuinely new, a new understanding for the individual, a new concept placed before the larger community.
>
> (Davis and Hersh, 1980, pp. 283–4)

More recently, Rota (1997), like Poincaré, linked insight with the appreciation of mathematical beauty:

> ... we think back to instances of appreciation of mathematical beauty as if they had been perceived in a moment of bliss, in a sudden flash like a light bulb being lit. The effort put into understanding the proof, the background material, the difficulties encountered in unravelling an intricate sequence of inferences fade and magically disappear the moment we become aware of the beauty of a theorem. The painful process of learning fades from memory and only the flash of insight remains.
>
> (Rota, 1997, p. 130)

Many of the mathematicians interviewed by Burton (1999a, 1999b) described, sometimes in almost lyrical terms, feelings of joy, excitement or euphoria accompanying the sense of 'Aha!'. Making a new discovery, or finding a new connection were compared with a light switching on, climbing a mountain and seeing the view from the top, finding a new path through unfamiliar terrain, or seeing how to fit pieces into a jigsaw.

Only a few mathematics educators have written about the 'Aha!' experience, but those who have done so have stressed its importance. For example, McLeod (1989), writing about affective responses to mathematical problem-solving, claimed that although frustration is the most common emotion encountered, the 'Aha!' experience is also perceived very intensely. He stressed the positive emotions that accompany the moment of insight, and suggested that 'emotional responses can play a significant role in students' learning of mathematics' (McLeod, 1992, p. 583).

A characterisation of 'magical' moments

Naidra, in the interview quoted earlier, described these moments as sudden flashes of understanding, adding 'It's great when it happens.' Another student, Simon, was asked about such moments, and said:

> It happens, it happens in most projects, when ... you're just looking and look-ing over again, and then it just happens and you're on your way again. ... I mean, you can just keep throwing forward ideas and stuff and then one – like a word or something – it might just click, I don't know, it's just really that.

I noticed that the students' descriptions had a great deal in common with those I had found in the literature. This led me to formulate the following characterisation of a 'magical' moment:

- There is a claim to a sudden realisation of new knowledge or understanding. Usually this new knowledge is 'seen' with great clarity, or experienced with a high degree of confidence or certainty.
- The realisation of new knowledge is accompanied by a positive emotional response, which may be described variously as joy, delight, pleasure, excite-ment, triumph, satisfaction, surprise or relief.

For the students, the sudden realisation of new knowledge was expressed when they spoke of 'a flash of understanding', 'it might just click' and 'different things can spark that off.' The positive emotional response was evident from the repetition in Naidra's statements – 'It's great when it happens' and 'When it happens, it's good.' Simon's emotional response gives a strong impression of anxiety followed by relief when 'you're on your way again.'

In what follows I first give some examples of 'magical' moments observed in one partic-ular classroom. I then reflect on these examples from the point of view of the learner, focusing on why these incidents might be regarded as important and how they come about. Following this, I give a description of the classroom context in which these incidents occurred, and use this to formulate some hypotheses about what mathematics teachers might do to encourage 'magical' moments. Finally, I draw some tentative conclusions and suggest some issues that I believe warrant further research.

Classroom examples of 'magical' moments

The observations reported here took place in an eleventh-grade class (students aged 16–17) in a co-educational high school in Melbourne. The students in this class had chosen to study an integrated mathematics course, which included some introductory calculus. I videotaped a few lessons in this classroom as part of a larger study and, after Naidra's remark had aroused my curiosity about 'magical' moments, I modified the questions for subsequent interviews and reviewed the taped lessons, to investigate the occurrence of this phenomenon.

To illustrate 'magical' moments observed in the classroom I have, for reasons of brevity, chosen examples from a single lesson. The group whose work is reported consisted of two boys, Simon and Naidra, and two girls, Maria and Lida (pseud-onyms chosen by the students). Simon and Naidra had worked together before but never with either of the girls. Lida had arrived from Europe about two months ear-lier, and her English was still very limited. She appeared to lack confidence and spoke rarely, but assured me that she was able to follow the discussions in the group. She claimed that she felt no need to say anything because she agreed with what the others were saying.

The problem

The class was working on 'The Theatre Confectionery Pack' problem (Williams, 1990, pp. 27–8). Briefly, each group was given a sheet of paper 20 cm by 30 cm, with instructions on how to fold it into an open box suitable for holding candy. Then they were asked to work out how to vary the positions of the folds to obtain a larger box. This problem is a more complex variant of the standard open-box problem familiar to calculus students. Figure 6.1 shows the diagram given in the instructions, with variables introduced by the group added. Figure 6.2 shows a completed box as seen from below.

It is important to note that the class had never had a formal lesson on maximum–minimum problems. This activity was the third of a series designed to have the students develop techniques for solving such problems and reflect on the concepts involved. Earlier in the year, they had worked on a project to find gradients of graphs. As a result, they knew the definition of a derivative and could differentiate polynomials, but their only knowledge about finding maxima and minima was what they had discovered in the course of the previous two activities. They had been given no rules or procedures, nor had the teacher attempted to summarise for the class what they had learned.

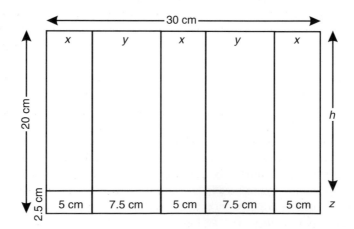

Figure 6.1 Net for the confectionery box

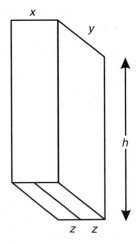

Figure 6.2   The finished box

Outline of the group's solution process

A summary of the group's steps in solving the problem is included to assist readers to follow the excerpts from the transcript which follows.

- During the previous lesson the group had made a box, following the instructions and using the measurements given.
- At the beginning of the lesson reported here, they introduced variables x, y, h, and z, as shown in Figure 6.1, and used these to write down the two equations $3x + 2y = 30$ and $h = 20 - z$. They wondered aloud whether x and y were related to z and h in some way.
- Next they rewrote the first equation in the form $y = -{}^3/_2 x + 15$ and graphed it, but were not sure what the graph told them.
- Simon noticed that they had two linear equations, and began to solve them simultaneously – ignoring the fact that the variables in them were different. He simply changed h to y and z to x. After a while, he realised that this gave meaningless results.
- Meanwhile, Maria noticed that z always had to be half of x if the two flaps were to fit together properly to form the base. She made a couple of attempts to point this out, and eventually the others listened to her. This was a key step, setting them on a pathway towards a solution of the problem.
- They realised they could make a table of values of x, y, z, h and V (the volume of the box) and used this in a systematic way to find the maximum volume.
- As they calculated entries for the table, they became aware that only some values of the variables made sense in the context. This led them to interpret the equation $y = -{}^3/_2 x + 15$ and its graph as giving information about the domain of the independent variable.
- Finally, they decided to use calculus to get a more precise answer, and after

some discussion they derived an equation for the volume as a function of x. They were expanding this in preparation for differentiating it when the lesson ended.

'Magical' moment 1: it's half of x

When the students were looking for relationships among the variables x, y, h, and z, Maria had an idea. After a couple of false starts, she managed to make herself heard.

M: It's half (*pointing to the model*) because like, it seems like, (*indistinct*), you see how, here, this is half of the base …
S: Is that just a coincidence?

No further attention was paid to Maria's remark, and she did not pursue it. Six minutes later, the group was still stuck, and discussed making another box with different dimensions. Simon read the instructions aloud again, then held the box and turned it over and over, while the rest watched. Maria tried again.

M: I just thought, it's got to be half of x, so it will fold up.
S: It goes, hang on, is this x? (*Four seconds pause, while he studies the model.*)
M: (*indistinct*)
S: You're right, it is! (*looks towards Maria and nods emphatically*).
N: (*to Maria*) So z has to be half of x.
S: (*to Naidra, excitedly*) Because look, this is z, and this is x, so it's always going to be half. (*turns to Maria*) It's not a coincidence. Well done!

Simon's reaction makes it clear that this was a 'magical' moment for him. He finally understood what Maria had been saying, and acknowledged this. His positive emotional response was indicated by his excited manner of speech, and the way he explain the whole thing again to Naidra, although Naidra had already acknowledged that he understood it.

Why did the boys not grasp this idea when Maria first pointed it out? My first thought was that they had not paid much attention to what Maria said – perhaps they were not expecting her to make a helpful observation, because they did not know her well, and were unaware of her mathematical and problem-solving abilities, or perhaps they held preconceptions about gender and mathematical competence. But this interpretation does not stand up to scrutiny. Simon's remark, 'It's not a coincidence,' indicates that he had indeed paid attention to what Maria said, and had kept it in mind during the ensuing six minutes of discussion.

An alternative interpretation is that when Maria first made her observation, the boys were not ready to take it in. The fact that Maria did not respond to Simon's question, 'Is that just a coincidence?' may indicate that she herself was unsure of the validity or significance of her claim. It is worth noting that they did not have a diagram like Figure 6.2 to study, but were working from Figure 6.1 and their model, which had not been labelled with the variables x, y, z, and h. When they began to consider how they could alter one dimension of the box, they re-read the instructions and studied the model more carefully. They then began to wonder about how any change would affect the other dimensions, and at this point Maria's suggestion may suddenly have made more sense.

'Magical' moment 2: restricting the domain

Very early in the session, the group derived an equation connecting x and y, expressed it as $y = -\,^3/_2\,x + 15$ and drew a graph of this in the x–y plane.

S: Um, but I don't know what the hell that gives us.
N: Well, it's the possible widths that it can be.

It could be inferred from this that Naidra had realised that the graph could be used to work out the domain of x. When the teacher joined the group, Simon explained it to her, saying:

S: … and we've got a graph, to show us where, if you pick an x value or a y value, you can find out what the other is.

This suggests that Simon saw the graph as useful only for finding x from y, or vice versa – he had just used it in this way to check their working. Since he was normally an articulate student, I assume that if he was aware of the more complex understanding hinted at by Naidra, he did not at that moment see it as relevant to the problem.

About 22 minutes later, the group had worked out how to express all of the variables in the problem in terms of x and were drawing up a table of values. Simon discovered that $x = 16$ gave a negative value for y.

S: And now I find out that y equals negative 9, which is impossible. Which means there's a domain and a range, x can't go over 10.
N: Of course it can't, it's unrealistic.

This was the first mention of the technical terms 'domain' and 'range'. For Simon, it appears to represent a shift from regarding the relationship simply in terms of ordered pairs of numbers to invoking some of the language and concepts associated with the idea of a function. The tone of Naidra's reply suggested that this was obvious to him and Simon had said nothing new.

Nearly two minutes later, the following exchange took place:

S: Why can't it go above 10? (five seconds pause)
N: 'Cos you get a negative y.

Later, the teacher joined the group again, and asked them to explain what they

gain, Simon was the spokesperson and explained what they had dis-
the domain.

s it have to be between zero and ten?
here's three of them, and if it was ten, there'd be thirty, and there's
no room for ys, and anything above. And on the graph it shows our domain,
… and our range, y can't be bigger than 15.

Naidra later described this series of exchanges as giving him insight. It seems here as though Simon and Naidra were thinking aloud, as they jointly constructed a deeper understanding of the connection between the dimensions of the box, the possible y values and their graph. This new understanding made such an impression on Naidra that, when it was the group's turn to report one interesting thing they had discovered to the rest of the class, this is what he suggested they should talk about. He mentioned this when interviewed.

I: I'm interested in moments when something became clear, or when you suddenly made sense of something. Can you tell me if that happened?

N: Oh, it happened on a few occasions.

I: … Can you tell me about one of them?

N: OK, how about what I said when I was at the board, um, restricting the domain.

I: Restricting the domain, yes. Now how did that become clear to you?

N: Well, Simon was the one who came up with it, and he just, I guess he just realised that if you solve for y, that'll give you a rule, make it possible to graph it, and therefore be able to see where there's a restricted domain. … Yes, well, once Simon showed it to us, and we could all see what he was doing with it, it just became clear.

I: So was there something particular made it clear?

N: Um, sometimes, it just presents itself, I think. And, this was one of those times, it just became clear, when it wasn't a second before. That's what happened.

This description satisfies all of my criteria for a 'magical' moment: Naidra claims to have achieved a new understanding, experienced it as 'clear, when it wasn't a second before' and his emotional response is evidenced by his desire to explain the newly grasped idea to the class.

When the group first discussed the meaning of the equation, Naidra appeared to understand better than Simon what it told them, and said so three times, but from his own account it was not until later, when he heard Simon explain it, that he realised the full significance of the idea. In the initial exchanges, this incident may not seem like a 'magical' moment. It appears that coming to know is sometimes so gradual that students fail to recognise *that* they know, or *what* they know. Yet, when something is finally seen clearly, they experience a moment of illumination, and the former uncertainty is completely forgotten. Here, although Naidra himself first articulated the idea that the equation told them about 'the possible widths', it was not until Simon linked this with the formal language of domain and range *and* the physical shape of the box that he experienced a moment when 'it just became clear'.

'Magical' moment 3: too many variables

Early in the discussion, Simon worried that there were too many variables:

S: ...we can't have three variables in an equation.
N: Why can't you?
S: No, I mean, in a graph like, you can't graph something with three variables (*Naidra nods.*) You have to get it down to two, so you have a y and x (*gestures, begins to draw*).

Much later, after the group had realised that z is half of x, they began to discuss making a table so as to calculate the volume systematically. Simon began to draw up the table using values they had already calculated. Naidra interrupted him:

N: Could I suggest that we ... choose one variable to work it around, and then work from the lowest to the highest possible one, using integers in the table. In that way we get a really good table, you know, that we can see.
S: We could, yeah, okay, I was just – so like, to start with our height as being 1, and then do 2, and then 3, and then get up to 19. Okay we'll do that. I'll just work out these two volumes. How much was this?
N: No hang on, I think we should work around x, because, um, z is x over 2, (*one second pause*) ... alright? ... We can say that x is the variable and the rest are dependent variables.
S: Oh but what about y? I think –
N: Yeah, y is a dependent variable, 'cos if you take, if you work around x.
S: Oh yeah, but I mean, you can say, there's another way of saying it, that if you work around y, you can work out the rest of them then. If I say y equals 5 –
N: But z is not y over 2.
S: You can work out what x is, through y, and then work out z, but yeah, we'll work around x, which is probably more neater, but I'm saying the only thing that we can't work around is height, although, you could probably get to all answers through height as well.
N: Yeah.
S: But I mean, x is probably the easiest, yeah.

When they began the table, Simon had not fully thought through how they would do it. His initial proposal was to start with height. This was contradicted in his later statement, 'but I'm saying the only thing we couldn't work around is height,' which he then immediately contradicted again. Simon, it seems, was only thinking of filling in numbers in a table.

Naidra raised the discussion to a more formal theoretical level by bringing in the idea of [independent] variables and dependent variables. This may have helped Simon to conceptualise the relationships between the variables in a different, and more powerful, way. By the end of the extract Simon was quite clear that any of x, y, z or even h could be treated as the independent variable, and the others expressed in terms of it. But he was still thinking of a chain of relationships enabling each variable to be calculated from the next. As the next extract shows, he had not realised that this implied that V, the volume of the box, could be expressed as a function of x alone (or of any of the other variables alone). Naidra, too, was probably thinking of a chain of relationships. His concern to 'work around' x seems to have been largely because he thought it would be more efficient.

The group proceeded with their table of values, and used it to find an approximate maximum volume. Finally, they began to think of calculus, and decided, 'We definitely have to do a derivative'.

S: Yes, but, we need an, an equation for the graph, which we don't have.
N: Yeah, that's it, exactly.
S: Do you want to try and graph the whole thing, try and, because we've got three variables, that's what I don't –
N: We don't have three variables.
S: Oh, because we can do x over two. (*very excitedly*) Look what we can do.
N: What can we … ?
M: That's for z.
N: All right, I'm looking.
S: Well basically volume equals x times y times h. So volume, if we want just one, we can relate it all to one variable, that's x and then we'll have two variables to graph. (*Simon then explained how to write an equation for the volume in terms of x alone.*) So that's what y equals –
N: Ohhh, that's brilliant –
S: And this is what height equals and our x value –
N: Oh, that's, that's brilliant –
S: Now we've got two variables, we can graph it! Just expand it, and we can graph it! Just expand it –
N: Oh, that is beautiful.

In the interview that followed, Naidra was asked about this incident.

I: OK, now there was another time, when you suddenly said, 'Oh, that's wonderful, that's brilliant, beautiful!' Now, what was that?
N: Um, I think that was Simon again, um, we, I could see where the volume was going to be x times y times 20 minus z (*He gave a detailed explanation.*) … Simon saw that, came up with it, and then I saw it … he explained it to me.

This was a 'magical' moment for both Simon and Naidra. For Simon, this is clear from the statement, 'Look what we can do,' his excitement as he said it, the many repetitions, and the way he kept talking over Naidra's interjections, until in the end he had explained the whole thing twice. And Naidra's response leaves no doubt as to how he felt.

Notice that Naidra first pointed out that they could treat x as the independent variable and the rest as dependent variables. Simon then developed this, saying that any of the three variables could play the role of independent variable. Later, when they began to derive an expression for the volume, Simon's feeling that they had too many variables returned, and Naidra had to remind him that this was not so. But when Simon adopted his suggestion, the final result came as a revelation to Naidra. In the interview he was certain the whole thing was Simon's idea. It is as though he 'knew' at some preliminary level, but did not know that he knew until he heard it explained by Simon.

Was this a 'magical' moment?

As the students made a table, starting with $x = 1$ and increasing by one at each step, they noticed that y, z and h changed by constant amounts from row to row but V did not. Naidra suggested that this was because V was a cubic function. When the table was complete, Naidra looked at it and said, 'Um, that's beautiful, that table, it really is, it really gives you insight,' and about 30 seconds later, 'but I've got a very happy feeling about this problem, I do, I've got to say.'

These reflective statements express aesthetic appreciation and strong positive affect, but the claim to new knowledge is less clear. Naidra's use of the word 'insight' seems to be more a reflection on what he had observed earlier than a claim to a new understanding at that instant. Thus it may not be a 'magical' moment according to my definition, but it certainly demonstrates the close relationship for this student between learning, aesthetic appreciation and positive emotions.

Reflections on the learning context

Should we value 'magical' moments?

Are 'magical' moments important enough for us to be concerned about recognising and encouraging them?

I believe that the pleasure and excitement which these events produce are of value both for their own sake, and because they may influence students' continued participation and performance in mathematics. Burton noted the importance of moments of insight for the mathematicians in her study, reporting that the excitement and euphoria experienced are 'what holds them in mathematics' (Burton, 1999a, p. 135). We may surmise that learners who experience similar feelings will also be profoundly influenced.

McLeod (1992) pointed out that 'emotional responses can play a significant role in students' learning of mathematics' (p. 583). He explained that although an emotional response may be fairly transient, if students repeatedly encounter similar emotions in mathematics, this can lead to the development of positive attitudes.

Attitudes are more stable than emotions, however intensely felt. Naidra's 'happy feeling' quoted above may illustrate the effect of repeated positive feelings beginning to produce positive attitudes.

The confidence and clarity with which new knowledge is perceived in a 'magical' moment are important. Rather than interpreting other people's explanations, the students have constructed the knowledge for themselves – they have 'authorship' of the ideas. This provides an important element of self-affirmation, encouraging them to have confidence in their capacity to master new mathematics in the future. It may also mean that the new knowledge is better understood and recalled than knowledge achieved without the same struggle and flash of insight.

How do 'magical' moments happen?

In each of the examples cited, the moment of insight was associated with *changing the way of looking at the problem* or with *making a connection between the immediate problem and more general mathematical concepts or structures* or both.

For example, the first 'magical' moment involved seeing the box in a new way – instead of concentrating on the net diagram given in the instructions, the students began to study in detail the box they had made, and this helped them to see that when the two little flaps, each of width z, were folded up, they met in the middle, and together equalled the width of the box. The second 'magical' moment was associated with a shift from thinking of the equation they had derived as giving information about pairs of numbers, to noting how it related to the way the paper had to be folded, and to seeing the equation as a function and linking it with properties such as domain and range. And in the third example the students made a shift from seeing the set of relationships they had derived as rules for calculating entries in a table, to thinking of them as functions, linking this to the idea of independent and dependent variables, and realising that they could use these relationships to express the volume as a function of a single variable. Thus 'magical' moments appear to involve seeing things from a new perspective, and may also be associated with increased formalisation.

Received wisdom from many mathematicians (Hadamard, 1945; Davis and Hersh, 1980) suggests that, after an initial period of intensive work on a problem, one can put it aside, relax and think of other things, and a moment of insight may come 'out of the blue'. Rota (1997), on the other hand, stressed the process of struggle, eventually culminating in a flash of insight, and suggested that the effort and the difficulties may often be forgotten in the euphoria of the 'Aha!' experience.

The incidents I have described fit better with Rota's description, although occasions when insight came 'out of the blue' could have occurred at times when the students were not being observed. As Naidra remarked, 'It doesn't have to happen in a lesson.' According to their own reports, the students I observed certainly experienced the 'magical' moment as a sudden insight, but the process of groping towards it was quite long and confused. Understanding seemed to develop through uncertainty and struggle, but there came a moment at the end when everything was suddenly clear. In each example described, a process of preparation seemed to be necessary before the insight could occur, but the data are insufficient to indicate what forms of preparation might be most helpful.

Reflections on the pedagogical context

The teaching approach in the class observed

While many instructional strategies may lead to the occurrence of 'magical' moments, the teaching approach employed in this study was sufficiently structured to warrant a description of its key features.

Challenging problems

The usual procedure in the class was for groups of four students to work for three or four lessons on a challenging, open-ended investigation. The teacher designed these activities with the aim of enabling students to develop for themselves the mathematics needed, by working on the activity in small groups and then discussing and comparing their ideas with the rest of the class. Before such an activity began, there was no formal teaching of the mathematical content. At most 10 minutes might be used to introduce the topic.

Group composition and teamwork

The teacher chose the groups for each activity, taking into account the complexity of the task and her knowledge of the students' personalities and mathematical capabilities. Groups were expected to work together as teams and to resolve their problems by collaborative efforts.

The teacher's role

As groups brainstormed and developed their ideas, the teacher moved around, listening to and sometimes joining in group discussions. She asked questions to elicit progress, to help students clarify their understanding, to prompt them to elaborate explanations, to help groups refocus and so facilitate a breakthrough, to encourage generalisation or extension of the original problem, or to elicit evaluation. She avoided answering questions, giving hints or indicating whether an explanation or an approach was 'correct'. She made a habit of asking a question and then walking away, leaving the group to think about it for themselves.

Reporting

After about 20 minutes' work on a problem, each group was asked to report its progress to the whole class. The teacher decided the order of reporting, and sometimes nominated which parts of their material groups should report on, to ensure that each group would have something new to contribute. After a reporting session, students returned to their groups for further work on the problem, and the cycle continued. The reporting session allowed students to see how other groups approached problems and to realise that there is no single 'correct' method. The students were encouraged to ask questions of the student at the board, either to clarify their own understanding or because they suspected a flaw in the justification, but were not permitted to criticise until it was their own turn to present.

Related activities

Between problem-solving sessions, the class might work on other mathematical activities, perhaps even on a different topic. Where possible, these activities were designed to introduce ideas that might help in solving the problem – but the students were not made aware of this.

Classroom norms

The teacher's approach strongly emphasised social norms which she believed would help to create a supportive learning environment in which all students would feel able to take risks. These included collaborating effectively within groups, showing consideration for other people's feelings and acknowledging other people's contributions. In addition, she stressed certain socio-mathematical norms (Yackel and Cobb, 1996) such as the need to justify assertions and an appreciation of aesthetic aspects of mathematics.

What might teachers do to promote 'magical' moments?

Anyone may experience occasional flashes of insight while trying to solve an unfamiliar problem, or seeking to understand mathematics in a coherent and meaningful way. From time to time a breakthrough will be experienced, when something is seen in a new way, and its significance becomes clear, or its links with some other part of mathematics are understood. Such events happen no matter what the teacher's level of competence, or what style of teaching is used. We might surmise, however, that 'magical' moments would be less likely to occur in expository teaching, where work on problems is preceded by carefully-structured preparatory explanations and guided practice. If instruction progresses by small, simple steps, and the teacher anticipates difficulties and provides immediate clarification, students will have less need to struggle and less occasion to make efforts of their own to achieve understanding and insight.

The level of challenge in the task seems to be critical. With too much challenge, many students will be unable to make headway and will become frustrated; with too little, a solution will be too easily attained, and students will have little need to strive for insight. Since closed tasks are less likely to meet the needs of all students, open-ended problems with a variety of entry and exit points are indicated.

Interaction among students can reveal different ways of thinking about a topic, and may provide some with the key to solving a problem or understanding a new concept. This is perhaps what Simon was referring to when he said, 'A word or something ... might just click.' Discussing problems in small groups should increase the chance of any one student experiencing a flash of insight, because more talk should mean a greater variety of ideas being proposed.

A focus on understanding processes rather than on getting answers quickly may also be important. Each individual needs to be made responsible for ensuring that (s)he has understood and can explain the method of solution. One way of ensuring that students accept this responsibility is to require them to justify their solutions to the rest of the class, as happened in the class I observed. If it is the responsibility of the other students to validate the justifications provided, everyone must think seriously about them. At the same time a wider range of approaches to each problem is placed before the class. In these ways, each student's opportunity to have a moment of insight may be increased.

The class in the study had a rule, 'Don't spoil things for others,' which I believe was directly related to the frequent occurrence of 'magical' moments. Students were asked to avoid telling other groups how to do something until the teacher decided that it was time for sharing, and indicated how much should be shared. Co-construction was valued, but not direct telling.

Encouraging reflection may be another important way to facilitate 'magical' moments. A problem that can be solved in a short time provides less opportunity for this, because one quick thinker in a group may see immediately how to solve it, and leave little work for the rest. Extended problems requiring work over a longer period provide more scope for reflection, and make it easier for less quick-thinking group members to contribute.

Conclusion

The episodes I have described clearly have an important motivational value. Although a single event may not make a great difference to students' attitudes, the cumulative effect of many such moments has the potential to influence profoundly their dispositions towards mathematics. If we want students to learn to love mathematics, and to experience joy and self-affirmation through doing mathematics, I suggest that we should endeavour to structure our classrooms so as to cultivate 'magical' moments. There is also a probable cognitive benefit. My examples indicate that 'magical' moments may be associated with understanding an idea with great clarity, gaining a new perspective on a mathematical concept and, possibly, with increased levels of formalisation and perceiving links between hitherto unrelated ideas.

Many metaphors have been used to describe moments of insight in mathematics: a flash of lightning, a spark, things fitting together with a click. My preferred metaphor captures the idea of sudden illumination leading to deeper understanding: it is the image of someone stumbling around in a dark room, bumping into objects and failing to realise what they are, and then finally finding the light switch. When the light goes on, they are not only able to see clearly where they are going, but can also see where they have been, recognise the objects they bumped into on the way and see how they are placed in relation to one another.

Acknowledgments

I should like to thank David Clarke and Leone Burton for their helpful advice and comments on earlier versions of this manuscript, and Gaye Williams for the privilege of observing and videotaping her classroom and for many valuable conversations about her teaching approach. I am grateful to the students for allowing me to videotape their discussions and for sharing with me their reflections on their learning.

References

Burton, L. (1999a) 'The practices of mathematicians: what do they tell us about coming to know mathematics?', *Educational Studies in Mathematics* 37: 121–43.

Burton, L. (1999b) 'Why is intuition so important to mathematicians but missing from mathematics education.' *For the Learning of Mathematics* 19(3): 27–32.

Davis, P.J. and Hersh, R. (1980) *The Mathematical Experience*, Boston, MA: Birkhäuser.

Hadamard, J. (1945) *An Essay on the Psychology of Invention in the Mathematical Field*, Princeton, NJ: Princeton University Press.

McLeod, D.B. (1989) 'The role of affect in mathematical problem solving', in D.B. McLeod and V.M. Adams (eds) *Affect and Mathematical Problem Solving: a new perspective*, New York:Springer-Verlag: 20–36.

McLeod, D.B. (1992) 'Research on affect in mathematics education: a reconceptualization', in D.A. Grouws (ed.) *Handbook of Research on Mathematics Teaching and Learning*, New York: Macmillan: 575–96.

Polya, G. (1965) *Mathematical Discovery: on understanding, learning and teaching problem solving*, 2 (Combined edition, 1981), New York: Wiley.

Rota, G-C. (1997) *Indiscrete thoughts*, Boston, MA: Birkhäuser.

Williams, G. (1990) *Change and Approximation: problem solving and projects related to course content*, St Arnaud, VI: Gaye Williams Publications.

Yackel, E. and Cobb, P. (1996) 'Sociomathematical norms, argumentation, and autonomy in mathematics', *Journal for Research in Mathematics Education* 27: 458–77.

7 Open and closed mathematics approaches

Student experiences and understandings

Jo Boaler

Introduction

There is a growing concern within mathematics education that many students are unable to use the mathematics they learn in school, in situations outside the classroom context (Masingila, 1993; Nunes, Schliemann and Carraher, 1993). This has led educators to suggest that teachers depart from 'drill and practice' methods of teaching, and engage students in mathematical problem-solving. It has been recommended that students are given open-ended, practical and investigative work that requires them to make their own decisions, plan their own routes through tasks, choose methods, and apply their mathematical knowledge. The reported benefits generally relate to increased enjoyment and understanding (Silver, 1994; Winograd, 1991; Perez, 1985), to equality of opportunity (Burton, 1986), and even to enhanced transfer (The Cognition and Technology Group at Vanderbilt, 1990). Research into the effectiveness of problem-oriented teaching (see, for example, Cobb *et al.*, 1992; Charles and Lester, 1984) is, however, limited, partly because such teaching approaches are rare.

In recent years in the UK there has been an official legitimisation of open approaches to mathematics teaching, through the Government-sponsored Cockcroft report of 1982 (Cockcroft, 1982) and then through the National Curriculums of 1989 and 1991 (DES, 1989, 1991) which made the teaching of process-based work statutory. In the US the 'NCTM Standards' (National Council of Teachers of Mathematics, 1989, 2000) offered a similar legitimisation of process-based approaches. More recently, we experienced a Conservative backlash in the UK against all forms of progressive education and a set of policies that politicians and the media have termed 'back-to-basics'. These policies include support for learning by rote, an emphasis upon arithmetic and numeracy and the following of set methods and rules (Ball, 1994). These 'back-to-basics' policies stand as a direct threat to the emergence of a new form of mathematics education that many believed was going to change school mathematics into a subject that students would find more enjoyable, understandable, and relevant (Burton, 1995, 1986).

Research methods

In order to investigate the experiences and understandings students develop in different teaching environments, I conducted ethnographic, three-year case studies (Eisenhart, 1988) of two schools. As part of the case studies, I performed a longitudinal cohort analysis of a 'year group' of students in each school, as they moved from Year 9 (age 13) to Year 11 (age 16). To understand the students' experiences of mathematics, I observed between 80 and 100 lessons in each school, usually taking the role of a participant observer. I interviewed approximately 20 students and four teachers each year; I analysed comments elicited from students and teachers about classroom events; I gave questionnaires to all of the students in my case study year groups ($n = 300$) and I collected an assortment of background documentation. These methods, particularly the lesson observations and student interviews, enabled me to develop a comprehensive understanding of the students' experiences and to begin to view the world of school mathematics from the students' perspectives. In addition to these methods, I gave the students various assessments during the three-year period. Some of these I designed myself, but I also analysed school and external examinations, such as the GCSE mathematics examination. All of these methods, qualitative and quantitative, were used to inform each other in a continual process of interaction and re-analysis. In order to validate emerging perspectives, I made extensive use of triangulated data and the analyses developed in this chapter were generally based upon three or more different data sources.

The two schools

The two schools in the research study were chosen because their teaching methods were very different but their student intakes were very similar. The two schools both lie in the heart of mainly white, working-class communities located on the outskirts of large cities. Neither school is selective, and most parents choose the schools because of their proximity to their houses. Amber Hill is a secondary school which begins with Year 7. There were about 200 students in the year group I followed: 47 per cent of these were girls, 20 per cent were from single-parent families, 68 per cent were classified as working-class, and 17 per cent were from ethnic minorities. Phoenix Park is an upper school, which begins with Year 9. There were approximately 110 students in the year group that I followed: 42 per cent of these were girls, 23 per cent were from single-parent families, 79 per cent were classified as working-class, and 11 per cent were from ethnic minorities. A comparison of the students' mathematical attainment at the beginning of Year 9, using standardised NFER (National Foundation for Educational Research) tests, showed that there were no significant differences in the performance of the two sets of students. Seventy-five per cent of Amber Hill students and 76 per cent of Phoenix Park students were below the national average. In Years 7 and 8 both sets of students followed the same mathematics approach – SMP 11–16 individualised booklets. At the beginning of Year 9 and the beginning of my research study, the students had therefore experienced the same mathematical approaches and reached similar levels of attainment. At that point they encountered a huge divergence in their mathematical pathways, with one set of students moving to the SMP textbooks and the other students moving to a school that used open-ended projects. In the remainder of this chapter I will describe the students' experiences over the next three years and the ways that the different approaches impacted their developing beliefs and understandings, starting with a description of the students experiences in the more 'traditional' school.

Amber Hill school

Amber Hill is a large, mixed, comprehensive school. During my research study the school was run by an 'authoritarian' (Ball, 1987) headteacher who tried to improve the school's academic record by encouraging and, where possible, enforcing, traditionalism. As a result, the school was unusually ordered and orderly, and any visitor walking the corridors would observe quiet and calm classrooms with students sitting in rows or small groups, usually watching the board or working through exercises. In mathematics lessons from Year 9 onwards the teachers all used the same approach – they would start each lesson by explaining methods and procedures on the board, then give students questions from SMP textbooks to work through for the remainder of each lesson. The teachers used this approach in every lesson apart from two weeks of each year when the students worked on an open-ended project. The eight teachers of mathematics at Amber Hill were all committed and experienced. The students were grouped into eight sets, based upon their entry scores and teachers' beliefs about their abilities; Set 1 contained the highest-ability students.

In my lesson observations at Amber Hill school I was repeatedly impressed by the motivation of the students, who would work through their exercises without complaint or disruption. In a small quantitative assessment of their time on task (Peterson and Swing, 1982), I recorded the numbers of students who were working 10 minutes into, halfway through, and 10 minutes before the end of each lesson. I observed eight lessons, each with approximately 30 students and found that 100 per cent, 99 per cent, and 92 per cent of the students appeared to be working at these three respective times. The first of these figures was particularly high because at this early point in lessons the students were always watching the teachers work through examples on the board.

Unfortunately, control and order in the mathematics classroom do not, on their own, ensure effective learning. My lesson observations, interviews, and questionnaires all showed that many students found mathematics lessons in Years 9, 10, and 11 extremely boring and tedious. In the lessons that I observed, students often demonstrated a marked degree of uninterest and uninvolvement with their work. Thus, although the students worked hard and stayed on task throughout their lessons, they were extremely passive in their approach to their work and would sit and dutifully complete exercises in lessons without any apparent desire to challenge or think about what they were doing (Boaler, 1997a). At the end of their

Year 9 all of my case study cohort completed a questionnaire that asked the students to write about aspects of lessons that they liked, disliked, or would like to be improved ($n = 160$). This prompted many students to write about the similarity of their mathematical experiences and the dominance of textbook work. In response to the question, 'What do you dislike about the way you do maths at school?' 49 students (31 per cent) criticised the lack of variety in the school's approach, 77 students (48 per cent) also reported a lack of practical or activity-based experience. For example:

> Maths would be more interesting if we had some practical or group work. We barely ever do class activities; for example, we have done [only] one all year.

The students believed that their mathematical experiences lacked variety, not only because they worked on textbooks for the vast majority of the time, but also because they regarded the questions within the books as very similar to each other:

> I wish we had different questions, not three pages of sums on the same thing.

In interviews conducted with students in Years 10 and 11, the students also referred to the monotony of their mathematical experience:

JB: Can you think of a maths lesson which you really enjoyed?
D: No.
P: They're all the same.
D: I'm just not interested in it really; it's just boring; they're just all the same; you just go on.

(Danielle and Paula, Year 10, Set 2)

The student comments noted in this chapter represent a very small selection of those I received, but they were not unusual in any way. Indeed, comments were chosen because they typified the views presented by multiple students on several occasions. A large proportion of the students in the year group believed that mathematics lessons were too similar and monotonous. These beliefs were consistent across the eight mathematics sets, even though the teachers of these groups were quite different individuals who varied in popularity and experience. The aspect that united the teachers was their common method of teaching: a 15–20 minute demonstration of method, followed by the students working through questions in their textbooks, either alone or with their seating partners.

Rule-following behaviour

As a result of approximately 100 lesson observations, I classified a variety of behaviours that seemed to characterise the Amber Hill students' approach to mathematics. One of these, I termed rule-following (Boaler, 1997a). Many of the Amber Hill students held a view that mathematics was all about memorising a vast number of rules, formulas and equations and this view appeared to influence their mathematical behaviour:

N: In maths, there's a certain formula to get to, say from A to B, and there's no other way to get to it, or maybe there is, but you've got to remember the formula, you've got to remember it.

(Neil, Year 11, Set 7)

L: In maths you have to remember; in other subjects you can think about it.

(Louise, Year 11, Set 1)

The students' views about the importance of remembering set rules, equations, and formulae seemed to have many negative implications. For example, in mathematical situations the students did not think it was appropriate to try and think about what to do, they thought they had to remember a rule or method they had used in a situation that was similar. However, because, in mathematics lessons, they were never encouraged to discuss different rules and methods or think about why they may be useful in some situations and not others, the students did not know when situations were *mathematically* similar. This meant that questions that did not require an obvious and simplistic use of a rule or formula caused students to become confused.

The predominance of the students' belief in the importance of remembering rules was further demonstrated by a questionnaire devised in response to my field-work and given to the students in Year 10 ($n = 163$). In one item of this questionnaire students were asked which they believed to be more important when approaching a problem, remembering similar work done before or thinking hard about the work at hand. Sixty-four per cent of students said that remembering similar work done before was the more important. This view appeared to be consistent with the strategies they employed in class and was, in many ways, indicative of their whole approach to mathematics. The belief of many of the Amber Hill students that mathematics was all about learning set rules and equations seemed to have stopped them from trying to interpret situations mathematically. The Cognition and Technology Group at Vanderbilt (1990) note that when novices are introduced to concepts and theories they often regard them as new 'facts or mechanical procedures to be memorised' (1990, p. 3). The Amber Hill students rarely seemed to progress beyond this belief. This belief also led to a second, related aspect of their behaviour that I have referred to as cue-based (Boaler, 1997a).

Cue-based behaviour

Often during lesson observations I witnessed students basing their mathematical thinking on what they thought was expected of them, rather than on the mathematics within a question. Brousseau has talked about the didactical contract (Brousseau, 1984, p. 113), which causes pupils to base their mathematical thinking upon whatever they think the teacher wants them to do. I was often aware that the

Amber Hill students used non-mathematical cues as indicators of the teacher's or the textbook's intentions. These sometimes related to the words of the teacher, but students would also use such cues as the expected difficulty of the question (what they thought should be demanded of them at a certain stage), the context of the question, or the teacher's intonation when talking to them. The following extract is taken from my field notes of a Year 9 Set 1 lesson:

> Helen has her hand up and I go over. The question says that '58.9 tonnes of iron ore has 6.7 tonnes of iron in it. What percentage of the ore is iron?'. While I am reading this, Helen says, 'I'm just a bit thick really.' I ask Helen what she thinks she should do in the question, and she immediately tells me, correctly. When I tell her that she is right she says, 'But this is easier than the other questions we have been doing: in the others we have had to add things on and stuff first.' A few minutes later two more girls ask me for help on the same question: both of these girls have already completed more difficult questions.
>
> (Amber Hill, Year 9, Set 1)

In this extract the girls gave up on the question on iron ore because the mathematical demand was different from what they had expected. The previous exercise had presented a series of abstract calculations in which the students were asked to work out percentages that required them to 'add things on and stuff first.' In the next exercise the questions were mathematically simpler, but they were contextualised. The writers of the textbook obviously regarded these as less difficult, but the girls were thrown by this, because they expected something more mathematically demanding. This expectation caused them to give up on the question. It is this sort of behaviour that I have termed cue-based, because the students were using irrelevant aspects of the tasks, rather than mathematical sense-making or understanding, to cue them into the right method or procedure to use. Schoenfeld (1985) asserts that this sort of cue-based behaviour is formed in response to conventional pedagogic practices in mathematics that demonstrate set routines that should be learned. This sort of behaviour, which was common amongst the Amber Hill students, meant that if a question seemed inappropriately easy or difficult, if it required some non-mathematical thought, or if it required an operation other than the one they had just learned about, many students would stop working.

To summarise, the students at Amber Hill were highly motivated and hard-working, but many of them found mathematics lessons tedious and boring. A large number of the students also appeared to be influenced by an extremely set view of mathematics that they essentially regarded as a vast collection of sums, rules and equations that needed to be learned. This meant that when situations were slightly different from what they expected, or when they did not contain a cue suggesting the correct rule to use, many did not know what to do.

Phoenix Park school

Phoenix Park school was different from Amber Hill in many respects; most of these derived from the school's commitment to progressive education. The students at the school were encouraged to take responsibility for their own actions and to be independent thinkers. There were few school rules and lessons had a relaxed atmosphere. In mathematics lessons at Phoenix Park, the students worked on open-ended projects, in mixed-ability groups at all times, until January of their final year when they stopped their project work and started to practise examination techniques. At the beginning of their projects the students were given a few different starting points to choose between, for example, 'The volume of a shape is 216, what can it be?' or 'What is the maximum-sized fence that can be built out of 36 gates?' The students were then encouraged to develop their own ideas, formulate and extend problems, and use their mathematics. The approach was based upon the philosophy that students should encounter a need to use mathematics in situations that were realistic and meaningful to them. If a student or a group of students needed to use some mathematics that they did not know about, the teacher would teach it to them. Each project lasted for two to three weeks, and at the end of the projects the students were required to give in descriptions of their work and their mathematical activities.

In the mathematics lessons I observed at Phoenix Park, there was very little control or order and, in contrast to Amber Hill, no apparent structure to lessons. Students could take their work to another room and work unsupervised if they wanted to, as they were expected to be responsible for their own learning. In many of my lesson observations I was surprised by the number of students doing no work or choosing to work only for tiny segments of lessons. A study of the number of students working on tasks 10 minutes into, halfway through, and 10 minutes before the end of 11 lessons showed that 69 per cent, 64 per cent and 58 per cent of students (approximately 30 in each lesson) were on task at the three respective times. What these figures do not show is that there were a few students in each class who appeared to do almost no work in any lesson. In Year 10 the students were given questionnaires in which they were asked to write a sentence describing their mathematics lessons. The three most popular descriptions from Phoenix Park students ($n = 75$) were: noisy (23 per cent), a good atmosphere (17 per cent), and interesting (15 per cent). This contrasted with the three most popular responses from Amber Hill students ($n = 163$) which related to difficulty (40 per cent), their teacher (36 per cent), and boredom (28 per cent). When I asked students at Phoenix Park, in interviews, to describe their lessons to me, the single factor that was given the highest profile was the degree of choice they were given:

T: You get a choice.

JB: A choice between … ?

L: A couple of things; you choose what you want to do and you carry on with that, and then you start another, different one.

JB: So you're not all doing the same thing at the same time?

Both: No.

JB: And can you do what you want in the activity, or is it all set out for you?

L: You can do what you want, really.

T: Sometimes it's set out, but you can take it further.

(Tanya and Laura, Year 10)

Students also talked about the relaxed atmosphere at Phoenix Park, the emphasis on understanding, and the need to explain methods:

I: It's an easier way to learn, because you're actually finding things out for yourself, not looking for things in the textbook.

JB: Was that the same in your last school do you think?

I: No, like if we got an answer, they would say, 'You got it right.' Here you have to explain how you got it.

JB: What do you think about that? – explaining how you got it?

I: I think it helps you.

(Ian, Year 10)

During lesson observations at both schools I frequently asked students to tell me what they were doing. At Amber Hill most students would tell me the textbook chapter title, and, if I enquired further, the exercise number. It was generally very difficult to obtain any further information. At Phoenix Park students would describe the question they were trying to solve, what they had discovered so far, and what they were going to try next. In lessons at Phoenix Park the students discussed the meaning of their work with each other and negotiated possible mathematical directions. In response to the questionnaire item concerning remembering or thinking, only 35 per cent of Phoenix Park students prioritised remembering, compared with 64 per cent of Amber Hill students. At its best the Phoenix Park approach seemed to develop the students' desire and ability to think about mathematics in a way that the Amber Hill approach did not:

J: Solve the problems and think about other problems and solve them – problems that aren't connected with maths, think about them.

JB: You think that the way you do maths helps you to do that?

J: Yes.

JB: Things that aren't to do with maths?

J: Yes. It's more the thinking side to sort of, look at everything you've got and think about how to solve it.

(Jackie, Phoenix Park, Year 10)

The students' enjoyment of their mathematics teaching, at the two schools, appeared to be quite different. At Amber Hill there was a strong consensus about the problems of the school's approach, but the Phoenix Park approach really seemed to divide the Year group: some loved it, most liked it, a few hated it. The consensus at Amber Hill primarily related to the monotony of doing textbook work and the lack of freedom or choice the students were given. In Year 9, 263 students completed a questionnaire that asked them to describe what they disliked about mathematics at school; 44 per cent of Amber Hill students criticised the mathematics approach, and 64 per cent of these students criticised the textbook system. Other common criticisms included the constant need to rush through work, the tendency for books to go 'on and on', the lack of freedom to work at their own level and the lack of choice about topics or order of topics. At Phoenix Park 14 per cent of students criticised the school's approach and the most common response, from 23 per cent of students, was to list nothing they disliked about mathematics at school.

A second important difference between the two schools related to gendered preferences for ways of working (Boaler, 1997a, 1997b). In questionnaires given to students in the two case study year groups in Years 9, 10 and 11, the boys were always significantly more positive and confident than the girls at Amber Hill, but there were never any significant differences between girls and boys at Phoenix Park.

I have attempted to depict the primary distinguishing characteristics of the two school approaches and the students' responses to them. More detail on the two school approaches and the students' achievement can be found in Boaler (1997a, 1997b, 1999, 2000). Ultimately, the success or otherwise of either of these two approaches must be ascertained through a consideration of the students' understanding of mathematics. In the next section I present the results of applied assessment activities and formal, closed examinations.

Student assessments

In each of Years 9 and 10 I gave the students an applied task and a short written test that assessed all of the mathematics they would need to use in the task. For example, in Year 9, the students were asked to consider a proposed house and decide whether it would pass some local authority design rules. They were given a model of the house and a scale plan of the house and they had to consider angles, areas, volumes and percentages. They were also given a short written test in which they had to use the same mathematics. These different assessments showed that students at the two schools were equally capable on short, written mathematics tests, but the scores of the Amber Hill students were significantly lower than those of the Phoenix Park students on the applied activities. The reason for the lack of success of the Amber Hill students seemed to be that they did not know which methods to use in the applied assessments. For example, at one point students had to decide whether the angle at the top of the roof was 70° or more – it was actually 45°. The students were capable of estimating the angle, but over ¾ of the students in the top set at Amber Hill responded incorrectly because they tried to use trigonometry and used the methods inaccurately. The students at Amber Hill did not appreciate that trigonometry was inappropriate in the context of the activity.

The fact that the Phoenix Park students gained higher grades in applied, realistic situations may not be considered surprising, given the school's project-based approach. However, in traditional, closed questions the Amber Hill students did not perform any better than the students at Phoenix Park. In their GCSE examinations, 11 per cent of the Amber Hill cohort attained an A–C grade, and 71 per cent passed the examination. At Phoenix Park 11 per cent of the cohort attained an A–C grade, and 88 per cent passed the examination. Significantly more of the Phoenix Park students than Amber Hill students attained an A–G pass ($n = 332$, chi-squared $= 12.54$, $p < 0.001$), despite the fact that the GCSE examination was markedly different from anything the students were used to at Phoenix Park.

At Amber Hill there were also significant differences in the attainment of girls and boys; 20 per cent of the boys and 9 per cent of the girls who entered the examination attained grades A–C ($n = 217$, chi-squared $= 3.89$, $p < 0.05$). At Phoenix Park there were no significant differences in the achievement of girls and boys, with 13 per cent of the boys and 15 per cent of the girls who entered the examination attaining grades A–C ($n = 115$, chi-squared $= 0.12$, $p < 0.80$).

Discussion

The relative underachievement of the Amber Hill students, in formal test situations may be considered surprising, both because the students worked hard in mathematics lessons and because the school's mathematical approach was extremely examination-oriented. However, after many hours of observing and interviewing the students I was not surprised by the relative performance of the two groups of students. The Amber Hill students had developed an *inert* (Whitehead, 1962) knowledge that they found difficult using in anything other than textbook questions. In the examination, the students encountered difficulties because they found that the questions did not only require a simplistic rehearsal of a rule or a procedure; they required them to understand what the question was asking and which procedure was appropriate. They required them to apply the methods they had learned to new and different situations. In interviews with the Amber Hill students following their GCSE examinations, the students were clear about the reasons for their lack of success. The students agreed that they could not interpret the demands of the different questions and they could not see the relevance of the procedures they had learned, to the questions asked:

L: Some bits I did recognise, but I didn't understand how to do them, I didn't know how to apply the methods properly.

(Louise, Year 11, Set 3)

In their mathematics lessons the students had not experienced similar demands, for the textbook questions always followed on from a demonstration of a procedure or method and the students were never left to decide which method they should use. If the students were unsure of what to do in lessons, they would ask the teacher or try and read cues from the questions or the contexts they were presented in. In the examination the students tried to find similar cues but they were generally unable to do so:

G: It's different, and like the way it's there like – not the same. It doesn't like tell you it, the story, the question; it's not the same as in the books, the way the teacher works it out.

(Gary, Year 11, Set 4)

T: You can get a trigger, when she says like *simultaneous equations* and *graphs, graphically*. When they say like – and you know, it pushes that trigger, tells you what to do.

JB: What happens in the exam when you haven't got that?

T: You panic.

(Trevor, Year 11, Set 3)

The success of the Phoenix Park students in the examination was enhanced by their desire and ability to think about different situations and work out what was required:

T: I think it allows – when you first come to the school and you do your projects, and it allows you to think more for yourself than when you were in middle school and you worked from the board or from books.

JB: And is that good for you, do you think?

T: Yes.

JB: In what way?

T: It helped with the exams where we had to … had to think for ourselves there and work things out.

(Tina, Year 11)

Indeed, it was this perceiving and interpreting of situations that seemed to characterise the real difference between the learning of the students at the two schools. When the students were presented with the angle problem in the architectural task, many of the Amber Hill students were unsuccessful, not because they were incapable of estimating an angle, but because they could not interpret the situation correctly. The Phoenix Park students were not as well versed in mathematical procedures, but they were able to interpret and develop meaning in the situations encountered:

JB: Did you feel in your exam that there were things you hadn't done before?

A: Well sometimes, I suppose they put it in a way which throws you. But if there's stuff I actually haven't done before I'll try and make as much sense of it as I can and try and understand it as best as I can.

(Arran, Phoenix Park, Year 11)

This flexibility in approach, combined with the students' beliefs about the adaptable nature of mathematics and the need for reasoned thought, appeared to enhance the students' examination performance. Another major difference between the learning of the students related to their reported use of mathematics in real-world situations. The students at Amber Hill all spoke very strongly about their complete inability to make use of any school-learned methods in real situations, because they could not see any connection between what they had done in the class-room and the demands of their lives outside of the classroom (Boaler, 1997a).

JB: When you use maths outside of school, does it feel like when you do maths in school or does it feel … ?
K: No, it's different.
S: No way; it's *totally* different.

(Keith and Simon, Year 11, Set 6)

The students at Phoenix Park did not see a real difference between their school mathematics and the mathematics they needed outside of school.

JB: Do you think in the future, if you need to use maths in something, do you think you will be able to use what you're learning now or do you think you will just make up your own methods?
G: No, I think I'll remember. When I'm out of school now I can connect back to what I done in class so I know what I'm doing.

(Gavin, Year 10)

In the following extract Sue contrasted her project-based work with the few weeks of examination preparation the students received prior to their GCSE at Phoenix Park:

JB: Do you think, when you use maths outside of school, it feels very different to using maths in school, or does it feel similar?
S: Very different from what we do now; if we do use maths outside of school, it's got the same atmosphere as how it used to be, but not now.
JB: What do you mean by 'it's got the same atmosphere'?
S: Well, when we used to do projects, it was like that, looking at things and working them out, solving them – so it was similar to that, but it's not similar to this stuff now; it's, you don't know what this stuff is for really, except the exam.

(Sue, Year 11)

Sue's comment seems to capture the essence of the value of Phoenix Park's approach. When the students worked on projects they needed to think for them-selves, interpret situations, choose, combine and adapt different mathematical procedures and this 'had the same atmosphere' as the mathematical demands of the real world. The students at Phoenix Park had been enculturated into a system of working and thinking that appeared to advantage them in new and unusual settings.

Conclusion

At Amber Hill school the mathematics teachers were not unusual. They were dedicated teachers, who were effective at teaching textbook, mathematical methods. The students worked hard to learn the methods they were taught. Schoenfeld (1985) describes this type of textbook approach as widespread, and it is certainly the predominant model adopted in the UK. The results of this research reveal some important limitations of this type of teaching. At Amber Hill school the students developed an inert, procedural knowledge that was of limited use to them in anything other than textbook situations.

There were many indications from this study that the traditional back-to-basics mathematics approach of Amber Hill was ineffective in preparing students for the demands of the real world, and was no more effective than a process-based approach for preparing students for traditional assessments of content knowledge. There were problems with the Phoenix Park approach, including the fact that some students spent much of their time not working. Despite this the Phoenix Park students were able to achieve more in test and applied situations than the Amber Hill students, they also developed more positive views about the nature of mathematics that I have not had space to report upon in this chapter. It would be easy to dismiss these results or to attribute them to some other factor, such as how good the teachers were at Phoenix Park. But part of the value of ethnographic studies is the flexibility they allow researchers to investigate the influence of different factors, using the data that is most appropriate. After hundreds of hours spent in the classrooms at the two schools; after hearing the students' own accounts of their learning; after analysing over 200 questionnaire responses each year and after consideration of the results of traditional and applied assessments; I have been able to isolate factors that have and have not been influential in the students' development of understanding. One important conclusion that I felt able to draw from this analysis is that a traditional, textbook approach that emphasises computations, rules and procedures, at the expense of depth of understanding, disadvantages students, primarily because it encourages learning that is inflexible, school-bound and of limited use.

References

Ball, S.J. (1987) *The Micro-politics of the School*, London: Methuen.

Ball, S.J. (1994) 'Culture, crisis and morality. the struggle over the national curriculum', in P. Atkinson, S. Delamont and W.B. Davies (eds) *Discourse and Reproduction: a Festschrift for Basil Bernstein*: 85–102.

Boaler, J. (1997a) *Experiencing School Mathematics: teaching styles, sex and setting*, Buckingham: Open University Press.

Boaler, J. (1997b) 'Reclaiming school mathematics: the girls fight back', *Gender and Education* 9(3): 285–306.

Boaler, J. (1999) 'Participation, knowledge and beliefs: a community perspective on mathematics learning', *Educational Studies in Mathematics* 40: 259–81.

Boaler, J. (2000) 'Exploring situated insights into research and learning', *Journal for Research in Mathematics Education* 31(1): 113–19.

Brousseau, G. (1984) 'The crucial role of the didactical contract in the analysis and construction of situations in teaching and learning mathematics' in H.G. Steiner (ed.) *Theory of Mathematics Education ICME 5 Topic Area and Miniconference*, Bielefeld, Germany: Institut für Didaktik der Mathematik der Universität Bielefeld: 110–19.

Burton, L. (1986) 'Femmes et mathematiques: y-a-ul une intersection?', unpublished chapter presented at the conference: *Femmes et Mathematiques*, Quebec, Canada.

Burton, L. (1995) 'Moving towards a feminist epistemology of mathematics', in P. Rogers and G. Kaiser (eds) *Equity in Mathematics Education: influences of feminism and culture*, London: Falmer Press: 209–26.

Charles, R., and Lester Jr, F. (1984) 'An evaluation of a process-oriented instructional program in mathematical problem solving in grades 5 and 7', *Journal for Research in Mathematics Education* 15(1): 15–34.

Cobb, P., Wood, T., Yackel, E. and Perlwitz, M. (1992) 'A follow-up assessment of a second-grade problem-centred mathematics project', *Educational Studies in Mathematics* 23: 483–504.

Cockcroft, W.H. (1982) *Mathematics Counts. Report of inquiry into the teaching of mathematics in schools*, London: HMSO.

DES (1989) *Mathematics in the National Curriculum*, London: HMSO.

DES (1991) *Mathematics in the National Curriculum*, London, HMSO.

Eisenhart, M. (1988) 'The ethnographic research tradition and mathematics education research', *Journal for Research in Mathematics Education* 19(2): 99–114.

Masingila, J. (1993) 'Learning from mathematics practice in out-of-school situations', *For the Learning of Mathematics* 13(2): 18–22.

NCTM (1989) *Curriculum and Education Standards for School Mathematics*: Reston, VA.

NCTM (2000) *Principles and Standards for School Mathematics*: Reston, VA.

Nunes, T., Schliemann, A.D. and Carraher, D.W. (1993) *Street Mathematics and School Mathematics*, New York: Cambridge University Press.

Perez, J. A. (1985) 'Effects of student generated problems on problem solving performance', unpublished doctoral dissertation, Teachers College, Columbia University.

Peterson, P.L. and Swing, A.R. (1982) 'Beyond time on task: students' reports of their thought processes during classroom instruction', *The Elementary School Journal* 82(5): 481–91.

Schoenfeld, A.H. (1985) *Mathematical Problem Solving*, New York: Academic Press.

Silver, E.A. (1994) 'On mathematical problem posing', *For The Learning of Mathematics* 14(1): 19–28.

The Cognition and Technology Group at Vanderbilt (1990) 'Anchored instruction and its relationship to situated cognition', *Educational Researcher*: 2–10.

Whitehead, A.N. (1962) *The Aims of Education*, London: Ernest Benn.

Winograd, K. (1991) 'Writing, solving and sharing original math story problems: case studies in the cognitive behaviour of fifth grade children', unpublished doctoral dissertation, University of Northern Colorado.

Section 4

Teaching Mathematics

8 Landscapes of investigation

Ole Skovsmose

In his observations in English classrooms, Cotton (1998) has noticed that a mathematics lesson is divided into two parts; first, the teacher presents some mathematical ideas and techniques, then the students work with selected exercises. He has also noticed that there are variations of the same pattern, reaching from a full-lesson teacher presentation to a full-lesson student occupation with exercises. According to this and many other observations, traditional mathematics education falls within the *exercise* paradigm. Most often, the mathematical textbook represents a 'given' for the classroom practice. Exercises are formulated by an authority external to the classroom. This means that the justification of the relevance of the exercises is not part of the mathematics lesson itself. Furthermore, a central premise of the exercise paradigm is that one and only one answer is correct.

The exercise paradigm can be contrasted with an *investigative approach*. Such an approach can take many forms, one example being project work. In general, project work is located in a 'landscape' that provides resources for carrying out investigations. Project work represents a learning milieu, different from the exercise paradigm.

My interest in the investigative approach is related to critical mathematics education, which can be characterised in terms of different concerns (Skovsmose and Nielsen, 1996), one of which is the development of *mathemacy*, seen as a competence similar to literacy, as characterised within the pedagogy of Freire (1972). Mathemacy refers not only to mathematical skills, but also to a competence in interpreting and acting in a social and political situation structured by mathematics. Critical mathematics education includes a concern for developing mathematics education in support of democracy, implying that the micro-society of the mathematics classroom must also show aspects of democracy. Critical mathematics education emphasises that mathematics as such is not simply a subject to be taught and learnt. Mathematics itself is a topic which needs to be reflected upon, as mathematics is part of our technology-based culture, and it exercises many functions, which may best be characterised by a slight reformulation of 'Kranzberg's First Law' (1997): What mathematics is doing is neither good nor bad, nor is it neutral. D'Ambrosio (1994) has used a more harsh formulation emphasising that mathematics makes part of our technological, military, economic and political structures, and as such it becomes a resource for wonders as well as for horrors. Making a critique of mathematics as part of mathematics education is a concern of critical mathematics education (Skovsmose, 1998b, 2000). Such concerns seem better taken care of outside the exercise paradigm.

The following presentation is partly based on my work on project-based mathematics education, and it is related to my work with teachers, with whom I have discussed these ideas – teachers working in very different political, economic and cultural contexts in Colombia, South Africa, Norway, Brazil, England and Denmark. I always start with an example.

An example

A landscape which can support investigative work, I call a *landscape of investigation*. (The following example is inspired by Ole Einar Torkildsen's lecture at the NOMUS-Conference in Aalborg (Denmark) in 1996.) We take a look at the good old table of numbers, which has certainly decorated the walls of many mathematics classrooms and served as basis for a variety of exercises. We concentrate on a rect- angle drawn on the table. If the numbers in the corners of the rectangle are labelled a, b, c and d, it is possible to calculate the value of F determined by

$F = ac - bd$

The rectangle can then be translated to another position, and the value of $F = ac - bd$ can be calculated again.

1	2	3	4	5	6	7	8	9	10
11	12	13	14	15	16	17	18	19	20
21	22	23	24	25	26	27	28	29	30
31	32	33	34	35	36	37	38	39	40
41	42	43	44	45	46	47	48	49	50
51	52	53	54	55	56	57	58	59	60
61	62	63	...						

Figure 8.1 The good old table of numbers

For instance, we observe that $22 \times 34 - 24 \times 32 = -20$, and that $37 \times 49 - 39 \times 47 = -20$. Let us try to translate the rectangle to a different position and again calculate the value of F. By the way, what will happen if we rotate the rectangle 90° and make the same calculation? Well, ... ? What is going to happen, if we choose a bigger rectangle and make a similar translation? What will now be the value of $F = ac - bd$? How does the value of F depend on the size of the rectangle?

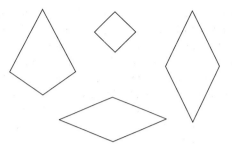

Figure 8.2 Other figures to be translated

Naturally, it is possible to investigate translations of other figures. What will happen if we calculate the values $F = ac - bd$, and a, b, c, and d refer to the numbers determined by the corners of the shapes shown in Figure 8.2? Which of these figures can be 'translated' without the value of F being changed?

Why not investigate a function different from F? For instance, what will happen if we permutate the operations 'subtraction' and 'multiplication' and instead of $F = ac - bd$ calculate

$$G = (a - c)(b - d)$$

(a, b, c, and d still refer to the corners of a rectangle)? Would G be constant under translation? What about the other figures shown at Figure 8.2? Do other functions exist that are rectangle-translatable (meaning that the value of the function is kept constant during a translation)? Yes, of course a function H defined as $H = 0a + 0b + 0c + 0d$ satisfies this condition. But do more 'interesting' rectangle-translatable functions exist? If we succeed in finding such a function, would it, then, also be rhombus-translatable? Would, in fact, any rectangle-translatable function be rhombus-translatable? In more general terms: what functions make which figures translatable?

What if we consider negative numbers? Thus, the number table from Figure 8.1 could be extended adding numbers to the left and to the right of each line, so that we have to deal with number lines placed on top of each other. We could then consider translations that bring the figures into areas with negative numbers. Incidentally, what would happen if the table was set up as shown in Figure 8.3 (overleaf)? It must also be possible to carry out the calculation in a different number base. Would the quality of 'translatability' depend on which number base we are considering?

Naturally, we need not concentrate on configurations of numbers determined by the corners of a figure with four corners. We could consider any configuration of numbers, $a_1, \ldots, a_n$, and any function, $F = F(a_1, \ldots, a_n)$. The question would then be: what functions defined on a configuration of numbers are constant with respect to translation of the configuration? And why not consider rotation as well? Or any other movement of the figure? Furthermore, up to now we have concentrated on a particular property of the function F, being constant or not, but we could observe many other properties of the function F. This leads to the question: what functions defined on a configuration of numbers exhibit 'nice' properties under translation?

1	2	3	4	5	6	7
8	9	10	11	12	13	14
15	16	17	18	19	20	21
22	23	24	25	26	27	28
29	30	31	32	33	34	35
36	37	38	39	40	41	42
43	44	45	...			

Figure 8.3   A different set-up for the table of numbers

What if … ?

We imagine that this example has occupied some students and a teacher for a while. We have been observing their conversation. The teacher has asked 'What if … ?' and later we hear again his or her 'What if … ?' The students might be surprised by some of the mathematical properties indicated by the questions. Mumbling is heard all around. Later it becomes possible to hear students' voices more clearly. 'What if … ?' '… Yeah, what if … ?' Maybe the teacher asks, 'Why is it that … ?' which leads to more mumbling and, maybe, longer periods of silence. Later on some of the students voices can be heard, 'Yes, why is it that … ?'

A landscape of investigation invites students to formulate questions and to look for explanations. The invitation is symbolised by the teacher's 'What if … ?' The students' acceptance of the invitation is symbolised by their 'Yes, what if … ?' In this way the students become involved in a process of *exploration*. The teacher's 'Why is it that … ?' provides a challenge, and the students' 'Yes, why is it that … ?' illustrates that they are facing the challenge and that they are searching for *explanations*. When the students take over the process of exploration and explanation in this way, the landscape of investigation comes to constitute a new learning milieu. In a landscape of investigation the students are in charge.

Is the example about the translation of figures then, in fact, a landscape of investigation? Maybe, maybe not, because a landscape only becomes a landscape of investigation if the students *do* accept the invitation. Being a landscape of investigation is a relational property. Acceptance of the invitation depends on the nature of the invitation (the possibility of exploring and explaining pure mathematical properties of a number table might not appear so attractive to many students). It depends on the teacher (an invitation can be presented in many ways, and to some students an invitation from a teacher might sound like a command). And it depends certainly on the students (they might have other priorities for the time being). What might serve perfectly well as a landscape of investigation for one group of students in one particular situation might not provide any invitation to another group of students. The question whether a certain landscape might support an investigative approach or not is an empirical one which has to be answered through an experimental educational practice by the teacher and students involved.

Learning milieus

Classroom practices based on landscapes of investigation contrast strikingly with the exercise paradigm. The distinction between the two can be combined with a different distinction that has to do with the 'references' which might provide the mathematical concepts and the classroom activities with some meaning to the children.

Different types of reference are possible. First, mathematical questions and activities can refer to mathematics and to mathematics only. Second, it is possible to refer to a semi-reality – not a reality that we actually observe, but a reality constructed by, for instance, an author of a mathematical textbook. Christiansen (1997) refers to a 'virtual reality' as a reality that is established by the mathematical exercise itself. I use the notion 'semi-reality' in a similar way. Finally, students and teachers can work with tasks referring to real-life situations. Combining the distinction between the three types of reference and the distinction between two paradigms of classroom practices, one gets a matrix showing six different types of *learning milieus* (Figure 8.4).

	Paradigm of exercises	*Landscapes of investigation*
References to pure mathematics	[(1)]	[(2)]
References to a semi-reality	[(3)]	[(4)]
Real-life references	[(5)]	[(6)]

Figure 8.4 Learning milieus

Type (1) is positioned in a context of 'pure mathematics' as well as in the paradigm of exercises. This learning milieu is dominated by exercises, which can be of the form:

$$(27a - 14b) + (23a + 5b) - 11a =$$
$$(16 \times 25) - (18 \times 23) =$$
$$(32 \times 41) - (34 \times 39) =$$

Type (2) is characterised as a landscape of investigation located in numbers and geometric figures. The introductory example about the translation of geometric figures in a number table illustrates this type of milieu.

The type (3) milieu is located in the paradigm of exercises with references to a semi-reality. The nature of such a semi-reality can be illustrated by the following example (see Dowling, 1998):

Shopkeeper *A* sells dates for 85p per kilogram. *B* sells them at 1.2 kg for £1. (a) Which shop is cheaper? (b) What is the difference between the prices charged by the two shopkeepers for 15 kg of dates?

Certainly there is talk about dates, shops and prices. But I do not suppose that the person who constructed this exercise made any empirical investigation of how dates are sold or interviewed a person in order to find out under what circumstances it would be relevant to buy 15 kg of dates. The situation is artificial. The exercise is located in a semi-reality.

However, the practice of mathematics education has established specific standards for how to operate in such a semi-reality. If, for instance, a student asks the teacher about the distance between the shops and the home of the person who is going to buy the dates, and if the student wants to figure out how far it is possible to carry a bag of 15 kg by making an experiment in the schoolyard, and if the student asks whether both shops can be expected to deliver the dates or not, and whether it can be assumed that the qualities of the dates from the two shops are the same, then the teacher would most likely regard the student as trying to obstruct the whole mathematics lesson.

Certainly, such questions generate obstruction considering the general 'agreement' between teacher and students operating in the exercise paradigm. Solving exercises with reference to a semi-reality is an elaborated competence in mathematics education, based on a well-specified contract between teacher and students. Some of the principles from the agreement follow. The semi-reality is fully described by the text of the exercise. No other information is relevant in order to solve the exercise. Further information is thus totally irrelevant, the sole purpose of presenting the exercise being to solve it. A semi-reality is a world without sense impressions (to ask about the taste of the dates is out of the question), only the measured quantities are relevant. Furthermore, all quantitative information is exact, as the semi-reality is *defined* in terms of these measures. Thus, the question whether it is okay to negotiate the price or to buy, say, a little less than 15 kg of dates is devoid of meaning. The exactitude of the measurement, combined with the assumption that the semi-reality is fully described by the information provided, makes it possible to maintain the 'one, and only one, answer is correct' assumption. The metaphysics of the semi-reality makes sure that this assumption can be maintained, not only when references are made exclusively to numbers and geometric figures, but also when references are made to 'shops', 'dates', 'kilograms', 'prices', 'distances' as well as other seemingly empirical entities. If it is not realised that the way the mathematics fits the semi-reality has nothing to do with the relationship between mathematics and reality, then the ideology of certainty has found a habitat (Borba and Skovsmose, 1997). In particular, this metaphysics has structured the communication between teacher and students.

It has been considered irrelevant to make actual observations of how mathematics is operating in real-life situations to being able to construct exercises of type (3), but recently, much more careful studies of mathematical practices in different work situations have been carried out (e.g. Wedege, 1999). Real-life based exercises provide a learning milieu of type (5). For instance, figures concerning unemployment can be presented as part of the exercise, and based on such figures questions can be asked about the decrease or the increase of employment, comparisons can be made between different periods of time, different countries, etc. (see, for example, Frankenstein, 1989). All figures referred to are real-life figures, and this provides a different condition for the communication between teacher and students, as it now makes sense to question and to supplement the information given by the exercise. The activities remain settled in the exercise paradigm.

Like milieu (3), milieu (4) also contains references to a semi-reality, but now this semi-reality is not used as a resource for a production of exercises, but as an invitation for the students to make explorations and explanations. The 'big horse race' can serve as an example. The racecourse is drawn on the blackboard, and eleven horses: 2, 3, 4, … , 12, are ready for the start. Two dice are thrown, the sum of the number of spots shown is calculated and a cross is made on the diagram. As Figure 8.5 shows, the sum 6 came out three times before any of the other sums. Horse 6, therefore, became the lucky winner, followed by horse 7 and horse 10.

This horse race can be developed into a greater classroom activity. Imagine that you are working with a Year 7 or 8 class. Two bookmaker agencies are set up behind desks in corners of the classroom. A small group of students runs each agency. Independent of each other, the agencies announce their odds. The rest of the class, the very wealthy gamblers, make their bets: 'Look, agency A pays back 8 times the money on horse number 9. But look at agency B! They pay back 40 times for horse number 10!' Placing the bets has to be done in a hurry, as the next race is soon going to start. Another group of children is in charge of the race, they ring the bell, and (a kind of) silence enters the classroom. The dice are thrown, the sums are calculated, crosses are made, the horses race towards the goal line. Some of the gamblers smile broadly.

Agency A has only a few customers. Their odds seem far less favourable than those provided by agency B. However, a new race is going to start. New odds are suggested. The gamblers are surprised: 'What marvellous odds this agency A is now

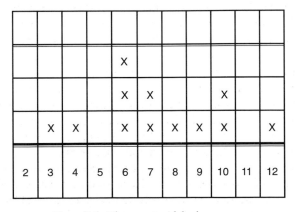

Figure 8.5 The terrain of the horse race

offering!' New bets, new races, new winners, new losers. The horses are not anonymous any more, and horse number 2 is called 'The Turtle'. Suddenly, one agency loses its whole fortune. Anyway, a new millionaire sets up a new agency.

The teacher suggests that it is time for a Derby. Up to now the races have been 3 units, but a Derby must be 5 units, at least. Odds are produced by the agencies. After the second Derby, some of the gamblers start wondering: Could horse number 7 possibly be particularly fit for long distances?

Even after several races, there is no smell of horses in the classroom. The great horse race takes place in a semi-reality, but not in the exercise paradigm. And the many remarks about the abilities of the different horses ('Horse number 11 needs some vitamin pills') are not perceived as obstructions. The strict logic governing the semi-reality of learning milieu number (3) is no longer in operation. The whole activity is located in a landscape of investigation. Many discoveries are waiting for the children. Strategies are to be produced and improved. And, as I have chosen to describe the activity, the children certainly accepted the invitation to participate in the big horse race. (I wrote this description while I was a visiting scholar in England. Had I stayed in Denmark, I would most likely have described the 'big cycling race'!)

Naturally, it is possible to develop landscapes of investigation with a greater degree of reality involved than the big horse race. An example of milieu (6) (see Neilsen, Patronis and Skovsmose, 1999) is 'The Interior Design Project', initiated by students' concerned with organising their common room at their school in a better way. During the project the students were split into groups. Partition walls were placed in the classroom in order to create small offices for the different groups of 'architects'. The first task of each group, now operating as a small company, was to design a logo. One company used a bottle opener, as their slogan was: 'We open for new ideas'. One important task for the 'architects' was to provide a scale drawing of the common room. They also spent time clarifying the principles of perspective drawings. They presented their ideas to other classes of the school to get an impression of the general opinion before 'The Interior Design Project' concluded with a presentation to the school's governors. On this occasion the 'architects' had also provided small three-dimensional models illustrating the idea of their proposals. Naturally, they also knew that the governors would be most concerned about money, so each company had to prepare their budget in detail including: cost of paint for decorating the room; cost of installing lockers in the common room; cost of some new furniture, etc. The different suggestions were well received, and after the meeting the chair of governors wrote a letter to the class: ' … it was exciting to see your presentation … In my opinion there were a lot of specific ideas, which could be realised, if we could find the money.' In this final aspect the project became very realistic – unfortunately, the money for the students' project was not found!

The project 'Planning a Major Road' included the students' reaction to the Government's planning of a major road through the suburbs of the city close to the school. Public protest had been voiced, and the students' task was to improve the planning of the positioning of the road. The project 'Jobs of Young People', involved the students in statistical investigations concerning the salaries of young people. The results were presented in a small newspaper distributed in the school and among students from neighbouring schools. 'Designing a Bridge' included a careful consideration of 'slope', while 'The Traffic Project' concentrated on public and private transport, with a special focus on the connection between a small village and a major city close by. Such projects, all described in Nielsen, Patronis and Skovsmose (1999), also offer opportunities to consider: students' interests; democratic life in the classroom; interdisciplinary factors; mathematics and common sense; and the teacher as supervisor. All of these are issues are important to consider when transitions between the different learning milieus are planned. Other examples of project work are presented and analysed in Skovsmose (1994).

Moving between different learning milieus

Naturally, the matrix in Figure 8.4 represents a strong simplification. The division between the exercise paradigm and landscapes of investigation is certainly very broad, representing a huge terrain of possibilities. Some exercises can provoke problem-solving activities, which might turn into genuine mathematical investigations. Problem-posing means a further step into landscapes of investigation, although problem-posing activities can be very different from project work. No doubt the horizontal divisions are also 'woolly'. My point, of course, is not to try to provide any clear-cut classification, but to elaborate the notion of milieus of learning in order to facilitate discussion about making changes in mathematics education.

A good deal of mathematics education is switching between milieus (1) and (3). In this sense the exercise paradigm provides a foundation for 'tradition' in mathematics education. However, I do not want to make the claim that milieu (6) is the only essential alternative to the exercise paradigm. In fact, I do not want to suggest that a particular learning milieu can become designated to represent the ultimate goal for mathematics education, critical or not.

I support a mathematics education moving between the different milieus as presented in the matrix. In particular, I do not regard it as an aim to abandon exercises from mathematics education altogether. It might make good sense after, say, the big horse race to use a period for 'consolidation' in which the students work with exercises related to the notion of probability. It is important that students and teacher together find their route among the different milieus of learning. The 'optimal' route cannot be determined in advance but has to be negotiated by students and teacher. The matrix of learning milieus can also be used as an analytic tool. For instance, it is possible for the students and the teacher to reconsider last year's route: Which learning milieus did we experience? Have we spent all the time in one or two milieus? In which milieu did we experience a particular success? Did some moves from one milieu to another cause difficulties? Many considerations of planning can be referred to the matrix.

Long ago, I was engaged in a mathematical project involving young children, about seven years old. The main aim of the project was to plan and to construct a playground outside the windows of the classroom where there was a small piece of ground available for the class. Certainly, this activity took place in a learning milieu of type (6), and, as a result of the project, a small playground was in fact set up outside the windows of the classroom with the active help of parents during a few weekends. Before that, however, much activity had taken place. First, the children visited other playgrounds in order to test what made a 'good' one. Seven-year-olds are experts in carrying out this kind of test! More difficult, however, was specifying the exact quality of the good playground. How tall are the swings? How much sand is needed? etc. Many things have to be measured, and in order not to forget such measures it becomes important to make notes about the observations. Not an easy task!

Such periods of intense activity are very fruitful and important, but other more relaxed types of activities are important as well, both for the teacher and for the children. As part of the project about the playground (which lasted for a few months), there were organised periods of 'office work', which actually looked like an excursion into the learning milieu of type (1). The children were organised in small groups working in their 'offices'. As in any public office, voices were low. The children had juice or lemonade in plastic cups standing on their desks, which, by some magic, now looked like real office desks. Sometimes the 'office staff' ate biscuits while they added up numbers. Sometimes the radio played low, soft music. From the outset, the papers scattered around the desks contained exercises in addition and subtraction. The point is that the children, during the more intensive periods of project work, had recognised the importance of being able to add numbers, and to add them correctly. During office hours, these kinds of skills could then be consolidated, and reasons for doing such office work were found in the previous periods of the project work. The actual set-up of 'office work' broke the pattern of the normal exercise paradigm, although the activity as such was of type (1). This illustrates that the route between the different milieus might help to provide the students' activities with new meaning. The office work did not take place in an atmosphere of the school mathematics tradition, although it took place in the exercise paradigm. In particular, the communication between teacher and students in the office, was not governed by the same logic as the communication between teacher and students adjusted to the school mathematics tradition. In general the pattern of communication between students and teachers and among students are of special importance for the learning milieu (Alrø and Skovsmose, 1996a, 1996b, 1998).

The consolidation provided by office work also serves as a preparation for being engaged in a new project. The creation of harmony between project work and course work has been a big challenge to project-based mathematics education – no matter whether we have to deal with project-based university studies in mathematics or with elementary school mathematics (Vithal, Christiansen and Skovsmose, 1995).

Sometimes, in discussions with teachers, it has been suggested to me that before trying to investigate any landscape the students should be equipped with some understanding and techniques that, most efficiently, can be produced within an exercise paradigm. The big horse race illustrates why, in my opinion, this is not generally the case. Had the children, before the race, been introduced to some basic notions of probability illustrated by the canonical diagram – the number of eyes of the red dice is shown on the x-axes, the number of eyes of the blue dice is shown on the y-axes, and the sum … – then the fascination of the game could be lost. However, an opposite route is relevant in many cases, i.e. the route from (4) to (3). When the game has been tried out and the children have become familiar with the strengths and weaknesses of the different horses and they have got an idea about the reliability of odds, then the children and the teacher can start making particular observations and finding explanations. And exercises can be used as a means of clarifying half-made discoveries.

The risk zone

French research in mathematics education has paid much attention to the notion of didactical contract (see, for instance, Brousseau, 1997). With reference to the notion of learning milieu, a didactical contract can be defined in terms of 'balance in a learning milieu'. Thus, a didactical contract refers to an established harmony between the parameters of the learning milieu, i.e. a harmony between the way meaning is produced, the tasks are organised, the textbook is structured, the communication is carried out, etc. And, furthermore, this harmony must be recog-nised and accepted by both teacher and students. That a didactical contract is established does not, however, reveal anything about the quality of the learning milieu. It first of all indicates that teacher and students have a shared understand-ing and acceptance of the priorities of the learning milieu. Their interaction is not problematic as long as both parties recognise the contract.

A didactical contract can be broken in many ways, for instance when students start asking about details of a semi-reality, as described previously. The contract can be broken if the evaluation is drastically changed. In general, improvement of mathematics education is closely linked to breaking the contract. And when, initially, I suggested a challenge to the paradigm of exercise, it can also be seen as a suggestion for breaking the contract of the school mathematics tradition.

From the teacher's perspective this might appear as moving from a comfort zone into a *risk zone*. This notion has been introduced by Penteado (1999, 2000) in her study of teachers' experiences in a new learning environment where computers play a crucial role. Moving between the different possible learning milieus, and paying special attention to landscapes of investigation, will cause a great deal of uncertainty. My point is that uncertainty is not to be eliminated. The challenge is to face uncertainty.

Computers in the mathematics classroom have helped to establish new landscapes of investigation (although some closed programs try to eliminate uncertainties by adjusting the activities to the exercise paradigm). The computer will immediately challenge the authority of the (traditional) mathematics teacher. Students working with, say, dynamic geometry will easily come to face situations and experi-ence possibilities not foreseen by the teacher as part of the planning of the lesson. A student's eager clicking on the mouse might quickly lead to an unknown corner of the program: What to do now? How to get out of here? The teacher must always be ready to face questions that cannot easily be answered. The traditional teacher authority can be broken within seconds. The degree of unpredictability is high. One epistemological reason for this is that computers are not simply tools which 'extend' our way of thinking; instead computers reorganise our way of thinking (see, for instance Borba, 1995, 1999).The whole idea of 'reorganisation' links closely to the idea of 'risk zone'.

When students are exploring a landscape of investigation, the teacher cannot predict what questions may come next. One way of eliminating this risk is, for the teacher, to try to guide everybody back into the exercise paradigm and into the comfort zone. Thus, the whole exploration of translatability of geometric figures in the number table could be reorganised as a sequence of exercises. And instead of letting the students play around with a dynamic geometry program, the teacher could specify each step to be taken: 'First you select a point. Yes, all of you! This point we call A. Then you select another point. This other point we call B ... ' By organising the activities by means of such orders, the teacher can bring about (almost) the same picture on all the screens in the classroom. When students are moving slowly forward in columns and rows in this way, the teacher can prevent the occurrence of the unpredictably events and challenges. By doing so, however, many learning opportunities are lost as well. In particular, leaving the 'risk zone' also means eliminating learning opportunities linked to computers-as-reorganisers.

Any landscape of investigation raises challenges to a teacher. A solution is not to rush back into the comfort zone of the exercises paradigm, but to be able to operate in the new environment. The task is to make it possible for the teacher and students to operate in cooperation within a risk zone, and to make this operation a productive activity and not a threatening experience. This means, for instance, accepting that 'What if ... ' questions can lead the investigation into unknown territory. According to Penteado, an important condition, that allows teachers to operate in a risk zone, is the establishment of new forms of cooperative work, in particular among teachers, but also along the line of students-parents-teachers-researcher.

However, why bother about operating in the risk zone? Why not simply accept the didactical contract of the school mathematics tradition that has been so carefully elaborated? Cobb and Yackel (1998) refer to 'intellectual autonomy' as an explicitly stated goal for their efforts to establish an enquiry-mathematics tradition in contrast to a school mathematics tradition. Intellectual autonomy is characterised 'in terms of students' awareness of and willingness to draw on their own intellectual capabilities when making mathematical decisions and judgements' (p. 170). Intellectual autonomy can be associated to the activities of exploration and explanation as facilitated by landscapes of investigation. It is difficult to see this autonomy rooted in those rules that constitute the adequate behaviour when operating in a semi-reality milieu (3).

How can we develop a mathematics education as part of our concern for democracy in a society structured by technologies that include mathematics as a constituting element? How can we develop a mathematics education which does not operate as a blind introduction of students to mathematical thinking, but helps students recognise their own mathematical capabilities and makes them aware of the way mathematics may operate in certain technological, military, economic and political structures? (These and related questions are discussed in Skovsmose, 1998b; Skovsmose and Valero, 1999; and Vithal, 2000.) I would never dare to claim that leaving the exercise paradigm in order to explore landscapes of investigation would provide an answer to these questions. Nor would I claim that it is sufficient to build mathematics education solely on real-life references. My only hope is that finding a route among the different milieus of learning may offer new resources, allowing students to both act and reflect, and so provide mathematics education with a critical dimension.

Acknowledgements

I wish to express my gratitude to Helle Alrø, Morten Blomhøj, Gunnar Bomann, Henning Bødtkjer, Linda Haggarty, Arne Astrup Juul, Miriam Penteado, Mikael Skånstrøm and Paola Valero for their critical comments and their suggestions for clarifying the 'landscapes of investigation'.

References

Alrø, H. and Skovsmose, O. (1996a) 'On the right track', *For the Learning of Mathematics* 16(1): 2–9 and 22.

Alrø, H. and Skovsmose, O. (1996b) 'The students' good reasons', *For the Learning of Mathematics* 16(3): 31–8.

Alrø, H. and Skovsmose, O. (1998) 'That was not the intention! Communication in mathematics education', *For the Learning of Mathematics* 18(2): 42–51.

Borba, M.C. (1995) 'Graphic calculators, functions and reorganisation of the classroom', in M.C. Borba, T. Souza, B. Hudson and J. Fey (eds) *The Role of Technology in the Mathematics Classroom*, proceedings of WG 6, ICME–8, Sevilla, Cruzeiro, Rio Claro.

Borba, N. C. (1999) 'Technologias informáticas na educação matemática e reorganização do pensamento', in M.A.V. Bicudo (ed.) *Pesquisa em Educação Matemática: concepções e perspectivas*, São Paulo: Editora UNESP: 285–95.

Borba, M. and Skovsmose, O. (1997) 'The ideology of certainty', *For the Learning of Mathematics* 17(3): 17–23.

Brousseau, G. (1997) *Theory of Didactical Situations in Mathematics: didactique des mathématiques, 1970–1990*, N. Balacheff, M. Cooper, R. Sutherland and V. Warfield (eds and trans), Dordrecht, The Netherlands. Kluwer.

Christiansen, I.M. (1997) 'When negotiation of meaning is also negotiation of task', *Educational Studies in Mathematics* 34(1): 1–25.

Cobb, P. and Yackel, E. (1998) 'A constructivist perspective on the culture of the mathematics classroom', in F. Seeger, J. Voigt and U. Waschescio (eds) *The Culture of the Mathematics Classroom*, Cambridge: Cambridge University Press: 158–90.

Cotton, T. (1998) 'Towards a mathematics education for social justice', unpublished Ph.D. thesis.

D'Ambrosio, U. (1994) 'Cultural framing of mathematics teaching and learning', in R. Biehler, R.W. Scholz, R. Strässer and B. Winkelmann (eds) *Didactics of Mathematics as a Scientific Discipline*, Dordrecht, The Netherlands: Kluwer: 443–55.

Dowling, P. (1998) *The Sociology of Mathematics Education: mathematical myths/pedagogic texts*, London: The Falmer Press.

Frankenstein, M. (1989) *Relearning Mathematics: a different R – radical maths*, London: Free Association Books.

Freire, P. (1972) *Pedagogy of the Oppressed*, New York: Herder and Herder.

Kranzberg, M. (1997) 'Technology and history: "Kranzberg's Laws"', in T.S. Reynolds and S.H. Cutcliffe (eds) *Technology and the West: a historical anthology from technology and culture*, Chicago, IL: University of Chicago Press: 5–20.

Nielsen, L., Patronis, T. and Skovsmose, O. (1999) *Connecting Corners of Europe: a Greek Danish project in mathematics education*, Århus: Systime.

Penteado, M.G. (1999) 'Novos atores, novos cenários: discutindo a inserção dos computadores na profissão docente', in M.A.V. Bicudo (ed.) *Pesquisa em Educação Matemática: concepções e perspectivas*, São Paulo: Editora UNESP: 297–313.

Penteado, M.G. (2000) *Risk Zone: introduction of computers into teachers' practice*, Rio Claro: Depto. de Matematica, State University of São Paulo.

Skovsmose, O. (1994) *Towards a Philosophy of Critical Mathematics Education*, Dordrecht, The Netherlands: Kluwer.

Skovsmose, O. (1998a) 'Aporism: uncertainty about mathematics'. *Zentralblatt für Didaktik der Mathematik* 98(3): 88–94.

Skovsmose, O. (1998b) 'Linking mathematics education and democracy: citizenship, mathematics archaeology, mathemacy and deliberative interaction', *Zentralblatt für Didaktik der Mathematik* 98(6): 195–203.

Skovsmose, O. (2000) 'Aporism and critical mathematics education', *For the Learning of Mathematics* 20(1): 2–8.

Skovsmose, O. and Nielsen, L. (1996) 'Critical mathematics education', in A. Bishop *et al.* (ed.) *International Handbook of Mathematics Education*, Dordrecht, The Netherlands: Kluwer: 1257–88.

Skovsmose, O. and Valero, P. (1999) *Breaking Political Neutrality: the critical engagement of mathematics education with democracy*, Denmark: Centre for Research in Learning Mathematics, Royal Danish School of Educational Studies, Roskilde University Centre, Aalborg University.

Vithal, R. (2000) *In Search of a Pedagogy of Conflict and Dialogue for Mathematics Education*, Aalborg, Denmark: Aalborg University.

Vithal, R., Christiansen, I.M. and Skovsmose, O. (1995) 'Project work in university mathematics education: a Danish experience', *Educational Studies in Mathematics* 29: 199–223, Aalborg, Denmark: Aalborg University.

Wedege, T. (1999) *Matematikviden og Teknologiske Kompetencer hos Kortuddannede Voksne*, Ph. D. thesis, Roskilde, Denmark, Roskilde University Centre.

9 Maximising energy in the learning of mathematics

Gillian Hatch

Working creatively

I believe that when they start school all children bring with them the ability to work creatively in mathematics. This ability needs be preserved in learners of all ages and abilities. Thinking and behaving creatively is an increasingly important skill in a world becoming ever more dominated by technology. Society needs a plentiful supply of adults who are mathematically literate and able to apply their mathematical knowledge. In the UK, at present, the extent of this supply is in some doubt, whether we look at the evidence from university teachers (Gardiner, 1995) or, at school level, at the results of international surveys (Lapointe *et al.*, 1992). I suggest that this is due to the loss of children's creative energy during their mathematical schooling and I shall offer some ways of working that may prevent this.

Often the loss of a creative approach to mathematics occurs quite early in a pupil's experience of learning mathematics in the school context. Some years ago I spent a summer term teaching in a secondary school and its two main feeder primary schools. This enabled me to compare a class of high-ability first year secondary pupils with the most able primary pupils from the year group below. The contrast was disturbing. The younger pupils were willing and able to attack any problem I chose to set them. They assumed that if they had been offered a task, then they could make some progress with it. I prepared material for the older pupils, looking for interesting ways to approach the ideas, but each week I had to accept that my selected material was too demanding, not in terms of content but in its demands on them to be relatively autonomous learners. Sadly, I remained in conflict with the class as to what they should be able to do for the whole term. I found it impossible to accept that I could not tap back into the behaviour they would have shown only a year before. All their energy for the learning of mathematics had been sapped. I believe that this change was caused by teacher behaviour and expectation. It seemed clear that the teacher concerned had made them dependent learners, who knew, or thought they knew, that they had to be told how to solve each new kind of mathematical problem. If we are to improve the quality of learning in our classrooms then teachers have to think clearly about the messages that their actions are giving to pupils.

How a teacher behaves in a classroom in a mathematical situation, and the habitual interaction which takes place speaks volumes to pupils about mathematics and the possibilities in it for them.

(Love and Mason, 1992)

Another perspective on this problem comes from university mathematics teachers who comment on the poor level of conceptual understanding amongst first-year students.

Our 18-year-olds no longer have any idea that if mathematical assertions are to have any value at all, statements must be formulated carefully and manipulated in precise, reliable, strictly defensible ways ... . In particular they have no idea that Mathematics has to be understood logically and manipulated correctly. More than ever before they long for rules and procedures.

(Gardiner, 1995)

While the increase in the percentage of young people going on to university must be a factor in this perceived change, it is clear that many find the transition to university work a traumatic one, and undoubtedly some of the reasons for this lie in school mathematics teaching. Mathematics graduates, when they begin an initial teacher education course, are often voluble about the difficulties they experienced adjusting to their degree courses. Anderson (1996) gives a detailed analysis of the causes of the problem but accepts the basic contentions. While I do not agree with all the arguments put forward by Gardiner and other critics, I fear that I do recognise some of the behaviours they describe when working with students following a degree course leading to qualification as a mathematics teacher.

My 12-year-old pupils, described above, also longed for rules and procedures. The problem was already discernible even at that age. The roles of problem-solving, investigation, the attainment of understanding, and the acquisition of appropriate fluency within the learning of mathematics need careful consideration. The UK political climate can make one feel that we are alone in finding the balance of these elements difficult to get correct. It is interesting, and in some ways comforting, to find similar concerns elsewhere. From Japan, Fujita *et al.* (1996) describe their students' dislike of mathematics and their lack of problem-solving skills.

I believe that the aim of mathematics teaching should be to keep all pupils in a high-energy state throughout their mathematical learning careers. Pupils in such a state will confront any problem, given to them or invented for themselves, with their previous learning in mathematics in an active and accessible state and with the assumption that they have the ability to make progress. It is clearly not easy to achieve this state, particularly with older or less able pupils, yet this is precisely the way in which pre-school children approach their learning. We need to find ways to preserve this attitude into formal schooling.

Such learners can be created only by providing high-energy classrooms for them. The task is made more difficult for teachers by the fact that most of them have not experienced such classrooms either at secondary school or university. Mathematics teachers have, however, retained enough of their early energy to decide to study Mathematics at university whether or not they experienced high-energy classrooms. Occasional individuals have even retained their own learning energy throughout the formalism of a university course. However, for most students learning to teach there is a need for a reawakening of energy. It is thus important to consider the nature of the high-energy classroom and how it may be created by the teacher.

What is lacking?

First let us consider the context and the influences on teachers of Mathematics in the UK which have led to classrooms showing high energy only rarely. Over the last twenty years teachers have been subjected to many studies, often conflicting with one another, and to criticisms of all kinds. So much advice has been given that it is unremarkable if they are bewildered and find it difficult to know which ideas to accept. There have, I believe, been two significant long-term results of the influential Cockcroft report (1982). The first is the 'bottom up curriculum', i.e. a curriculum designed to meet, as its priority, the needs of the average and below-average pupil. The second is the introduction into the curriculum of 'investigations'. I do not believe that either is an unqualified success. Philosophically, I agree strongly that the curriculum of the average or below-average child should not be driven by the needs of the more able child. We need a curriculum that supports all learners equally and enables all individuals to reach their maximum potential.

Pace

But it seems possible that the 'understanding of difficulty' approach has led to the loss of a sense of urgency to progress. Indeed, two Hungarian colleagues who visited British schools as part of a project with my university observed that:

> As a result of our experiences we formed the opinion that in an English school the underlying philosophy of teaching is quite different from ours ... Not to hurt the self 'image' of children is more important than to force them to achieve better results.
>
> (*Torok and Szeredi, 1993*)

Lesson pace has now become an issue for teachers in the UK as a result of the framework used to inspect our schools. Visiting schools in Hungary I felt that every lesson had this element of pace, but rarely do I observe the same quality in visits to UK classrooms. Pace, I believe, is not to do with the speed of movement through the curriculum but with a sort of tautness of expectation where all the pupils' energy is bent towards the learning task, whatever its nature. Pace is not to do with getting through more 'sums' per lesson but to do with the energy expended in understanding the meaning behind the sums and reflecting on the mathematics. The creation of a high-energy classroom will certainly involve the maintenance of pace.

Know-how

While the UK national assessment system is dominated by the techniques of mathematics there is a great temptation to teach through memory and not understanding (see Chapter 4 by Dave Hewitt). This means that our pupils do not acquire 'know-hows':

> But as soon as learning is stressed, everything changes. It seems that knowledge cannot simply be entrusted to memory; everyone must produce in one's mind the equivalent of that knowledge and replace it by a know-how ... Only know-hows can be counted on and do endure.
>
> (Gattegno, 1982)

Only 'know-hows', not memorised routines, can contribute to the high-energy state.

Investigating, conjecturing and proving

In many schools investigations have been, I believe, little short of a disaster. I have written about this elsewhere (Hatch, 1995). While the process of investigating is central to the kind of teaching that will create energy, it needs to be at the centre of the learning processes of mathematics and not undertaken as a separate topic or just to satisfy the requirements of an examination. The setting of investigations as assessment tasks, completed in a certain time span, which can be reliably marked using a numerical mark scheme, misrepresents the whole process of mathematical investigation which, as any mathematical researcher will confirm, proceeds at a definitely non-linear and unpredictable rate!

The average mathematics classroom that I visit may contain elements of investigational work, but these are not well integrated into the curriculum. They have little mathematical significance and often lead to poorly developed results. There is little sense that a well-tested conjecture is not the end of the road, that there remains a task to be undertaken before the conjecture becomes certainty. This ready acceptance of the truth of unproven conjectures may well be one of the root causes of the behaviour described by Gardiner. Alongside such investigational work I see much traditional chalk, talk and routine practice. As a teacher educator I work hard to present other models of the mathematics classroom. The problem in getting these accepted is that they are all harder to operate and student teachers often do not see them operating in schools, therefore the status quo tends to remain unchallenged.

Struggle

Many texts have been developed over the last ten years, aiming to make the learning of mathematics easier. Teachers have hoped that these would help pupils to enjoy mathematics more. However, when learning is broken down into minute steps the learner neither sees the overall picture nor learns to take bigger steps alone. The learner retains the information less well because the deeper parts of the brain do not become engaged. To internalise a concept in mathematics we need to engage with it in some real sense, we need to articulate it and reflect upon it, to relate it to other ideas. We need to educate our pupils to know that, out of difficulties encountered and overcome, emerges real 'know-how'. The high-energy state is characterised by the excitement of having struggled but yet won through (see Chapter 6 by Mary Barnes).

Challenging some assumptions about teaching

Little seems to have changed over the years despite the enormous volume of research and the many reports that have been produced. The same problems are described repeatedly. What can be said that might help teachers change what happens in classrooms? I have come to believe that there are two basic teacher assumptions that we need to question and perhaps to oppose actively in initial teacher education.

The importance of getting right answers

The first of these is hard to eradicate, especially in a system in which teachers and schools are judged by the performance of pupils in technique-based tests. It is that as teachers we feel happy when the pupils get the 'sums' right. We are not inclined to dig deeper and look for lack of understanding; we feel they are doing nicely and we feel good about it. Now, of course, we do need pupils to acquire appropriate levels of fluency. However we need also to be sure that pupils are facing difficulties of interpretation, discovering that the answers do not always drop out smoothly and that a struggle is sometimes essential. We need to develop strategies for helping pupils to work with difficult ideas.

Our pupils need to find mathematics offers something intellectually satisfying at an appropriate level for each of them if they are to value their progress. Above all, we have to believe that we are not failing if our pupils are not always succeeding easily.

As teachers we need to learn to probe their understanding, to uncover lack of clarity and misconceptions even if we do not like the results. As a teacher educator I ask student teachers and mentors in school to work with the classic conflict teaching question: 'Which is bigger: two-thirds or three-quarters?' The mentors are all convinced that the pupils will have so little difficulty that a lesson based on this is just not possible. They are almost always shaken by the misconceptions and failures in understanding that emerge. Conceptual problems need to be met head on rather than avoided if real understanding is to be achieved.

Teaching as explaining

The second assumption is that one of the main tasks of a teacher is to explain mathematics clearly to the pupils so that they understand it. When applicants to mathematics teacher education courses are interviewed they often suggest that they will enjoy explaining mathematics to pupils. Yet when I ask them to describe the characteristics of a good mathematics teacher they talk first about patience and humour. Only later do some speak of the ability to give multiple explanations of the same thing thereby tacitly acknowledging the fact that one explanation is rarely effective. As learners they seem to know that a lot more is involved than simple explanation. Yet as teachers they will usually feel that a major part of their job is to explain.

Dave Hewitt, in Chapter 4 of this volume, offers a useful approach to the issue of explanations. He divides mathematical knowledge into two categories. The first is that which is arbitrary, for example standard notation, definitions. The second is that which can be deduced from earlier knowledge or by working logically with the elements involved in the given situation. He argues strongly that to explain to pupils things which are non-arbitrary is to risk creating dependency on the teacher, to risk them ceasing to believe that they can work for themselves on the mathematics. It leads them to demand information as to how to approach the next step. Clearly the role of the teacher may include assisting the children to achieve their own explanations but in terms of autonomy this is very different from just supplying the correct explanation or answer.

Smith (1986) describes 'teaching without telling' as a process in which students' contributions are all valued as they are led to ask their own questions and are helped by the teacher only by the asking of more questions. The teacher in such a situation can often assist the pupils to move forwards just by asking them to review what they have done and reflect on it. In this way the pupils retain their self-confidence and the problem they are attempting to solve remains their own.

We need to withhold explanation unless there is no way pupils can create it for themselves. We need to monitor our behaviour carefully and try to perceive how we are using our explanations. We need to research the situations in which teacher explanation is valuable and necessary and those in which it is destructive. We need to enlarge our concept of explanation beyond simple verbal action. As a teacher educator I have to consider these two issues of teacher behaviour very seriously and seek ways for student teachers to become aware of their significance.

What is it that a teacher should be doing to improve the quality of learning in the classroom and ensure that the pupils are kept in a high-energy state? Schoenfeld (1994) gives a challenging description of what a classroom needs to be like to remain true to the nature of mathematics:

> If we believe that doing mathematics is an act of sense making; if we believe that mathematics is often a hands-on empirical activity; if we believe that mathematical communication is important; if we believe that the mathematical community grapples with serious mathematical problems collaboratively, making tentative explanations of these phenomena, and then cycling back through these explanations (including definitions and postulates); if we believe that learning mathematics is empowering and that there is a mathematical way of

thinking that has value and power, then our classroom practices must reflect those beliefs.

A mathematical ethos

In their recent review of research, Askew and Wiliam (1996), summarising the most recent international survey, speak of a 'mathematical ethos' in schools as linking with high achievement. This idea appears to connect strongly to the Schoenfeld description of high-quality learning. So our high-energy classroom needs to have such an ethos.

What might constitute a mathematical ethos in the classroom? I shall consider the areas of learning, reflection, practice and fluency, conjecturing, and memory, and the contribution that each can offer, to making our classrooms fit Schoenfeld's description.

Learning takes time

First of all we must convince teachers that one can never teach anyone anything; all one can do is to create a situation in which pupils may learn. The description given by Griffin (1989) of the need to allow time for learning to take place always catches the sympathy of classroom teachers, especially when given to them during a course that requires them to learn mathematics themselves. They recognise their need for that time to come to terms with the ideas and can relate this to children's needs.

> So what is the relationship between teaching and learning? I am drawn back to the conjecture behind 'teaching takes place in time, learning takes place over time', that learning is a process of maturation in the learner. The teacher cannot perform this process for the learner nor can the teacher force it upon the learner. Rather, it is the atmosphere and environment created in the classroom by the actions of the teacher which can raise the awareness of the learner and shift attention in such a way as to stimulate this process of maturation in the learner.
>
> (Griffin, 1989)

So we need to offer to pupils the chance to mature their understanding of a topic so that it will become part of their thinking and remain available to them.

Reflection

Maturation and reflection go hand in hand. A useful definition of reflection is given by Billington (1992):

> Reflection is the process by which one re-enters and focuses on a previous experience and as a result of that focusing confirms or makes changes to ideas previously held.

Davis (1988) relates reflection to the linking of significant moments and sharp experiences that can be held on to mentally and referred back to when a similar context occurs. So we need to give time to helping our pupils trace ideas back, to link them to previous experiences and draw out the commonalities. This is, in some sense, the reverse process to that in which pupils build up their own explanations. The rehearsal of the relation between new ideas and old supports the building of secure conceptual networks and implicitly suggests the idea of backtracking to firm ground if any ideas have become hazy. In the idea of reflection we can identify a resonance with Schoenfeld's phrase, 'cycling back through these explanations'. The purpose of reflection can thus be seen as that of making sense of what has been done, linking it to previous ideas. It can also include, in a classroom situation, sorting out differences of understanding between individuals.

Fluency and practice

The relationship between understanding and fluency is a complex one. A failure of fluency can cause much loss of energy. For example, it can cause such a delay in progress that the thread of the piece of work is lost. Able 13-year-old pupils who work out 18 + 5 on their fingers, or who are held up for perceptible amounts of time while they struggle to recall their tables, are liable to lose impetus in any work requiring a higher level of reasoning. I have watched pupils in the early stages of a sixth-form course, 17-year-olds who have chosen to study mathematics further, struggle with algebra and experience a feeling of total inadequacy. Yet they often need only to increase their algebraic fluency by doing some practice from a conventional algebra textbook to regain their energy. Bruce (1994), in a case study of three pupils aged 15–18, concludes that the student who progressed effortlessly to the higher level of mathematics was the one who not only showed robust concepts but had well developed skills in several key areas. The pupil who had not been given the time to achieve this mastery struggled and needed extra support to succeed. The most able pupil also had the capacity to refer back to internalised explanations of the automatic skills he had developed. These were certainly 'know-hows' as described by Gattegno.

Watching pupils play games as part of a research project, I became aware of the power of games to create what I call 'an unreasonable amount of practice', i.e. an amount of practice which would never be tolerated if pupil attention was on the practice rather than on the game. When applied to algebraic skills, for example, this kind of activity seems to lead pupils to learn to handle immensely complicated algebraic expressions apparently almost without noticing the complexity. The attention of the pupils is switched to the game not the difficulty of the algebra, and this appears to cause a subordination of learning of algebra to the excitement of the game. Hewitt (1994) gives an account of a similar, almost game-like activity, which results in comparable effects. He writes of 'a functioning – something which the learner knows so well that they hardly have to give it any conscious thought'.

In high-energy classrooms we should help pupils to become aware of the need to practise and achieve fluency. Pimm (1995) raises the issue of the awareness of the pupils to what they are doing:

> Children are very good at practising certain things until they have mastered them – they are willing, it seems, to pay the necessary attention. One thing is clear, however … it crucially matters how pupils approach practice in terms of what they get from it.

In any classroom that can be characterised as having a 'mathematical ethos' it seems that pupils should be expected to understand that fluency is in their own interests. We need to share this expectation with them and offer them ways to work at their perceived needs, perhaps in a semi-autonomous way. We need to help them to see that fluency can involve more than the mindless uncritical solution of routine problems. The activity of classifying routine problems, standing back and identifying what types of problem are involved and discerning what kind of approach is needed for each, constitutes a form of reflection on learning. As Pimm (1995) says:

> One key point is that if I approach a series of exercises with my eye out for the general, for what there is in common across all these activities, then I am better mathematically attuned to what is of importance. If I go through the exercises one after another, as something to get through, then my attention is crucially missing from the central focus, from the point of view of teaching. Sets of exercises where there is no connection between one and the next destroy the possibility of such focused practice.

As teachers we need to be sure that the tasks that we set for our pupils allow them to search for general structure within the particular exercises. We need to induct them into this process by discussing which problems are similar and which different.

Tasks of this kind can lead to the identification of general principles that might otherwise remain implicit. Within my work on algebraic games I became concerned as to whether the pupils thought that the rules for algebraic language changed with the letter used. I prepared a set of cards each of which had on it a linear equation. The pack contained sets of three cards showing the same equation but using a different letter for the variable. I asked a group of six to sort these cards into piles which had the same solution. Soon someone was saying that they had just solved this one and in response to my query I was told that it was just the letters that were different. When all the cards were in piles, I was able to tell them that it could not be correct as there should be the same number of cards in each pile. A quick re-examination led to the statement that 'It's the ones that are the same that should be in the same pile,' and the cards were rapidly sorted by 'sameness'. There was a great air of satisfaction and energy when this task was complete, yet it held within it quite a lot of routine practice, at least if your pedagogic philosophy allows you to accept the mental solution of simple equations!

Another possible way to create 'thoughtful practice' is to ask students, as a group, to set their own homework problems to practise something they have just learnt. This has two outcomes: one learns whether they have internalised the ideas sufficiently to be able to do this and in the next session the ones that were 'wrong' can be discussed, allowing further reflection on the task.

Conjecturing

Another element essential to this mathematical ethos is what has become known as 'conjecturing', that is the willingness to venture to state, for response by others in the group, a conjecture which is in the process of development. It invites comment from everyone as to its relevance, precision and truth. It involves all the pupils in the evaluation of ideas. When such an ethos has been established, the attitude of critical assessment permeates the situation:

> When a conjecturing atmosphere is established, pupils respond to exposition not as assertions to be 'learned' but as a stimulus to check out the ideas for themselves, to make sense for themselves through exploration and through explaining to each other.
>
> (Love and Mason, 1992)

The speaking out loud of a conjecture gains in several ways. To utter it at all, the conjecturer must clarify it sufficiently to express it in words that carry meaning for other people. Once it is uttered, it becomes a more objective object that itself may be criticised by the conjecturer. It is, by articulation, placed firmly in the arena for others to comment on, to make the attempt to refine or refute it. The teacher may play a part in this refining act, but in this atmosphere it is possible for the teacher's input to be subjected to the same critical comment. This process can be part of whole-class discussion as when the resolution of a piece of conflict teaching is in progress. Alternatively it may occur within small-group interaction, for example, during a piece of investigational work or when pairs of children play as a unit in a game. It embodies the idea of justification, which is at the heart of a true mathematical ethos, and allows contributions from different people as insight is developed. Pupils need to be helped to achieve this level of discourse, but the very fact that it is verbal makes it easier. In such a classroom the teacher's role is not just one of referee; there is much to be done in the thoughtful framing of questions, in the stressing and ignoring of certain aspects of the discussion, in the repetition of a pupil's statement, perhaps in slightly different words to establish whether there is agreement as to its meaning. The most significant contribution of all is probably the acceptance that everyone's ideas are of value and can be woven into the group progression in mathematics.

Watson (1994) describes how she works with the ideas that pupils offer in discussion. She believes that it is the teacher's task to be seen to value all pupils' contributions to discussion, to weave these into an account in which all the class have been involved. However, she also identifies a need to help the pupils, by her commentary on their results, to identify what is significant and the ideas that will contribute to the way forward in mathematics. In playing this role the teacher becomes a kind of consultant who is able to advise and comment but not take over authority over the totality of the knowledge constructed.

Know-how versus memorisation

Gattegno distinguishes knowledge from know-how and calls attention to the fact that we have to do more with knowledge than memorise it, if it is to become functional. As a pupil at school I enjoyed mathematics partly because it did not involve much memory work. However it is on just this issue of memory that many pupils founder as learners of mathematics. They become teacher-dependent memorisers of what to do in an ever-increasing number of meaningless situations. Hewitt (1994) (see also Hewitt in Chapter 4) discusses this need to avoid memorisation:

> Memory is an expensive way to ask people to learn. If the underlying structure can be made explicit, then a learner can be creative within that structure and generate their knowledge rather than being asked to memorise it.

The use of know-hows that can be re-accessed and recycled releases energy for intelligent action. Unless we use reflection to build such structures our pupils will not be able to retain their high-energy state. They will be using all their attention to hold on to meaningless rules, each existing independently of the others. Our high-energy pupils need to be helped to develop links and connections whenever possible. When an automated routine suddenly comes under question they need to be able to trace it back to its roots and re-establish it. They need to be able to respond to the question, 'How do you know that is correct?'

This indicates a strong relationship between the saving of memory energy and the idea of reflection. What then might help pupils to reflect and refine their understanding so that connections are made and retained? Talking mathematics both out loud and to oneself is crucial. Pimm (1987) speaks of the value of articulation:

> There is a world of difference between tacit and externalised knowledge. One force of talking aloud is that it requires the use of words, whereas merely talking to oneself allows words to be bypassed. It may be only when you discover a difficulty in expressing what you want to say, that you realise that things are not quite as you thought. Articulation can aid the process of reflection by affording better access to the thought itself.

An internal monitor

As we create opportunities for pupils to discuss or reflect we must keep in the forefront of our minds the need to support the development of conceptual structures by highlighting the interconnection of ideas. In the long term every mathematics learner needs to develop their own capacity to hear ideas in their head in such a way that they feel as if they were spoken out loud. Love and Mason (1992) speak of the 'internal monitor' who supplies a commentary on the mathematics being done, which all experts develop. They hold that pupils develop such a monitor by interac· tion with others whose own monitors are working well. It becomes, therefore, the responsibility of the teacher to seek opportunities to describe the functioning of their own monitor to help pupils to move outside their own work and criticise it. In the midst of mathematical work, experts may find themselves asking, 'Am I going in the right direction?' Their internal monitors are relatively well developed. By contrast a novice, with no internal monitor with which to maintain an overall picture, may be deeply embedded in the calculation and so keeps on struggling, getting deeper and deeper into the mire. Vygotsky was convinced that the only way that such a monitor will develop is through social interactions with others whose monitors are active. Watson's description of her way of working seems to include the demonstration of her internal monitor. Energised pupils certainly need to have this kind of monitor when working either as individuals or in a group.

There is a simple way in which we can start to work on this. My observation is that most pupils who obtain an obviously incorrect answer, even if they know it must be nonsense, hand in the work with no comment, hoping illogically, I believe, that the teacher will not notice the error. If teachers expect pupils to annotate their work with comments as to the reasonableness of their results and demonstrate that they value an incorrect answer with a clear evaluation of why it is incorrect as highly as the correct answer, then the process is at least started. When I say this is a simple way, I mean it is simple to describe. To persuade pupils to do this will need the kind of mathematical ethos in which errors are to be examined with interest as opportunities to progress, rather than mistakes to be carefully hidden.

Confidence and power

We need to create pupils who have confidence in their own mathematical powers. I have for many years now watched out for the moments when a learner of any age suddenly feels powerful, though it does not happen as often as I should like. I shall give some examples drawn from a range of contexts.

Some years ago a teacher on an in-service course said to me, 'Gill, come and tell me whether this is right – no, I know it's right, but come and let me tell you about it.' For him it was a moment of breakthrough. All learners need to experience feel- ings of power, confidence and control over mathematical situations in which they are working.

A student on the first year of a teacher education degree, who was very unsure of himself in mathematics, had achieved some progress with the problem on which the group was working. I asked him to present his results to the class. Thereafter, throughout a four-year course, he remained sure that he could do mathematics and at least once referred back to this as a turning point for him.

Mark, aged 9, had found a procedure that allowed him to win a simple strategy game. He said to me with immense pride and satisfaction, 'Just think, if you put 503 sticks on the table and the rule is that I can take one to nine sticks, all I have to do is take three sticks and I've won!' His pleasure in the generality of his solution involved an element of feeling in control of the situation. He had mastered it, he was really powerful.

Alice had discovered, in discussion, the possibility of using what she called 'take-away numbers'. She spent the rest of the afternoon creating more and more difficult examples of their use. Alice was exercising power over a newly acquired and well-understood skill. It seemed to me like a flexing of mental muscles whose power she really enjoyed. Highly energised students can greatly enjoy this muscle-flexing process. I remember at secondary school solving pages of quadratic equations just to enjoy my newly acquired power over them. Essential, however, is the provision of activities or time for this kind of power to develop.

This idea of feeling powerful is, I believe, strongly connected to the idea of a 'magical' moment discussed by Mary Barnes in Chapter 6. Experiencing a 'magical' moment certainly makes one feel powerful.

An agenda for conserving energy

So what is the agenda for beginning to work towards the conservation of energy in mathematics learning? Teachers need to accept two hard ideas:

- pupils need to experience challenge and struggle in their mathematics learning if they are to gain understanding;
- explanation is a two-edged and too easily accepted teacher weapon.

In working as, and with, teachers we need to pay attention to the following vital issues:

- how not to tell pupils things they can work out for themselves;
- how to create space for learning to mature;
- how to help our pupils to become reflective;
- how to avoid requiring pupils to overuse memory;
- what appropriate fluency is, particularly in the era of the symbolic manipulator, but also in relation to the ordinary calculator;
- how to create opportunities for pupils to talk about their mathematical ideas and develop internal monitors and rich conceptual structures;
- how to help our pupils to feel they are powerful learners of mathematics.

References

Anderson, J. A. (1996) 'The place of proof in school mathematics', *Mathematics Teaching* 155: 33–9.

Askew, M. and Wiliam, D. (1996) *Recent Research in Mathematics Education 5–16*, London: HMSO.

Billington, E. (1992) 'Beyond mere experience', unpublished MPhil. thesis, Open University, Milton Keynes.

Bruce, M. (1994) 'Failing A level Mathematics from the outset', unpublished MSc thesis, Manchester Metropolitan University.

Cockcroft, W.H. (1982) *Mathematics Counts*, London: HMSO.

Davis, J. (1988) 'Mathematics update', tutor notes, Open University, Milton Keynes.

Fujita, H., Itaka, S., Uctake, T. and Yokoehi, J. (1996) 'Mathematics education at risk' *Journal of the Japan Society of Mathematical Education*, reprinted in *The Mathematical Gazette* 488: 352–5.

Gardiner, A. (1995) 'Wrong way! Go back!' *Mathematical Gazette* 485: 335–46.

Gattegno, C. (1982) 'Thirty years later', *Mathematics Teaching* 100: 42–5.

Griffin P. (1989) 'Teaching takes place in time, learning takes place over time', *Mathematics Teaching* 126: 12–13.

Hatch, G. (1995) 'If not investigations, what?' *Mathematics Teaching* 151: 36–9.

Hewitt, D. (1994) 'The principle of economy in the learning and teaching of mathematics', unpublished Ph.D. thesis, Open University, Milton Keynes.

Lapointe, A.E., Mead, N.A. and Askew, J.M. (1992) 'Learning mathematics', *Report of the Second International Assessment of Educational Progress*, Princeton, NJ.

Love, E. and Mason, J. (1992) *Teaching Mathematics. Action and awareness*, Milton Keynes, Open University.

Pimm, D. (1987) *Mathematics, Symbols and Meanings*, Milton Keynes: Open University.

Pimm, D. (1995) *Symbols and Meaning in School Mathematics*, London: Routledge.

Schoenfeld, A.H. (1994) 'What do we know about mathematics curricula?' *The Journal of Mathematical Behaviour* 13: 55–80.

Smith, J. (1986) 'Questioning questioning', *Mathematics Teaching* 115(47).

Torok, J. and Szeredi, E. (1992) *Vade Mecum for Hungarian Students*, unpublished.

Watson, A. (1994) 'What I do in my classroom' in M. Sellinger (ed.) *Teaching Mathematics*, London: Routledge: 52–62.

10 Integrating computers into the teaching of mathematics

Ronnie Goldstein

Mathematics and IT – a pupil's entitlement (NCET, 1995) describes six major opportunities which ICT offers to those learning mathematics: learning from feedback, observing patterns, seeing connections, working with dynamic images, exploring data and teaching the computer. Some of these opportunities stress the mathematics, some focus on the ICT and some are about learning in general. A few years ago a similar document might have been structured by a consideration of major software applications such as spreadsheets, databases, dynamic geometry, graphic calculators and the Logo programming language. But it is not good enough these days just to consider the ICT. When a technology is unfamiliar it may be necessary to start by looking at it out of context and to consider what it can do rather than what we can do with it. But, as time moves on, we begin to understand that ICT must be integrated into the curriculum if it is to have any purpose in schools. This is not a new idea but nevertheless current practice suggests that it is appropriate to reiterate it here.

The computer is a tool and as such it must usually be secondary to the task in hand, a servant of the curriculum. In most secondary schools today there are not yet enough computers for them to be accommodated in all teaching rooms and also in computer rooms where all children can gain access. For various reasons, computer rooms have taken priority and, inevitably, students do not always appreciate the connection between their computer activities and the curriculum. When computers are more prevalent, we shall all benefit in the way that some owners of laptops or graphic calculators benefit today. The students will be using a personal, flexible tool, which is always accessible to them and yet never dominates their attention. It will be used only when there is an appropriate context and, when it is no longer needed, it will be put away.

A number of classroom activities where the computer has an important role are described in this chapter. In each case the benefit of additional work away from the computer is stressed. We start with a particular topic, locus, then we consider the classroom activity of tiling, which can be used to cover several National Curriculum topics; and finally we discuss the general notion of pattern in mathematics and the need for explanation. In each case, the computer provides only one approach amongst many that might be valuable. The computer activities do not stand alone and they must be fully integrated with the rest of the mathematics curriculum if the full potential of the medium is to be realised.

Locus at the computer

Understanding geometrical objects (a circle, a perpendicular bisector and so on) as the locus of points constrained by a rule enriches the geometrical conception of those objects and also provides students with an opportunity to experience the idea of mathematical constraint. Dynamic geometry software[1] can be used to draw loci in various ways. Perhaps the simplest is to plot particular points that are known to lie on the locus. For instance, to find the locus of points that are twice as far from one fixed point, A, as they are from another, B, the students could move a third point, C, around on the screen and measure the distances (CA and CB).

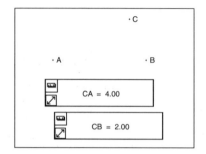

Figure 10.1 CA = 2CB

When the condition of the locus is met, the point can be kept in the correct position and then the exercise can be repeated for a number of other points in different positions. Alternatively, the students could use Blu-tack to mark the positions of the points (Figure 10.2). This gives messages about the status of the data on the screen in terms of accuracy and, because you cannot print a screen full of Blu-tack, students have to make sketches of their work, which encourages them to discuss their work away from the computer.

Figure 10.2 A child uses Blu-tack to record points on the screen that lie on the locus

Simple loci for younger students to explore at the start include the points that are a given distance from a fixed point, the points that are a given distance from a fixed line and the points that are equidistant from two fixed points or two fixed lines. In addition, most dynamic geometry packages also allow locus definition by constant area to be explored.

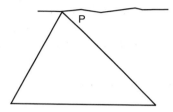

How can you move P so that
the area of the triangle always stays the same?

Why should this be?

Here the traditional approach is to start with the line parallel to the base of the triangle and note that the area is constant. Working with the computer, however, allows the teacher to adopt a problem-solving approach that will be more exciting for many of the students. Another example of approaching a problem back-to-front and using Blu-tack or some other means to locate particular points, is given below.

Quicksand

You are walking towards some quicksand. There are two posts in the ground.
If the angle between you and the two posts is more than 90°, you will be in the quicksand.
If it less than 90° you will be safe.

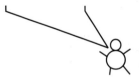

Find the edge of the quicksand.
Explore what happens for other angles.

Usually, pupils start with circles and learn the angle properties associated with them. Here, the pupils start with a particular property and they discover the circle for themselves.

An alternative approach for some students might be to start with a geometrical object – a circle, a square, an angle bisector – and to ask whether or not it can be generated as a locus. This would involve determining a property that defines the shape.

Older students might be able to understand a method for constructing the path traced by a locus. The methods employed above for tracing loci are valuable but they are not precise. They can be used to form helpful pictures of the results but it may be necessary to *construct* the loci. A picture might fail to reveal that a locus that looks circular is actually an ellipse. If the locus has been constructed it should be possible to test extreme cases and learn more. The following approach uses the idea of a 'handle'. For example, if the required locus is the set of points equidistant from a fixed point and a fixed straight line, the handle only needs to be an independent line segment.

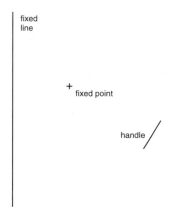

Figure 10.3   A line segment is used as the 'handle'

The handle is used to construct the two equal lengths. Start by constructing all the points whose distance from the fixed point is the length of the handle (a circle). Then construct all the points the same distance from the fixed line (a parallel line). The intersections of the circle and the parallel line must be two of the points that lie on the locus.

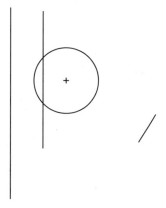

Figure 10.4 The intersections are the same distance from the point and the line

The users can then alter the length of the handle and see the intersections move as the diagram changes. The software can also be used to trace the locus of the intersections.

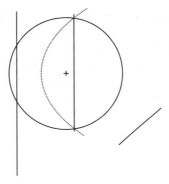

Figure 10.5 Changing the length of the handle generates the locus

The result in this case is a parabola.

Other locus activities

The approaches considered above for the teaching of locus all involve dynamic geometry software. While it has been appropriate to elaborate on these (the software has not been with us for too many years yet), there are many other classroom activities that might also be valid. For example, plotting particular points might be done with a large sheet of paper and counters, using a ruler to measure the distances and find points that lie on the locus. If the teacher wants to work with small groups of children this might be more expedient than the use of a computer, which is more suitable for pairs.

An important method, which has no equivalent approach at the computer, is the body-centred approach. This involves the students themselves moving around in the playground or the school hall. They must each act as one of the points and obey the rule, in order that they form the locus (Figure 10.6).

Figure 10.6 Children standing the same distance from the dustbin and the wall

The teacher can ask all the students to move so that they are standing at a point that is twice the distance from one chair as they are from another. This forces every student to be central and active. The activity is usually successful because the students cannot fail. Even if they do not fully understand where they should position themselves, they will not be out of line if they follow their friends. The students will appreciate that the results of such an exercise are very approximate and this may be a good reason to move on to a different approach. Indeed, getting the students to participate is a good way to start the topic of locus.

An entirely different approach is to encourage the students to form a mental image:

> Close your eyes. In your mind can you see two points? Put a cross near one of the points and move it slowly towards the other one until it is the same distance from each. Now move the cross further, so that it is twice as far from one of the points as it is from the other …

Forming pictures in the mind is easier for some people than it is for others. However, it is an important mathematical process that we need to stimulate in all our students (see also Bills, 2001).

Finally, as we complete this array of different classroom approaches to the study of locus, there is software specifically designed for the topic: for instance, *Arms* is from the SLIMWAM[2] collection and it shows two line segments each rotating about one of its end-points. The computer traces the locus of the mid-point of the line joining the rotating end-points of the arms.

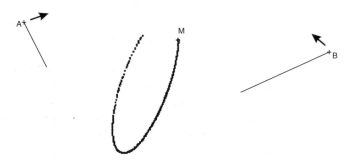

Figure 10.7 The two arms rotate and the locus of M, the mid-point of AB, is traced

The user of the computer is free to change many of the factors that alter the locus, such as the lengths of the arms and the speed and direction of their rotation. Using software such as *Arms* encourages conjecturing as the students struggle to identify the impact of these different factors. However, this means that the students must reflect, and sometimes when they work independently, they are more likely to press the 'go' button and see the final picture before they have given themselves the chance to ponder the all important questions. Perhaps *Arms* and other software which encourages students to ask, 'I wonder what would happen if … ?' should be driven by the teacher and run on a single machine in the classroom.

It may not be appropriate to use all of the methods above during a child's education at secondary school. (Given a free choice, which approaches would you adopt, and when?) It will surely be beneficial, however, to use more than one, in which case it is vital that they are connected somehow. If one of the methods involves the computer, it must be seen by the students to be directly related to any non-computer approach.

Tiling at the computer or with cardboard?

Tiling is another topic which can be very fruitful in the secondary curriculum and there is very good software[3] enabling students to design their own patterns. The topic itself is not mentioned in the National Curriculum but it is very attractive to students and it can be used to address many aspects of transformation geometry and angle. When computers are used to serve the curriculum the relative merits of the technology and other resources can be considered. A student using software to design tiling patterns will undoubtedly benefit from the speed and accuracy of the microcomputer and will be able to create several different shapes and test them all to see if they form tiling patterns. But, on the other hand, the student may need to do some things more slowly, so that there is time to understand the rationale of an approach. If the student has never used scissors and card, or at least plastic shapes, to make tiling patterns, a full understanding may never be reached of the design of the pattern that the computer achieves so quickly. This does not imply, however, that the computer can only be used when the student fully appreciates all the concepts. Forming partially understood patterns quickly and easily can motivate students to understand what is happening.

Work with scissors and card should be happening alongside the computer. Perhaps the most important message we can learn from all of this is the obvious one: don't let the students try to learn anything by using one approach alone. Learners need a variety of contexts in which to experience new concepts. The computer can be exciting and worthwhile but it is one road among many to a full conceptual understanding.

In discussing the relative merits of computers and other resources there is a danger of assuming that the results for the student are the same and that the same mathematical content is being addressed. Let us consider tiling activities in a little more depth in order to illustrate how false this can be. *Put and take* is an idea well known in the primary school.

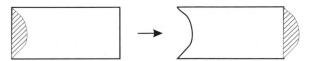

Figure 10.8 A piece of the card is moved

The essence of the activity, when it is done with card and scissors, is to cut a small piece from one side of a tile and stick it on the opposite side. This produces a new shape and, provided the original shape can be used as a tile, so, too, can the new one.

At first glance *Reptile*[3] might appear to offer a similar experience, but there are important differences. When children work with card and scissors, the emphasis is on the piece of card to be repositioned and the topic of area can be addressed. With *Reptile*, however, the students have to manipulate the edges of the tile. The same final result is achieved by distorting one of these edges and then copying it, so that two of the tile's edges are identical. At no point is the student likely to be considering the area of the tile – the emphasis is on the identical edges.

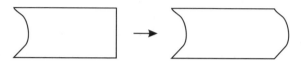

Figure 10.9 The computer copies the distorted edge

It has often been observed that the medium of any activity fundamentally affects the message, and it is important to be aware that different approaches in the classroom will not produce identical results. Hopefully, they will be complementary.

Observing patterns

The notion of pattern is not often a topic in its own right but it has a central position in mathematics and computers can facilitate the process of spotting patterns. One of the opportunities computers provide for learners of mathematics is *observing patterns* (NCET, 1995). When exploring mathematical problems, the speed of computers and calculators enables students to produce many examples and this means that they may be more likely to observe patterns and make generalisations. A very simple example arises when a young student is using a calculator to multiply different decimal numbers by 10. The pattern of the results becomes clear very quickly. Without the technology, using the standard written algorithm to multiply would surely be ineffective for some of the children. In the space of a lesson they might not be able to achieve more than a few results and so the pattern would not be so obvious. One or more wrong results would certainly render the activity worthless! With the technology the answers are always correct (we often need to concentrate on the correct questions) and so the pattern is clear. It is, of course, assumed here that the teacher's purpose in this activity is to stress the pattern – if the aim of the lesson is for the students to learn to multiply numbers on paper or mentally then the calculator will not be very helpful.

Another example in which students notice regularity in the data generated by the technology, comes from the use of dynamic geometry software. It is a very simple matter to set up a triangle and to instruct the software to display the sizes of the interior angles (Figure 10.10 overleaf).

As the students distort their triangles, they may notice that the sum of the angles always remains constant at 180°. They may be motivated to ask about the sum of the interior angles of other polygons and the software will help the students to see that the angle sum increases regularly as the number of sides increases.

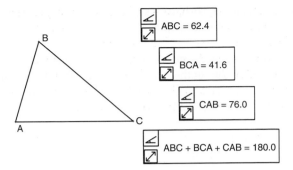

Figure 10.10 The measurements show that the angle sum is constant

Explanation

Pattern is a fundamental aspect of mathematics and computers can often make the patterns clearer. But is this enough? Should we be content when a pattern has been spotted? In his article, *Trainspotters' paradise*, Dave Hewitt (1992) informs us why the answer is a resounding 'No!' Students of mathematics need to understand and explain the patterns that they find. The students in the class working on decimals need to realise why the digit in the hundredths column is bound to appear in the tenths column when the number is multiplied by 10. The students who have noticed that the angle sum of a triangle is 180° have not finished either. Why must the angle sum be a constant 180° for all triangles? The students might continue by tracing the path of a triangle, rotating through each angle in turn. They will move forwards along the first side, rotate through the angle, walk backwards along the second side, rotate again, walk forwards, and then rotate through the third angle. They might then recognise that all three rotations were in the same direction and they finished facing in the opposite direction from their start. Whichever triangle they used they always turned through half of a complete turn.

While computers and calculators are wonderful tools for enabling students to explore freely and allowing them to make conjectures, there is more to mathematics than pattern-spotting. In both of the examples above the explanations needed to be made away from the computer and abandoning a machine is not always a simple matter in school. When the pupils are working with computers they usually want to stay precisely where they are. ICT is only available on rare occasions and so it makes little sense not to use it when it is available. The following sections consider further reasons why work involving pattern might not always be straightforward.

Who needs to explain?

A student who has seen a pattern may not appreciate the need for any further action. The following fictional conversation is between a sixth-former (SF) and her mathematics teacher (MT). The sixth-former has been using a graph-plotter. She has drawn two graphs on the same screen; one was for the function cos 2x and the other for 2 cos²x − 1. They appear to coincide and so she is quite sure that the two functions she had entered must have been identical, but her teacher has a pure mathematical bent and she is not convinced so easily.

MT: The two lines on the screen might appear to be on top of one another, but what happens further away from the origin, outside the limits of the small screen?

The sixth-former is not deterred by this.

SF: But I can easily tell the machine that I want to look at a different section of the graph. Look, if I alter the range on the *x*-axis from 100 to 110, the graphs are still the same.

MT: But after you've altered the range, I can still ask the same question. What happens from *x* = 1000 to 1010? You can alter the ranges of both axes as many times as you like, but you won't convince me that it always works. Even if you could, just because the lines look the same on the screen doesn't mean that they are identical. Your knowledge is limited by the accuracy of the machine.

SF: It's the same thing here. I can zoom in on the graph as much as I like and the graphs are always identical. I may not be able to zoom indefinitely, but I certainly can go as far as you want me to. Surely that convinces you that the lines are the same.

MT: No, I'm sorry, calculators and computers simply cannot prove anything. They can verify results with lots of examples, but that's not proof.

SF: 'Lots' is an understatement, isn't it? Supposing I create a spreadsheet with three columns:

	A	*B*	*C*
1	*a*	a^2	$(a + 1)(a - 1)$
2	1	1	0
3	2	4	3
4	3	9	8
5	4	16	15
6	5	25	24
7	6	36	35
8	7	49	48
9	8	64	63
10	9	81	80
11	10	100	99

I agree with you that the information here is not enough to prove that $a^2 - 1 = (a + 1)(a - 1)$ but I can alter the first column in any way I like and the number in the second column is always 1 more than the number in the third column. If I change the number 1 at the top of the first column to 11, I can show that the identity works for $a = 11$ to 20. Or, by inserting -57, I can show that it works for $a = -57$ to -48. I can show that the identity works when $a = 61.47$ or any other awkward number you care to choose. This would convince anybody that it is always true. That's what proof means, you know, convincing people.

	A	B	C
1	a	a^2	$(a + 1)(a - 1)$
2	61.47	3778.5609	3777.5609
3	62.47	3902.5009	3901.5009
4	63.47	4028.4409	4027.4409
5	64.47	4156.3809	4155.3809
6	65.47	4286.3209	4285.3209

MT: Well, I'm not convinced. If someone wants to prove a theorem she has to show it always works. It's not good enough for her to say that she *could* type any numbers into the computer and then the theorem *would* hold for those numbers.

SF: One final example – have you used a dynamic geometry package? Imagine you have a triangle on the screen and it has been constructed so that one of its sides is the diameter of a circle and the opposite vertex lies on the circumference of the same circle.

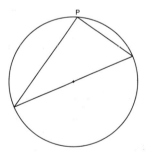

Figure 10.11 A triangle inscribed in a circle, with one of its sides as the diameter

You can move the point P anywhere around the fixed circle and, as long as you don't destroy the triangle, the angle at P remains at 90°. The software makes it obvious that it always works. Convinced?

MT: When you drag a point around with your mouse you may think that you're testing all the points on the journey, but the computer is fooling you. It's really drawing several still pictures and, because they're drawn so fast, you think that it's a dynamic model. So you haven't actually tried every position in the plane for each of the points, and you never can. It's just like the spreadsheet – lots of examples don't make a proof.

Explaining the results

Consider now the student who has noticed that a^2 always seems to be 1 more than $(a - 1)(a + 1)$ in the spreadsheet. In order to explain the result and really understand it, she needs to leave the computer and, if she can cope with the formal algebra, manipulate the symbols and prove that it is always true.

Alternatively, a geometric model might be utilised. The square with the corner missing represents $a^2 - 1$ and, when one strip is moved, a rectangle representing $(a + 1)(a - 1)$ is formed.

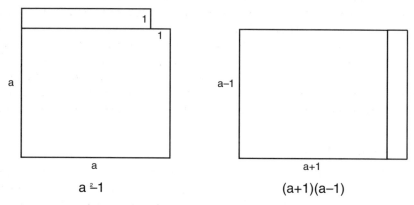

Figure 10.12   A geometric model to explain an algebraic identity

To understand the result about the angle in the semicircle, the student needs to leave the computer and show how logic demands that the angle at the circumference is equal to the sum of the other two angles which comprise the original triangle (Figure 10.15). (The new line passes through the centre of the circle and the marked angles are equal because the triangles are isosceles.)

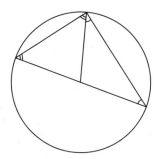

Figure 10.13   The angle of the original triangle that is opposite the diameter must be 90°

The explanations above are not only important because they start to satisfy the pure mathematician's desire to justify the result universally, for all numbers or for all the points in the plane. The explanations also get closer to the heart of the mathematics being studied. The computer has allowed the students to explore, with all the freedom to be wrong. Indeed, it is through exploration with the computer that the results may have been suggested in the first place. But when a student is able to argue and convince someone else, then some new mathematics has been understood.

The computer sometimes encourages us to work in ways that do not necessarily lead to analytical solutions. The machine is a workhorse which can generate so much data so quickly that we may be tempted to simply spot patterns without any analysis of the situation under consideration (Goldstein and Pratt, 1994). The computer offers many powerful opportunities for generalisation based on experimental evidence and the process of exploration leading to such generalisations can be a vital component of students' learning. In some cases the exploration may lead naturally to the justification but where this does not happen, the teacher may have to intervene. Indeed, teachers need to try to find opportunities to ask students why results are true whenever they stumble across them. If such opportunities arise through the work with the computer, all well and good; if not, it is vital that exploration on the computer and the explanation away from it are seen to be connected.

Misleading patterns

This penultimate section is used to remind the reader that we should never be content in mathematics just because we've seen a pattern. Patterns can sometimes be misleading. The example given below is not from the computer and, unless you are familiar with the situation, please take the trouble to do a little counting – you will be surprised at the result.

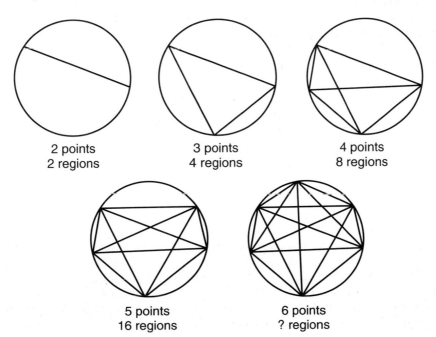

2 points
2 regions

3 points
4 regions

4 points
8 regions

5 points
16 regions

6 points
? regions

How many regions do you think there will be when there are six points on the circumference of the circle? Use the number pattern to decide.

Now count the regions on the diagram. (You may need to draw your own diagram, in which case make sure you get the maximum number of regions by locating the points on the circle strategically.)

The number of regions is not what the obvious number pattern suggests. If you have not seen this before, your conviction in the pattern may have been so strong that you thought you had miscounted. This example demonstrates how dangerous it is to rely on a number pattern. (The numbers of regions do, of course, form a well-defined sequence but it is too complex to include here.) There's a clue, though, in Chapter 5 on proof in the companion volume *Aspects of Teaching Secondary Mathematics*, Rodd and Monaghan (2001)! Students are often tempted to look at number patterns and not relate them to the mathematics. Number patterns do not always lead to incorrect mathematics. They can be very informative and they can suggest sensible hypotheses, but they are only ever part of the story. To appreciate the full picture we must always try to look behind the simple pattern. When students see patterns in their work, a good rule of thumb for you, the teacher, is to ask them why the pattern works. This is not only true for the able students; all students should be challenged continually to justify what they are doing and to explain all of their results.

Implications for the future

It may be that some smaller pieces of educational software can be used profitably on their own, without reference to other classroom activities, but as soon as the computer is used in more significant ways it becomes important that the work happens alongside other related activities. In schools today work at the computer often happens in computer rooms and so the teacher needs to be particularly careful to ensure that the work is integrated into the mathematics curriculum.

In the future we might expect computers to be available just about everywhere. There are likely to be a few laptops available in the cupboard in every classroom in the school. Further machines will be stationed in clusters in many areas and compatible machines will also be available in the library and at home. Furthermore, students will probably all carry their own personal machines that will also be compatible with those in the school. While the computer is not so prevalent it is often the main focus of attention when it is used. This, too, will change in the future and the computer will be just another resource in the classroom to be used only when it is appropriate.

There will be further issues to consider when computers are more prevalent. If they are to be fully integrated with other mathematical activities and if they are to become resources to be used naturally and frequently, it will be important for the students to learn to make their own decisions about their use. Pupils will need to learn *whether* or not to use a machine at any stage; if so, *when* should it be used and *which* software is the most appropriate (NCET, 1994).

Computers and calculators can often be very supportive; but there are also times when they make no significant contribution to the mathematics that is being studied; indeed, they may even intrude. Pupils need to decide whether or not a machine would be helpful and when to use it. Preliminary work may be appropriate before the machine is switched on, and at some stage the machine may need to be discarded for the work to progress. In an ideal situation it is likely that the student will need to move freely between many resources, some of them electronic. Deciding which software may also be a crucial issue. In mathematics there are many situations in which a computer might be helpful but it is certainly not always clear which software application is the most appropriate. For instance, many modelling activities could involve the use of calculators, spreadsheets, Logo, graph-plotters and possibly symbol manipulators too.

Much current software is sophisticated and it takes considerable time to become familiar with it. Few students know even one application well and they are certainly not familiar with enough to be able to make choices. Of course this obstacle may always be present to some extent. Even people who are very familiar with the latest technological developments have their favourites.

While it is likely that we will be compelled to address all these issues in the future, it is important never to forget what we can do now. Computers should be used in mathematics lessons to serve the curriculum and, if this is to happen, it is vital that the work at the keyboard is always fully integrated with the mathematics that is being learned.

Notes

1 Dynamic geometry software enables the user to create points, lines and circles and then draw geometrical constructions such as parallel lines or tangents. It is more than a drawing package, though, because the computer remembers the mathematics. If one constructs the perpendicular bisector of two points and then moves one of the points, the perpendicular bisector also moves so that it remains in the correct position. In addition the software can be used to measure lengths, angles and areas. The better known programs available are:
   - Apollonius Geometer. Dial Solutions Ltd, 0113 294 5111, http://www.dialsolutions2.demon.co.uk
   - Cabri-Géomètre II. Chartwell-Yorke, 01204 811001, philip@chartwel.demon.co.uk, http://www.chartwellyorke.com
   - A version of Cabri-géomètre is also available on the TI–92 graphic calculator from Texas Instruments, 01234 213394, http://www.ti.com/calc
   - Geometer's Sketchpad. QED, 0345 402275, 01707 396698, QEDBooks@aol.com
   - Geometry Inventor. TAG, 01171 357350, http://www.tagdev.co.uk
2 SLIMWAM (Some lessons in maths with a micro) is a collection of programs available from ATM. See http://www.atm.org.uk/pub/software/slim.htm
3 Listed below are three items of small software that will make a significant contribution to lessons on the theme of tiling.
   - *Newtiles*. Compose tiles from standard shapes and replicate them. SMILE, 0171 221 8966, smile@rmplc.co.uk, http://www.rmplc.co.uk/orgs/smile/index.html
   - *Reptile*. Allows the creation of tiles by deforming a square, an equilateral triangle or a regular hexagon. Previously marketed as *Escher*. Kudlian Soft, 01926 842544, support@kudlian.demon.co.uk
   - *VersaTile*. Longman Logotron, 01223 425558, http://www.logo.com

References

Bills, C. (2001) 'Mental mathematics', in L. Haggarty, (ed.) *Aspects of Teaching Secondary Mathematics*, London: RoutledgeFalmer.

Goldstein, R. and Pratt, D. (1994) 'Mathematical elegance', in *Micromath* 10(3): 25–7, Association of Teachers of Mathematics.

Hewitt, D. (1992) 'Trainspotters' paradise', in *Mathematics Teaching* 140: 6–8, Association of Teachers of Mathematics.

NCET (1994) *Whether, When and Which, choices for students when computers are more prevalent.*

NCET (1995) *Mathematics and IT – a pupil's entitlement, description of six major opportunities provided by ICT when students are learning mathematics*, see http://vtc.ngfl.gov.uk/resource/cits/maths/entitlement/index.html

Rodd, M. and Monaghan, J. (2001) 'Aspects of mathematical proof', in L. Haggarty, (ed.) *Aspects of Teaching Secondary Mathematics*, London: RoutledgeFalmer.

Section 5

Assessing learning in Mathematics

11 What does it mean to understand something and how do we know when it has happened?

Anne Watson

Words which appear to describe cognition, such as 'understanding' and 'knowing', are used throughout educational literature, and in teachers' shared discourse, with flexibility and fluency. When we try to use them precisely they become problematic, as they can take slightly different meanings, but we communicate effectively about them by elaborating what we mean. However, once they enter the statutory language through official documents which describe what education should be achieving they can no longer be used casually. Teachers are accountable for the ways in which they fulfil the statutory requirements, and need to have a worked-out and justifiable view of what 'understanding' means. Phrases such as 'knowledge and understanding' and 'mathematical understanding' are used in the Initial Teacher Training National Curriculum (ITTNC) (TTA, 1999), and the Mathematics National Curriculum (NC) (QCA, 1999) refers frequently to pupils' 'ability to use and understand concepts' and to assessing such ability. These requirements suggest that there is a state called 'understanding' and we can know when it exists and when it does not exist.

Understanding as a state

In this chapter I am going to argue that the idea that pupil progress in mathematics can be seen by assessing recognisable states of understanding is an over-simplification of how learning happens.

It is very common for new teachers to find themselves thinking, 'I never really understood addition of fractions (or calculus, or graph-plotting etc.) until I had to teach it!' In other words, the thinking involved in planning to teach (such as working out how to explain or exemplify and predicting what pupils will find difficult) has enabled the teacher to re-examine existing knowledge and look at it in a new way that is recognised as being deeper, more connected and more secure than previous experience. Possibly the teacher has easily remembered how to add fractions, but thinking about how to teach has led to considering why it is done that way and brought new insights into the importance of equivalence, or has raised an awareness of the numerical value of the fractions. And yet the teacher has been able to add fractions, pass examinations involving this skill and be thought of as 'understanding adding fractions'. What is being recognised here is that, even when one is extremely competent in a mathematical technique, there are still ways in which understanding can grow in a new situation, when one looks at the topic differently. Understanding is not static.

Marton and Saljö (1997) classify learning as surface (learning procedures and descriptions) or deep (learning about connections and relationships with previous knowledge). This kind of distinction can be useful when planning how to teach, but fails to take account of the fact that mathematical procedures consist of strings of simpler procedures which could be described as previous knowledge. To continue the example of adding fractions, one has to multiply and to add, to identify multiples and factors, to find common multiples and common factors … all dependent on previously acquired knowledge and skills. In this sense, learning mathematical procedures inevitably involves connecting and employing previously-learnt procedures. What is missing from this observation, but is implied in Marton and Saljö's distinction, is a sense of underlying meaning allowing us to explain why we add fractions this way and justify the answers we get.

Nevertheless, most mathematicians do not explain their actions when adding fractions. It is usually enough to know how to do it and to understand that the method works, but being able to reconstruct explanations, if needed, can contribute to future learning. So here we have two meanings of understanding: 'I understand that in situation X I need to do Y' and 'I understand why I need to do Y in situation X.' Ryle (1949), in describing types of knowledge, referred to these as *knowing-that* (factual, definitional) and *knowing-why*. He also describes a third type, *knowing-how*, which is the knowledge required to carry out the chosen action.

Examples of *knowing-that* can be found in the NC, for example 'Understand that "percentage" means "number of parts per 100" ' (p. 59). In this case understanding appears to mean 'knowing a definition of a word', where the definition gives us some clues (but very few) about what we can do with it mathematically. Some students may be able to construct everything they need to do with percentages from this fact, others may need much more help, but all can be tested on whether they can repeat definitions and correctly use procedures in particular circumstances. There is widespread agreement that what is being tested is not 'understanding', which relates to more complex forms of knowledge, but whether pupils can act in a certain way in the very precise circumstances of the test – a very localised *knowing-that*.

A state of understanding would include knowing facts and procedures, but might also include a sense of underlying meaning, some connection to previous knowledge and, possibly, the ability to explain. However, as shown above in the description of previous knowledge links in adding fractions, making connections is not dependent on a sense of meaning or *knowing-why*. It is possible to progress in mathematics to some extent by performing increasingly complex procedures and hence displaying a kind of behavioural, fluent, automatised understanding of how to enact mathematical algorithms.

Understanding as meaning and connection

Skemp (1976) points out that knowing what it is appropriate to do, and when to do it, involves a different kind of understanding than knowing how to do it. He reports that Mellin-Olsen described two kinds of understanding: 'instrumental' as the application of rules without reasons and 'relational' as knowing what to do and why. His enthusiastic embrace of the importance of relations has influenced mathematics education hugely, but a cautious reader might well ask, 'Relate to what?' and notice that possible reasons in mathematics can range from the purely pragmatic, 'It works in these circumstances, I can check by other means' to the purely logical, 'Given these axioms and these rules of logic, this will always work.'

Repetition of a definition does not imply that the pupil attaches any meaning to what is being said. Understanding requires more than rote-learning or following procedures correctly, although these could form the basis for future work to develop understanding. A poem learnt by heart can be brought back to mind and reconsidered many times. But the development of meaning is a personal process, dependent on what the pupil makes of successive experiences of a word or concept.

> Understanding is a personal thing ... The prize is the greater meaning that can flow from the union of isolated thoughts. All it takes is a connection but making it may not be easy. Understanding is not something that can be passed or transmitted from one person to another. No one can make the connection for someone else. Where there are connections to be made, the mental effort has to be supplied by the learner.
>
> (Newton, 2000, p. 2)

The meanings pupils develop about a concept, the relationships and reasons they attach to it, are inevitably obscure to others. Even in the education profession the nature of understanding is unclear and requires elaboration. For example, the NC contains the requirement that pupils should 'understand equivalent fractions' (p. 59). Clearly this would not be a matter of simply knowing they exist, nor is there anything to explain in this statement; it seems to be more an instruction to know-about. But what should be known? A teacher preparing to teach about them might know that they give alternative ways to represent the same numerical value, or proportion, or ratio; that, plotted as ordered pairs on a coordinate grid, they lie on a straight line; that the traditional rule 'what you do to the top, you do to the bottom' can be easily misunderstood and used to justify adding something to both the numerator and denominator, rather than only scaling. The teacher would know how to generate them, how they relate to each other and how this knowledge would contribute to later work. Given all these possible components of understanding, some of which are fortuitous, some pedagogic and some procedural, how can one assess whether a pupil understands equivalent fractions or not?

Growth of understanding

The above example suggests that understanding can change and develop, becoming more complex. Locke (1690), in his classic essay about understanding, proposed that ultimately everything is connected to everything else, hence growth of understanding relates to an increase in the number of links one makes. This a useful metaphor in mathematics because ultimately the links themselves can be named as mathematical objects (such as are expressed through abstract algebra, morphisms, networks, etc.). Since we do not know how much there is to know, there is no end to the growth of understanding.

Pirie and Kieren (1994) have developed a theory of the 'growth of mathematical understanding as a whole, dynamic, levelled but non-linear, transcendentally recursive process' (p. 62). This hierarchical model has been used to relate different levels of understanding to what can be observed in pupils' behaviour, i.e. descriptions of observable actions of mathematical understanding that express background processes. It provides a structure for considering questions such as 'What can be said about the understanding of a pupil who chooses to use symbolic forms, or manipulates familiar formats to adapt them to a new situation, or derives a new fact from some previous knowledge?'

They describe stages of primitive knowing, image-making and -having, property-noticing, formalising, observing, structuring and inventising. *Primitive knowing* is what is known so far, making distinctions in existing knowledge and using it in new ways leads to formation of new *images*. Images can be manipulated and compared and lead to new *properties* being noticed by the learner who then abstracts something to be said about them, thus moving to a level of *formalising*. Reflecting on, and expressing, such formal thinking is called *observing*, and developing these observations as a theory is called *structuring*. After this the learner can create new questions and new lines of enquiry, which they call *inventising*. These processes, although increasingly complex, do not necessarily follow each other. In practice there is a lot of toing and froing between levels.

In secondary school mathematics it is rare for teachers to have the opportunity to observe pupils closely enough to be so precise about their understanding. The simpler models of Bruner (1960), who sees learning as a process of developing *iconic* and then *symbolic* representations of *enacted experiences*, with the help of interaction with others or Floyd *et al.* (1981) who see learning mathematics as a process of *manipulating, getting-a-sense-of* and *articulating*, might be easier to use in the classroom. Once learners can articulate or symbolise a mathematical idea, they are ready to manipulate it further to gain more understanding, or to treat it as the raw material for abstraction or more complex manipulations.

Understanding in context

Some teachers may interpret 'relational understanding' to be entirely about appropriateness in a context, which could be mathematical or 'real world', while others may look for generalised arguments or descriptions of underlying structure.

To interpret 'understand' as 'able to use in a real context' implies that all mathematics *can* be useful outside classrooms, which is dubious, and that pupils can apply what is learnt in one place to another, dissimilar situation. The implication is that relational understanding enables instrumental use of mathematics. But formal mathematics is rarely used outside classrooms (Nunes, 1993; Watson, 1998b), so the requirement to use it might be artificial and unrealistic. Further, Mason and Spence (1999) point out that none of the components of relational understanding (knowing that, how and why) necessarily lead to doing the most appropriate, sophisticated or efficient action in a particular situation. For a variety of ad hoc reasons the features of the situation just may not trigger a particular pupil to use the hoped-for mathematics. Cooper (in Chapter 13 of this volume), Christoforou (1999) and Watson (1999), among others, show that students' responses may be as much due to their social backgrounds and the way the mathematical question is structured as they are to understanding. Understanding appears to depend on the situation, different understandings being contingent on circumstances.

Understanding as overcoming obstacles

Sierpinska (1994), speaking of advanced mathematics, describes understanding as the overcoming of particular obstacles in mathematics. Such obstacles include common difficulties in learning mathematics, inherent difficulties in the subject, errors, misunderstandings, overextending ideas that only work in a restricted domain, and unhelpful ways of thinking, such as generalising with too little data or failing to discriminate between opinion and fact. She sees these obstacles as arising from 'unconscious, culturally acquired schemes of thought and unquestioned beliefs about the nature of mathematics' (p. xi). In other words, some obstacles are to be expected and taken into account when teaching. It is sensible to include overcoming identifiable obstacles as a component of understanding; the ITTNC pays significant attention to this aspect but on its own this approach may do little for the development of deeper knowledge.

The example of multiplication

To illustrate that understanding is dynamic, contingent and local I shall now look at typical meanings of 'understanding multiplication'. It is possible to write $5 \times 6 = 30$ from a variety of viewpoints, each one adequate for some purpose:

- a learnt statement with no underlying number sense, from rote-learning;
- a representation of grouped counting of objects, either five lots of six or six lots of five;
- an example to show a general grasp of commutativity;
- an example of number patterns in the five-times-table;
- an example of number patterns in the six-times-table;
- a learnt statement, with underlying number sense;
- an example of multiplying two positive numbers;

- multiplication as repeated addition;
- a way to work out the answer to a problem;
- multiplication as scaling;
- multiplication by numbers greater than 1 causes increase;
- a representative of a binary operation.

In this list are hidden several potential obstacles, for example the need to understand cardinal numbers, to use numbers as objects in their own right, to have an image of what happens when one multiplies and to shift from specific examples to general properties. The list also presages future obstacles: the inadequacy of seeing multiplication as repeated addition, or grouped objects, when multiplying by negative numbers or by numbers less than 1; the successive levels of abstraction which remove the learner further and further from images of addition or scaling; multiplying vectors or matrices require a more abstract notion.

For each viewpoint above apart from possibly the first, one can imagine a teacher legitimately saying the pupil understands multiplication. And yet the image of grouped objects is significantly unhelpful if one is trying to multiply matrices. Understanding, therefore, depends not only on the mathematical context but also the pedagogic situation; there is a sense in which one can understand 'enough for the moment'.

What teachers mean by understanding

If we cannot be specific about understanding, then we are unlikely to pinpoint particular moments when pupils achieve it as an attainable, definitive, stable state. When teachers say they are teaching for understanding they rarely mean that they want their students to know about formal logical systems. More often they are talking about pupils having a sense of the form and purpose of the mathematics, and the places where it is likely to be useful. They may want students to be able to 'generate' or reconstruct an appropriate response in new situations, not just mechanically repeat back what they have learnt by heart. Some typical statements from teachers are:

I know they understand when:

- they can say it to me in their own words;
- they can tell me how they did it;
- they can use it in context without being told;
- they use it without prompting;
- they can answer a question which comes at it in a slightly different direction.

(Watson, 1998a)

All of these indicate that teachers want pupils to have enough of an overview of techniques and procedures to be able to shift into another representation, generalisation or transformation which allows use in unfamiliar ways, explanations, general descriptions and applications (Dreyfus, 1991). Teachers, therefore, are recognising the abilities to generalise, represent and transform as components of understanding mathematics. Even given the temporary and local nature of understanding, it might be possible to say something about whether a pupil has generalised, represented or transformed some mathematical concept in given circumstances. But these are mental actions, so how can a teacher collect evidence of pupils' understanding?

How do we know what a pupil understands?

In order to recognise such generalisations, which are crucial in all mathematics, teachers have to rely on what they can see, hear and read. Hence there is no room for intuitive understandings in the above statements (Fischbein, 1987; Claxton, 1997), except those intuitions that might enable pupils to apply mathematics in new places. Instead there is much importance placed on verbal expressions of methods, although an essential aspect of mathematics is that structures can be expressed and manipulated in non-verbal ways. Another emphasis, which teachers might make, is that successful performance of mathematics in given contexts might indicate certain kinds of understanding. But observing pupils' actions in the classroom is difficult to manage systematically, and in the end one might only have the outcomes of written work to see.

The ITTNC says that new teachers should know:

> …how to use formative, diagnostic and summative methods of assessing pupils' progress in mathematics, including (ii) undertaking day-to-day and more formal assessment activities so that specific assessment of mathematical understanding can be carried out …. (and) (iii) preparing oral and written questions and setting up activities and tests which check for misconceptions and errors in mathematical knowledge and understanding … and understanding of mathematical ideas and the connections between different mathematical ideas.
>
> (TTA, 1999, p.14, 9aii and iii)

In order to achieve this a teacher must have a very clear idea of what kind of understanding is being assessed: instrumental, contextual, procedural, relational within mathematics, transformable, generalised, logical or abstract, with obstacles successfully overcome. Also required is an awareness of how such understanding can be assessed.

Is it possible, for instance, to find out if a pupil's understanding is relational or instrumental? Or, if one believes all understanding to be relational, even if it is related to a fragmentary rule-performance view of mathematics, can a teacher find out to what is it related? There are problems with observations of students. Although such observations tell us something, they do not give us access to understandings that have not been expressed in accessible forms (Watson, 1997). In addition, all observations have to be interpreted by the teacher, and one may not know how such expressions were achieved. For example, a correct proof can be given because it has been learnt by heart; this may or may not mean that the student has an understanding of how the proof 'works'. The understanding could be relational, or could be an instrumental response to a request to 'prove'. Neither does it indicate that the student has learnt anything about that type of proof in general, even if the student has grasped the reasoning in the learnt proof. The teacher needs to be cautious not to impute levels of understanding without evidence, and needs to probe further if more inferences have to be made.

Oral evidence, though highly valued by all the teachers, is time-consuming to organise. Language difficulties, diffidence or fear might prevent some pupils from speaking. It is rare to overhear useful remarks in a busy classroom, although such remarks often give insight into a pupil's thinking before they are able to record what they think on paper. In addition, oral evidence does not give hard evidence to support a teacher's judgements, so that over-reliance on oral evidence may leave the teacher vulnerable to criticism when being inspected by others. Reliance on oral work ought also to be seen in the light of Bernstein's work (e.g. 1971) on how middle-class pupils are at an advantage in school because the elaborated codes of language are what they might be used to at home, where working-class pupils are expected to communicate at school in a way very unlike the codes used at home. This theory relies on a very stereotyped view of language use outside school, but it does prompt a closer look at language forms in mathematics classrooms. The request to 'explain how you did something', a common requirement in teacher–pupil discourse, is a rare form of speech outside school in any social grouping. Hence reliance on pupils' ability to demonstrate their understanding orally for assessment purposes is expecting a keen awareness of different discourses as well as mathematical ability.

Many teachers comment that *written work* on its own is not enough to convince them that pupils understand; they want oral evidence, or written workings and explanations as well. However, there is also wide recognition that many pupils have considerable difficulty in recording in writing what they could do mentally or practically. Assessment of written work, particularly where it involves explanations or extended exploration, has to be seen in the light of research into assessing coursework. Several writers have shown that pupils can be very selective in what they write down, so that written work represents a highly-edited view of their mathematical thinking (MacNamara and Roper, 1992). Sometimes this is an attempt to produce curtailed, terse, classical mathematics, but it can also be due to a failure to appreciate what is important or an inability to find ways to represent abstract or intuitive thought on paper.

Observation in a busy classroom is difficult to organise but can reveal that the pupil is using particular methods, such as counting instead of using number bonds. Observation of actions depends in part on the teachers' notions of how mathematical activity *might* be observable. Sometimes this is clear, such as when one sees a pupil use a ruler and read off a measurement correctly. At other times it has to be interpreted, such as when a pupil is trying to make a cube from six squares and may appear to us to be doing it in an obscure way, but nevertheless succeeds. Other times, there is little to interpret; the pupil who is gazing motionless at a problem may or may not be thinking about it, and the thought may or may not be productive. On the other hand, avid writing may not indicate anything useful is being done. How the teacher interprets the actions can be influenced by many factors. In the examples above, interpretation depends on what the teacher expects to see relevant to the mathematics, what the teacher expects from the particular pupil and what the teacher expects from pupils in general. It also depends on what is noted by the teacher that can be affected by previous impressions of the pupil's abilities.

In order to avoid the possible unfairness that can creep into assessment, given the warnings above, it is possible to:

- be prepared to be surprised – avoid forming firm views of a pupil's capabilities and achievements;
- use a variety of forms of assessment so that you accumulate a broad view of what a pupil can do;
- relate the way you assess, and what you record, to the purpose of the assessment;
- discuss your views and interpretations with colleagues;
- look for evidence which contradicts, as well as that which corroborates, your views;
- do not base irrevocable decisions solely on your own interpretations of what a pupil can do.

Purposes of assessment

Diagnostic assessment

This purpose of assessment assumes that you can find out something about the pupil's current state of knowledge in order to decide what and how to teach. As I have argued above, it is not possible to establish current understandings with any certainty because of the complex, dynamic and situated nature of mathematical understanding. There are commercially produced tests to help in the diagnostic process, but it is important to realise the results tell you about a pupil's response to a particular question on a particular day. Responses may indicate that common misunderstandings exist, or that the pupil was able to get the right answer using a specific method, and this is useful information when planning to teach, but general judgements about individuals made on the basis of such tests could be flawed. A more immediate way to assess the knowledge pupils bring to a mathematics lesson would be to set up an interactive situation in which pupils are somehow encouraged to reveal how they see a topic, perhaps by making up their own questions, or describing methods on the chalkboard, or telling each other what they already know. The more we can find out about how they already think about the topic, and what they know which is related to it, the more appropriately teaching can be planned and focused.

As Hawkins (1967) said, active and talkative lessons allow pupils to show us what they know, and what images they attach to concepts. When:

> children are rather passively sitting in neat rows and columns and manipulating you into believing that they're being attentive because they're not making any trouble, then you won't get much information from them. Not getting much information about them, you won't be a very good diagnostician of what they need. Not being a good diagnostician, you will be a poor teacher … When we fail in this diagnostic role we begin to worry about 'assessment'.
>
> (p. 23)

Since the purpose of diagnostic assessment is to find out what is not known, what is misunderstood, and to inform future teaching it is debatable whether keeping records permanently for individual pupils is of any use except to provide a base from which to assess their later progress.

Formative assessment

Teachers make judgements all the time about how pupils are responding to teaching, and what progress they are making. For progress to be observed, hierarchical criteria need to be used, such as level descriptors of the NC, or progress tests in a published scheme of work. Pupils can be made aware of such criteria and possibly be involved in assessing their mathematics against them. In this way, the teacher and the pupil are both informed about how they are responding to teaching, and what topics, concepts or teaching styles are causing problems. Progress is often seen to be a one-way process, but the Pirie–Kieren model expects pupils to return to 'lower' levels of knowing from time to time, and if pupils have not worked in a particular area of mathematics for some time they may need to revisit earlier ideas. Often, formative assessment is accompanied by target-setting in which pupils are given, or may suggest for themselves, some learning goals for the near future. This can be effective in helping to motivate pupils, but can work against the development of deep understandings, encouraging instead the desire to acquire more and more skills at the expense of higher levels of understanding and reflective approaches to consolidating learning.

It is clear from this description that formative assessment relates to what has been taught and what will be taught to those pupils, rather than to some overarching curriculum plan. Although the information may be of value to individual learners, it is also very important for teachers to use in order to monitor their teaching. Again, it is debatable how valid permanent record-keeping about individuals would be, and judgements made about pupils on the basis of formative assessment need to be temporary. Formative assessment does not necessarily provide useful baselines for describing progress, as it usually relates to current teaching and learning.

Summative assessment

At the end of a course, or at fixed points during the school career, pupils may be tested in a variety of ways to see how much they have learnt and identify their overall progress. These assessments are done by comparing pupil work to an overarching plan, such as a national curriculum or some course objectives, and summing up what has been achieved. This purpose of assessment is usually to categorise and grade pupils individually, thus influencing future educational choices, and to get data about a group or cohort for other purposes such as within-school or between-school comparisons.

Methods of assessment

Although there are published tests for all three purposes described above, and national statutory tests for summative purposes, there are many other assessment activities which are an integral part of classroom life. In addition, teachers' judgements of what pupils have achieved are included in statutory assessments. A systematic study of methods used by teachers to find out what their pupils know (Watson, 1998a) found that, although teachers knew that their assessment findings were dependent on circumstances, they nevertheless believed that there was some ultimate state of 'understanding' about which they could say something, if only they could get enough information about pupils. More usefully for our purposes here, they described a variety of ways of finding out as much as they could about pupils' understanding because it was of central importance for their decisions about what and how to teach, who needed special support, who needed further challenges, and so on.

There are dense links between choice of assessment method and choice of teaching (see Watson, 2001) or tasks, questions and interactive strategies (see Mason, 2001) so I shall not comment fully on the pedagogy associated with every method below. Instead, I shall highlight how each method contributes to the meanings of 'understanding' given at the start of this chapter, and also how it relates to the three main purposes set out above.

1 *Looking for how mathematics is used in the context of practical or investigational work, or more complex mathematics. Is a concept used where appropriate? Has it been adapted for use?*

   If the concept is used, this can demonstrate that the pupil has internalised it and generalised it enough to recognise where it may be useful, and to transform it for use. However, failure to use it does not mean it is not understood; it may only mean that it was not seen as appropriate, or was deemed too complicated for the context, or just failed to come to mind. How it is used can give formative information; successful use can contribute to summative assessments; a practical situation can give diagnostic information about a skill if it is specifically requested.

2   *Explaining to the teacher; explaining to another student*

Verbal explanation can be evidence of generalisation, or of noticing and formalising properties of a procedure or concept. Some pupils may be uncomfortable about verbalising; those operating at a highly abstract level may not see how words can express the mathematics. Others can transform their understanding into words and learn more by doing so. This method can give useful diagnostic and formative information.

3   *Response to teacher-led questioning or open prompts, e g. 'Tell me about … .'*

While closed questions may give information about understanding, they may also encourage instrumental, or learnt-by-heart responses. Additionally, some pupils are adept at guessing answers from the teacher's cues, while others may choose not to take part. Open prompts may reveal much more about a pupil's personally-constructed understanding, but may fail to provide enough structure to trigger the most sophisticated response possible. One prompt that appears to be effective is 'Make up the hardest example you can.' Such questions can generate useful information for formative assessment, and may incidentally allow the teacher to diagnose difficulties, but may not reveal the full extent of a pupils' knowledge and can only give summative information insofar as they reveal ways of working with mathematics.

4   *Pupil expressing insight while working on an intended area of mathematics; or while working on another area of mathematics; communication pupil-to-teacher or pupil-to-pupil*

This is the kind of incident which is very revealing when it is spotted, but cannot be planned and hence may not be systematically incorporated into assessment practices. What is demonstrated might be intuition, or a recognition of some mathematics that has been met previously in some other form. It is more likely to take its place in the mental picture that the teacher develops for each pupil. In that sense it is formative, in that it informs the teacher that this pupil may be able to cope with particular kinds of challenge in future.

5   *Response to similar, simpler, slightly different or harder examples, or examples where questions are asked in other ways*

If a teacher is trying to find the extent or depth of a pupils' understanding, slight alterations of a standard question-type are very useful, and can be systematically incorporated into worksheets, homework tasks and tests. These can be used to identify common misunderstandings, and show how far the pupil is able to adapt, manipulate and transform the concepts taught. Careful developments of questions can be used, therefore, to diagnose what needs to be taught, and to summarise what can be done in certain situations. The more open approach of asking pupils to make up their own hard questions, as in 3 above, can also be used.

6   *Self assessment*

A formative assessment method that also motivates and informs pupils is to ask them to assess their own progress. There are several ways of doing this, but to be effective pupils must have some understanding of what it is they are supposed to achieve, otherwise the exercise can degenerate into meaninglessness. Writing journals, in which they describe what they have learnt by giving instructions or examples and recording difficulties (Waywood, 1992), is one way. Such exercises can show teachers what pupils see as the important aspects of a topic, and their sense of underlying structure.

7   *Tests: teacher-written tests, impromptu questions, use of a bank of test items, test as part of published scheme, tests written by students for their class*

Answering test questions is an obvious way to assess understanding, but the circumstances of the test need to be taken into account when deciding how to use the results. Timed tests consisting of closed questions assess algorithmic competence, speed, accuracy, recall, the ability to identify what is needed to answer a question and the ability to adapt what is known to fit a situation. It matters, therefore, whether the test is covering what has been actually been taught, or what is supposed to have been taught. It matters also how it has been taught, because the difference between the questions on the test and the kinds of situation the pupil is used to working with is crucial to how the pupil can engage with the questions. For this reason, teachers wishing for the best possible test results may try to 'teach to the test', in order to give their pupils the advantage of not having to adapt their understandings too much. Sometimes teachers are criticised for doing this, particularly when it leads to an instrumental approach in which pupils' responses are triggered by certain language forms in test questions. One way to teach to the test, but also to pay attention to the development of deep knowledge, would be to regard test questions as problems to be solved and develop a critical, questioning approach to the task.

Tests are commonly used for all three assessment purposes, but there are many problems with their use as summative tools. The style of question can attract some students and alienate others, questions can be ambiguous, small details of language can lead to misinterpretation of what is required (think of the difference between 'subtract' and 'subtract from'), the pressures of the test situation can lead to underachievement and so on.

8   *Analysis or discussion of errors*

For formative and diagnostic purposes pupils can be asked to explain how they did some mathematics, thus showing what sort of reasoning led to incorrect answers. This is also helpful when answers are correct! This method requires close one-to-one attention and is hence difficult to manage. However, a teacher can use similar methods with a whole class in order to become better informed about a range of misunderstandings that they might have. In addition, working on common errors can aid understanding. This is an example (as are several of the methods above) of good assessment practice merging with good teaching. Mason's article on questioning (Mason, 2001) gives further examples of this.

9   *Activities which use knowledge or processes, or both, and are expressed through paper, observation, verbal, investigative or practical work*

Many teachers in my research said that they would know for sure that pupils understood if they could apply their mathematics, unprompted, in a new situation. The situation might be a new mathematical context, or a practical situation such as on the sports field, or in technology lessons. Transfer of mathematics from the classroom to other situations that have their own habits, ways of seeing things and ad hoc methods is complex and sophisticated, as has already been said. But application to later work in the mathematics classroom would indeed inform the teacher about how pupils see the meaning, uses and scope of a topic. As in all types of assessment, this is most effective if pupils are familiar with what is required of them. If a class commonly approaches new mathematics with the questions 'What do I know which is like this?' or 'How does this fit with what I already know?' then connecting and using new topics will become a working habit. Not only will the teacher be able to see *who* understands the mathematics that has to be used, but *how* it is understood. In addition, the ground can be prepared for helping pupils see mathematics in a connected way, relating one algorithm to another, and hence constructing a network of knowledge.

Knowing about understanding

Although commonly used in education, the word 'understanding' is complex and open to a variety of interpretations, particularly in mathematics with its multiple layers of generalisation, abstraction and use. Understanding depends on mathematical context and on what is expected of the pupil. It can also depend on how mathematics is taught. To find out what a pupil understands is dependent on what it means to 'understand' in a context, and how the teacher identifies, collects and interprets evidence. Teaching for understanding (Watson, 2001) and assessment can be intimately related.

References

Bernstein, B. (1971) *Class, Codes and Control*, vol. 1, London: Routledge and Kegan Paul.
Bruner, J.S. (1960) *The Process of Education*, Cambridge, MA: Harvard University Press.
Christoforou, A. (1999) 'National Curriculum aural tests, social class and equity', unpublished MSc. dissertation, University of Oxford.
Claxton, G. (1997) *Hare Brain, Tortoise Mind: why intelligence increases when you think less*, London: Fourth Estate.

Dreyfus, T. (1991) 'Advanced mathematical thinking processes', in D. Tall (ed.) *Advanced Mathematical Thinking*, Dordrecht, The Netherlands: Kluwer.

Fischbein, E. (1987) *Intuition in Science and Mathematics: an educational approach*, Dordrecht, The Netherlands: Reidel.

Floyd, A., Burton, L., James, N. and Mason, J. (1981) *EM235: developing mathematical thinking*, Milton Keynes: Open University.

Hawkins, D. (1967) 'I-thou-it', *Mathematics Teaching*: 22–8.

Locke, J. (1690) *An Essay Concerning Human Understanding*, London: Penguin.

MacNamara, A. and Roper, T. (1992) 'Attainment target 1 – is all the evidence there?' *Mathematics Teaching* 140: 26–7.

Marton, F. and Saljö, R. (1997 2nd edn) 'Approaches to learning', in F. Marton, D. Hounsell and N. Entwistle (eds) *The Experience of Learning*, Edinburgh: Scottish Academic Press.

Mason, J. (2001) 'Minding your Qs and Rs: effective questioning and responding in the mathematics classroom', in L. Haggarty (ed.) *Aspects of Teaching Secondary Mathematics*, London: RoutledgeFalmer.

Mason, J. and Spence, M. (1999) 'Beyond mere knowledge of mathematics: the importance of knowing to act in the moment', *Educational Studies in Mathematics* 38: 135–61.

Newton, D.P. (2000) *Teaching for Understanding: what it is and how to do it*, London: RoutledgeFalmer.

Nunes, T., Schliemann, A. and Carraher, D. (1993) *Street Mathematics and School Mathematics*, Cambridge: Cambridge University Press.

Pirie, S. and Kieren, T. (1994) 'Growth in mathematical understanding: how can we characterise it and how can we represent it?', *Educational Studies in Mathematics* 26: 165–90.

QCA (1999) *The National Curriculum: handbook for secondary teachers in England*, London: DfEE/QCA.

Ryle, G. (1949) *The Concept of Mind*, London: Hutchinson.

Sierpinska, A. (1994) *Understanding in Mathematics*, London: Falmer.

Skemp, R. (1976) 'Relational and instrumental understanding', *Mathematics Teaching* 77: 20–6.

TTA (1999) *Initial Teacher Training National Curriculum for Secondary Mathematics*, London: DfEE.

Watson, A. (1997) 'Coming to know pupils: a study of informal teacher assessment of mathematics', in E. Pehkonen (ed.) *Proceedings of the 21st Conference of the International Group for the Psychology of Mathematics Education* 4, University of Helsinki, Lahti, Finland: 270–7.

Watson, A. (1998a) 'An investigation into how teachers make judgements about what pupils know and can do in mathematics', unpublished D.Phil. thesis, University of Oxford.

Watson, A. (1998b) *Situated cognition and the learning of mathematics*, Oxford, Centre for Mathematics Education Research/QED.

Watson, A. (1999) 'Getting behind pupils' written test performances: what they did; what they thought they did; what they could have done', in *Proceedings of the 4th British Congress of Mathematics Education*, Northampton.

Watson, A. (2001) 'Teaching for understanding', in L. Haggarty (ed) *Aspects of Teaching Secondary Mathematics*, RoutledgeFalmer, London.

Waywood (1992) 'Journal writing and learning mathematics', *For the Learning of Mathematics* 12(2): 34–43.

12 Assessment in mathematics education

Kenneth Ruthven

Introduction

Understanding the place of assessment in mathematics education involves recognising that it extends far deeper than the formal evaluation of pupil achievement for public certification. Certainly, this is the visible tip of the assessment iceberg, standing out beyond the surface of schooling. Beneath, however, lies a massive substructure where assessment not only makes contact with everyday teaching and studying, but is embedded within them. In terms of its occasion and organisation, assessment ranges from *informal* – unobtrusive, incidental judgements made in the course of ordinary classroom activities – to *formal* – distinct activities explicitly organised for purposes of assessment. In terms of the kind of information it generates, assessment ranges from *diagnostic* – concerned with understanding pupils and their performance – to *evaluative* – focused on grading pupils and their performance. And in terms of the purposes to which this information is put, assessment ranges from *formative* – helping to guide teaching, studying and learning processes – to *summative* – serving to appraise the outcomes of such processes.

Assessment is centrally concerned with mapping the dispositions and capabilities of pupils, and with charting the changes in these, which are commonly referred to as learning. Although learning is necessarily incidental to some degree, it is also directly shaped by the intentions and actions of pupils and teachers, and indirectly by the influence of the educational system on these intentions and actions. Hence, the place of assessment in mathematics education can be examined at the three levels of studying, teaching and schooling. The most fundamental level is that of studying, taken as the process through which pupils assess and shape their own learning. The next level is that of teaching, taken as the process through which teachers assess and shape the studying and learning of their pupils. The final level is that of schooling, taken as the process through which educational institutions and agencies assess and shape teaching, studying and learning. The three main sections of this chapter will examine each of these levels in turn, focusing on pupil self-assessment and reflexive studying; teacher assessment and responsive teaching; and systemic assessment and effective schooling.

Pupil self-assessment and reflexive studying

This section examines the ways in which pupils actively manage, assess and assist their own learning, through their approaches to studying. This will be illustrated by the examples of Adam and Gareth, fellow pupils in an upper secondary mathematics class (Anthony, 1996). Both Adam and Gareth see mathematics as important for their future careers and are motivated to work hard at the subject, although neither regards it as his favourite. Both pupils engage in self-assessment while studying. They do so, however, with differing concerns, reflecting the contrasting approaches that they have developed to studying mathematics, and the correspondingly contrasting views that they have formed of mathematical thinking and learning.

Adam's approach to studying mathematics involves proactively creating opportunities to assess himself and pursue emergent possibilities for learning. Moreover, the assessment criteria and learning goals he sets for himself are shaped by his concern that mathematics should be systematic and make sense. For example, asked by his teacher to make a summary of a trigonometry unit on the sine and cosine rules, he reports on how he took this as an opportunity to monitor and extend his grasp of underlying lines of reasoning:

> I just revised all the proofs and then wrote them down on paper and ran through how to prove the three formulas. I went through to check to see if I understood them. If I forgot how to do it, I read through it and tried to work it out. I also looked in our other textbook to see if there was any other way of doing it.

Adam adopts a similar strategy in using other pupils' classroom questions as starting points for assessing and developing his own knowledge and understanding:

> I'm just thinking what sort of problem he [the pupil] is asking and see if I can do it.

He treats his teacher's working at the board likewise:

> I was thinking what is she [the teacher] doing. I was thinking she's having problems drawing the graph. I was thinking about how to draw it, about how else to do it.

Focusing on exploring alternative methods and interconnecting mathematical ideas, and taking the initiative in structuring his activity to help him to identify and pursue such learning, Adam considers that:

> Maths is a thinking and doing subject. It's not necessary for you to memorise. If you do lots of work then you just remember the maths.

Consequently, he is sparing and selective in revising for tests:

> I don't think it's necessary for you to revise; only if you don't understand something.

Gareth's approach to studying mathematics is a more reactive one, shaped by an immediate concern to complete assigned tasks successfully. In response to the request to summarise the trigonometry unit, for example, he copies out the formulae and some worked examples. Correspondingly, when tackling mathematical problems, Gareth's primary strategy is to identify a suitable model to follow:

> I looked through the book to see how they did it but couldn't find … a worked example the same.

He has developed supplementary strategies to deal with such breakdowns. He contrasts the strategies he uses in different situations:

> It's different learning at home 'cause if you're having trouble with something in class you've got the teacher there who can come and show, but at home you have to do it by yourself – so it's harder … If I've got a problem, I first go straight to the back of the book and see their answer and work backwards to the question.

Nevertheless, in class, Gareth calls on the teacher only reluctantly:

> I only call her if I'm really in trouble. I learn more by figuring out how they got it myself.

For Gareth, 'figuring out' means reconciling the steps of the model provided by a worked example with the answer stated for a problem exercise. In the shorter term, Gareth's self-assessment focuses on his progress in completing a task by adapting a given model. Correspondingly, in the longer term, his self-assessment focuses on his progress in mastering and memorising the method implicit in these examples:

> Learning maths is done by just looking through and reading your notes and doing problems non-stop.

Gareth finds this 'pretty hard as it involves mostly memory work.' The demands that this makes on him are starting to become apparent when it comes to test preparation:

> Last year my brain just couldn't handle all the examples … So now I don't go over the examples the night before because it doesn't really help me much.

Nevertheless, despite performing poorly in tests and feeling 'not very good' at the subject, Gareth continues to work hard in the hope of improving his grade.

Both Adam and Gareth aspire to accomplish assigned tasks successfully, but whereas Adam overlays them with a concern to (re)construct and (inter)relate methods through reasoning about their mathematical sense and structure, Gareth treats them primarily in terms of applying a procedural template. In effect, although studying alongside one another in the same classroom, Adam and Gareth are projecting themselves into quite different mathematical environments, are assessing themselves in correspondingly different terms, and are learning mathematics to a correspondingly different depth. Indeed, they illustrate the distinction that has been drawn between approaches to studying which lead to 'deep' and 'surface' learning (Marton and Saljö, 1976). Approaches associated with deep learning involve more reflexive searching for underlying principles, for linking structures and for flexible methods, whereas approaches associated with surface learning rely on treating material in a fragmented and mechanical way. Most pupils appear to be capable of some flexibility in their approaches to studying, and the approach adopted in a particular situation is influenced by factors such as interest in the topic, the way in which tasks are presented, the models provided by the teacher and other pupils, and expectations regarding course assessment. However, pupils who consistently adopt approaches associated with surface learning experience considerable difficulty in adapting to situations requiring deep learning, because they lack, (1) the necessary study strategies, and (2) concepts that organise and interrelate the mathematical material that they have already 'learned'. Indeed, there is a vicious cycle in operation here. Hence, while pupils following surface approaches can perform as well as their peers on predictably structured tasks, they perform much more poorly on tasks that do not offer such cues and supports (Marton and Saljö, 1976; Crooks, 1988).

During the process of studying, both Adam and Gareth assess themselves in terms of progress towards specific objectives – completion of tasks, resolution of enigmas – taken as representing learning achievements. This aspect of their self-assessment, then, is strongly *criterion-referenced*. Nevertheless, both have also formed summary assessments of 'how good they are' at mathematics, grounded in *norm-referenced* comparisons with other pupils as to how difficult they find the subject and how successful they are in mathematical tasks and tests. This distillation of comparative assessments into a simple single rating of mathematical 'ability' is commonplace amongst pupils, parents, teachers and examiners, and influential in much thinking about the subject. Certainly, there are important differences in the pupils' approaches to studying, and consequent differences in the processes and products of their mathematical learning. However, the assimilation of these to a notion of ability erases their nuance. In particular, it tends to pre-empt consideration of the part that teaching and assessment might play in encouraging – or overcoming – surface approaches. Whereas, at present, Gareth perceives improvement in his mathematical learning as a matter of 'working harder', the assessment offered here suggests rather that he needs help in 'working smarter', in the form of support in recognising and pursuing the kinds of strategies underpinning a deeper approach to studying mathematics. Such support is likely to be critical to Gareth's continuing constructive engagement with the subject in the face of his experience of increasing demand and diminishing success, despite his intensification of effort. Happily, this assessment has also pointed to two potentially valuable resources: Gareth's existing concept of – and commitment to – 'figuring out', which might serve as a springboard for developing more reflexive approaches to studying and Adam's established strategies – and his capacity to articulate them – which might provide a source of peer modelling and coaching.

This section has examined the self-assessment of pupils as part of their wider approach to studying. It has identified important differences in the degree of reflexivity of their approaches, and consequently in their capacity and opportunity to learn. What part, then, does teaching play in shaping – and in reshaping – the approaches to studying developed by pupils? This issue is pursued in the next section.

Teacher assessment and responsive teaching

This section examines the ways in which teachers assess, and the ways in which teaching influences, studying and learning. Different dimensions of assessment emerge from the accounts offered by two teachers of mathematics, TC and KM (Watson, 2000).

TC points to a process of informal assessment through which he builds mental images of particular pupils:

> I suppose it's building up a picture in my head all the time from what I see, what they say and what they can do … just from watching really.

TC presents the images he constructs in this way as rather personal ones:

> It's my own judgement, my own thoughts about him and from watching him work.

The first aspects he reports appear to be general ones:

> How much work he is able to do, his interest in it, his attitude

but he quickly relates these more concretely to issues of classroom management and organisation:

> How much supervision he needs, or encouragement. In particular, do I have to speak to him to stay on task. And then I would also record how he is prepared to work without my help or asking, who he works with, how well he works, whether he likes to work on his own or not.

Finally, he touches on the reflexivity with which a pupil engages with study:

> Whether he asks questions that are not prompted by me ... or being stuck.

In these extracts, then, TC describes a dimension of assessment focused on pupils' approaches to studying.

KM describes a systematic process of assessment through which he monitors pupils against curricular objectives:

> I have a system in which there are three levels of mark: one for 'has met', one for 'has done sometimes' and one for 'mastery'.

He suggests that while his system 'looks fairly mechanical', nevertheless 'there are elements which are just picked up day by day as you interact with the students.' Here, KM describes a dimension of assessment focused on mapping pupils' progress in learning. In simplifying this map of progress and achievement, KM is particularly alert to the ability of pupils:

> You get an overall impression of the ones who are bright.

However, mainstream modes of assessment may not reveal talent:

> You might miss some. There are some who shine in different contexts. Some did better in a maths challenge than they did in a test, and exams sometimes throw up odd results.

KM points also to a need for flexibility in judging pupils' mathematical approaches:

> It might be about ways of working. I have learnt to accept other ways of working than the one I was familiar with. For instance, we now have to value divergent thinking as well as convergent.

Nevertheless, the default is that pupils should follow the teacher's model:

> But I do expect them to use my methods if they don't have any of their own which work.

Here, then, we see an approach by which differential teacher intervention can result in the classroom experience of pupils becoming strongly contrasted in the way exemplified by the cases of Adam and Gareth in the previous section.

These two accounts capture some of the diversity in informal assessment practices reported by Watson. Whereas some teachers use detailed recording methods showing 'coverage', 'performance' and 'understanding', others report working in a much less systematic way. While some teachers see themselves as assessing all the time, others present assessment as something they do deliberately at particular times. This diversity reflects a variety of solutions to the common problem of reducing the complexity and multidimensionality of classroom learning. Nevertheless, the accounts offered by TC and KM identify two major dimensions of assessment which can inform teaching actions: a dimension concerned with understanding the propensities of pupils as regards studying, used to inform actions aimed at drawing pupils into classroom work and steering their approaches to study and a dimension concerned with charting the progress of pupils towards curricular objectives, used to inform the planning of teaching activities and the setting of learning targets.

A strong influence on the way in which teachers construe both these dimensions is the pervasive idea of ability, which offers an attractively straightforward model of pupil capacity for learning. Nevertheless, the basic idea can be elaborated in rather different ways, and these are associated with very different treatments of pupils. Some teachers emphasise – and act from – a view of ability as an evolving and malleable state, a convenient encapsulation of a matrix of cognitive and metacognitive capabilities remaining open to development. In particular, this leads such teachers to seek to develop these capacities in pupils. Other teachers, however, emphasise a view of ability as a more permanent trait, constraining the capacity for learning of many pupils. This encourages teaching approaches that 'protect' pupils by increasing the predictability of mathematical tasks and correspondingly reducing the degree of active interpretation and critical engagement expected. Consequently pupils are not supported towards deeper learning, or in developing the associated metacognitive capabilities. In addition, the attribution of achievement to an ability factor beyond the control of pupils and teachers, more powerful than other factors such as effort, produces a fatalistic appraisal of the potential of less successful pupils. The result is a loss both of incentive to study and of opportunity to learn (Good and Biddle, 1988; Brophy, 1998).

This issue of ability relates closely to the kinds of evaluative comparisons that are made within – and between – classes, particularly in constructing, presenting and interpreting the results of formal assessment (Crooks, 1988). Group-referenced comparisons, which focus on a pupil's standing in relation to peers, tend to undermine the motivation – and hence the learning – of many pupils, notably of those who are consistently less successful. Greatly preferable are self-referenced comparisons which focus on changes in specific aspects of pupils' performance, helping teachers and pupils to set appropriate objectives for learning. Such assessment can simply chart progress towards these objectives, providing feedback on specific gaps and gains in performance. However, it is more effective when it provides insight into the mathematical thinking underlying pupils' performance, indicating what kinds of reorganisation, development and refinement of this thinking the teacher should be aiming to promote. Aggregate marks or grades at test-level are clearly deficient in providing such information although, broken down and followed through at item-level, they can be of some value in identifying where the performance of individual pupils or classes is weak. More valuable is information about specific ways in which responses to an item could be improved, and underlying thinking changed (see Wiliam, 2001). However, concern with marks or grades may divert pupils' attention from opportunities to learn through reviewing their response in the light of the more informative feedback. Simple strategies through which the teacher can refocus pupils' attention on learning include expecting them to revise their solutions in the light of feedback, and/or to tackle a fresh item of a similar type. Positive results have been reported from use of 'two-stage' assessments in which pupils are given the opportunity to reconsider and revise their responses in the light of feedback from the teacher (Leal and Abrantes, 1993).

Feedback from assessment activities – such as insights into the strategies that pupils are using – can inform teachers' planning of future work. Much writing on assessment and teaching has promoted the idea that teachers should build up detailed knowledge of individual pupils, differentiating tasks and tailoring their teaching interventions accordingly. Yet, the current conditions under which the typical secondary mathematics teacher works – responsible for teaching from five to ten classes of between 15 and 35 pupils – clearly constrain the extent to which such an ideal, however desirable in principle, is realisable in practice. Indeed, highly effective teachers who employ the prevalent exposition-and-practice approach to mathematics teaching tend to focus on teaching the class as an entity rather than as a collection of individual pupils (Bromme, 1994). In particular, knowledge of prototypical pupils is embedded in the mental teaching schemes that teachers build up, largely through adapting to – and reflecting on – critical incidents experienced while teaching a topic on many occasions and to different classes (Leinhardt, 1988). These schemes anticipate pupil difficulties within a topic and how they can be addressed. Knowledge of the specific class to be taught – gained through informal and formal assessment – helps the teacher to tailor a specific lesson from the more generic teaching scheme. For example, in building review of prior knowledge and skills into a lesson, expert teachers will emphasise those elements they expect to be troublesome; in presenting concepts or methods, they will include examples or situations linked to anticipated mistakes, so that these can be recognised and corrected. In short, such teachers direct their diagnosis and intervention primarily towards teaching the class as an entity, rather than individual pupils.

Nevertheless, such teachers also incorporate considerable interaction into their exposition as a means both of engaging pupils and of providing feedback to assist both parties during the course of the lesson. For example, building questioning into exposition can help pupils to sustain their concentration, can help to identify key ideas, and can be used to monitor their understanding (Crooks, 1988). Equally, pupil response to questioning can offer guidance to the teacher in regulating the pace and direction of the lesson, and in identifying difficulties – anticipated or unanticipated – requiring further attention (Good and Biddle, 1988). However, concern to maintain the pace and direction of a lesson may lead to 'quickfire questioning' which focuses on surface issues and encourages unreflective answers. Even if questions are more probing, pupils may be reluctant to respond if there is an emphasis on evaluating rather than elaborating their replies, if insufficient time is given to offer a considered answer, and if an approved one will quickly be forthcoming regardless (see also Mason, 2001).

During periods of practice, it becomes more feasible for teachers to monitor and interact with pupils on an individual or small group basis without breaking the flow of class work for others. Yet, the tendency remains towards brief interactions in which pupils' ideas are assessed in terms of the teacher's preconceptions, and assistance from the teacher takes the form of 'piloting' pupils along a preconceived route towards successful completion of the task (Johansson, 1993). Here we see an important way in which pupils may be steered towards an unreflexive approach to studying; and, indeed, teachers towards an unreflexive approach to teaching. Consequently, where this form of teaching predominates, it is rare to find teachers engaging in any depth with pupils' conceptualisations, and misjudgements about the nature of pupils' difficulties are commonplace (Maher *et al.*, 1992). Strategies have been proposed to introduce a higher degree of reflexivity into this type of exchange, and to secure greater engagement of pupils: giving pupils more time to respond to questions; asking pupils to discuss their thinking before responding; asking pupils to vote on different options (Black and Wiliam, 1998; Wiliam, 2001).

Taking such suggestions further, if deeper learning depends on the intensity and reflexivity with which pupils engage in classroom activities, then teaching strategies other than exposition-and-practice may be better suited to facilitating this goal. In the problem-solving-and-discussion approach of diagnostic teaching, pupils are presented with a task without any prior indications of how they should tackle it (Bell, 1993). The task is designed so that anticipated differences in pupils' mathematical conceptions – some of which will be misconceptions – will result in differing answers being proposed. The teacher uses the presence of conflicting answers to motivate pupils to give accounts of their reasoning; the differences between these accounts are used in turn to stimulate deeper reflection and discussion; and the teacher then organises this material and relates it to mathematically accepted ideas. Finally, pupils are asked to devise similar problems as challenges for one another. For example, after work focusing on the comparison of fractions, pupils might be invited to compute $\frac{1}{2} + \frac{1}{6}$ in the expectation that the answers $\frac{2}{8}, \frac{2}{6}$ and $\frac{2}{3}$ would all be proposed, and a range of strategies elicited. Characteristically, these strategies would employ different representations or analogues of the problem. Pupils would be encouraged to discuss these and suggest others (for example, combining test marks, or parts of an hour, or squares on a chocolate bar), to propose analogous problems which highlight weaknesses in particular conceptions or focus attention on central principles (for example, $\frac{1}{2} + \frac{1}{2}$ or $\frac{1}{6} + \frac{1}{6}$), and to pose key questions (for example, 'Isn't $\frac{2}{8}$ less than $\frac{1}{2}$?', 'Is $\frac{4}{6}$ the same as $\frac{2}{3}$?'). The rationale for this approach is that it leads pupils to engage more intensively and thoughtfully with mathematical problems and the concepts underpinning them, and that it provides extensive explicit feedback focused on misconceptions. Evaluations have found that discussing the misconceptions actually proposed by pupils is more effective than alerting them to common misconceptions, and much more effective than not addressing misconceptions in any explicit way. It has also been found that most pupils rate this approach as challenging but interesting.

Experience of diagnostic teaching makes some pupils aware of deeper approaches to learning. As one more articulate pupil put it:

> I never realised that you could think about a problem and work out how to do it; I always thought that if you looked at it, you could do it straight away; that was the end of it.

This has led to further work aimed at increasing pupils' awareness of different types of classroom mathematical task, and at developing appropriate metacognitive strategies (Swan *et al.*, 2000). Activities with a specific focus on assessment include pupils being asked to assess a 'typical' piece of pupil work, correcting and explaining mistakes; to construct tests (with mark schemes) for other pupils; to observe other pupils working and discuss their problem-solving approaches; and to assess their own progress against different types of criteria. In particular, the first two of these activities aim to strengthen pupils' awareness of the formative value of feedback from classroom assessment and their use of it to support their learning, developing strategies of self-assessment and – in some cases – linking these to strategies for self-directed assistance.

This section has examined assessment by teachers as part of a wider approach to teaching. It has identified important differences between approaches in the style and extent of their responsiveness to pupil ideas and states, and in the degree to which pupils are encouraged and supported to develop more reflexive approaches to studying. What part, then, do systemic features of schooling play in shaping – and in reshaping – the approaches to teaching developed by teachers? This issue is pursued in the following section.

Systemic assessment and effective schooling

This section examines systemic assessment, and its influence on teaching, studying and learning. Systems of assessment are under reform worldwide (Ruthven, 1994), but this section will focus on the changing system of national curriculum and assessment introduced to England and Wales from 1989 onwards (Ruthven, 1995).

The task group appointed to consider assessment and testing (Task Group on Assessment and Testing, 1987) identified four purposes for a system of national assessment: a *formative* purpose concerned with recognising the positive achievements of a pupil and planning appropriate next steps; a *diagnostic* purpose concerned with analysing learning difficulties so as to provide appropriate remediation; an *evaluative* purpose concerned with assessing aspects of the work of an educational institution and a *summative* purpose concerned with recording the overall achievement of a pupil in a systematic way. The most significant proposal of the task group was that 'an assessment system designed for formative purposes can meet all the needs of national assessment' prior to the end of compulsory education, at which point 'the focus shifts from formative to summative'. To the purposes identified by the task group should be added one more: an *ameliorative* purpose, as proposed both by the

Education Minister in his briefing – 'to help to promote good teaching' – and the working group appointed specifically to consider mathematics (Mathematics Working Group, 1988) –'[to] act as a force in support of curriculum change to improve standards of attainment'.

The Education Minister envisaged the national assessment process 'supplementing the normal assessments made by teachers in the classroom with simply-administered tests'. The task group proposed that these teacher assessments should be moderated through more varied forms of standardised assessment: 'a mixture of standardised assessment instruments including tests, practical tasks and observations' so as 'to minimise curriculum distortion'. Nevertheless, teacher assessments were seen as very important because they were 'based on many occasions and different types of task', so taking account of the way in which 'pupils perform differently on different days and in different circumstances'. The working group for mathematics similarly argued that 'the greater the variety of approaches [to assessment], the more informative and reliable the results are likely to be'. It proposed a mix of short tasks 'focusing on a narrow range of attainment targets', long tasks 'test[ing] flexibility and enterprise in choosing and using appropriate knowledge and skills to tackle mathematical and practical problems', and extended tasks 'test[ing] the ability of pupils to use their skills and knowledge in practical applications and cover[ing] a broad range of attainment targets', adding that 'overemphasis on [short tasks] is unlikely to help pupils make the connections between the areas in mathematics which are vital if knowledge and skills are to be applied effectively'. This advocacy of a diversity of forms of assessment by the professional groups was grounded in two considerations: a concern for the generalisability of assessment judgements, recognising that pupil performance can be highly sensitive to the form, context and occasion of the assessment; and concern about backwash from assessment practice into classroom practice, recognising that broadening or narrowing the range of assessment modes produces a corresponding influence on the variety of classroom activities.

All three of these parties agreed on the importance of clarity and precision in setting assessment criteria. The Education Minister sought an assessment framework based on 'clearly specified objectives for what pupils should know, understand and be able to do' which would provide criteria 'against which pupils' performance and progress can be assessed'. The working group expressed this still more sharply: 'Attainment targets in mathematics have to be very tightly defined to avoid ambiguity, and the degree of precision required gives a very clear picture of the "content, skills and processes" associated with the targets'. The task group suggested that an important way of achieving this clarity was by providing exemplars: 'Attainment targets should be exemplified as far as possible using specimen tasks.' The minister saw the results of assessment as being reported in some detail, taking account of 'the need for a sufficiently detailed profile of a pupil's performance to give a full and fair indication of attainment'. Nevertheless, some means had also to be found of reducing this complex information to a simpler summary form, because of 'the need to present aggregated information in ways which will be useful to a wider public than the teacher, pupil and his or her parents'. Here, the task group proposed that the profile should be projected onto a simple scale, formed by a 'sequence of levels represent[ing] the stages of progression', on the principle that 'a pupil assessed as achieving a given level ... will have satisfied the criteria for [that] level ... and will be working towards the criteria for the [next level].'

This assessment framework was grounded in common sense theories of learning as stepwise progression and of assessment as direct measurement. What this framework did was to operationalise these theories more fully and transparently than had any previous assessment system. One way of treating the ensuing experience is to view it as a public experiment testing out these theories (Ruthven, 1995). The weaknesses that were revealed had been sensed to some degree by the working group for mathematics. Their suggestion that 'pupils should be expected to be able to apply the knowledge, skills and understanding that is being assessed in a variety of different contexts and over a period of time' anticipated the way in which many pupils would perform inconsistently on supposedly equivalent tasks. And their suggestion that 'the mathematical development of each pupil is different and is difficult to predict' because '[m]athematical concepts form a network through which there are many different paths' was borne out by the way in which many pupils met objectives placed at higher levels while failing to meet some at lower levels. Teachers found it difficult – and burdensome – to make summative judgements against specific objectives. Inspectors reported that one of their main concerns was the meaning of a statement of attainment and the extent to which – and consistency with which – it should be evidenced in a pupil's performance for the pupil to be judged to have mastered it. Often teachers' multiple sources of evidence conflicted, and they were reduced to recording in terms such as 'work covered', 'some degree of understanding' and 'mastery'. In assigning pupils to a level, however, teachers experienced fewer problems. They tended to interpret their evidence so that, justifiably or not, it corresponded to the level hierarchy. In effect, teacher assessment came closer to assessing pupils' 'ability' than their 'attainment'.

The resulting revision of the national framework (Dearing, 1994) moved in this same direction, prioritising the assessment of a general level of performance in mathematics for each pupil, and suppressing the anomalies highlighted by the original system. Each level of the assessment scale is now characterised in terms of stereotypical 'level descriptions' from which teachers are expected to find the 'best fit' for each pupil. In the words of its author, the new system: 'eliminates spurious refinement and thus renders the assessment process more credible.' A major concern of the revision, then, was to secure the *reliability* – internal consistency – of the testing system, rather than to ensure its *validity* – external correspondence – in terms of covering the curriculum and matching its stated aims. In particular, national tests do not address the component of *Using and Applying Mathematics*. Although an element of teacher assessment remains in place, it enjoys little status compared to national tests and examinations that play an increasingly important part in the evaluation of schools and teachers. These changes have effectively dismantled many of the basic principles of the original system of national assessment; notably that a variety of forms of assessment should be used, and that assessment should yield interpretable profiles of pupils' mathematical development. The reformed system is dominated by evaluative and summative concerns, and provides little substantive information that might contribute to formative or diagnostic purposes (Stobart, 1999). As far as its ameliorative purpose is concerned, this risks becoming self-referential as improvement comes to be defined in terms of implementing the systemic framework and pursuing strategies narrowly targeted on raising performance in statutory tests.

The evolution of national assessment illustrates a wider principle on which there is general agreement: that in assessment systems devised for both formative and summative purposes, there is invariably a drift towards emphasis on the summative function in response to managerial concerns for accountability and evaluation, and a correspondingly diminished concern to generate information helpful for the formative purposes of teaching and learning (Stobart, 1999). The influence of the system on the classroom experience of pupils can be appraised from annual survey reports based on school inspections. In the year that statutory tests became mandatory, inspectors reported 'an increase in the time spent on testing in class'. The widely observed treatment of *Using and Applying Mathematics* was as a matter for summative assessment but not for active development as an integral part of the curriculum: '[P]upils were assessed on the few pieces of investigative work they attempted, had little opportunity to develop relevant skills, and were often uncertain what was required of them' (Ofsted, 1993). The following year, the inspectors offered a more general picture of assessment practice in schools. They pointed to informal processes of assessment and assistance within teaching: 'Most teachers have a good general knowledge of the pupils' strengths and weaknesses and give appropriate oral advice on how to overcome short-term problems.' However, this did not extend to the use of written class work for diagnostic and formative purposes: '[T]he marking of written work is seldom used to diagnose specific conceptual problems or to inform teachers' planning for subsequent work.' Further evidence is offered of a sharp division between everyday teaching and formal assessment. On the one hand: 'Teachers use a range of tasks in their day-to-day assessments of pupils' progress but much of the information so gained is not used to contribute to pupils' records of attainment'; on the other: 'Teachers rarely build assessment opportunities into their planning of classroom tasks'. Finally, there appear to be important limitations in the evidence base on which formal records are based: 'Formal assessments ... rely heavily on tests incorporated into published schemes and other written tests. These tests are frequently narrowly focused and fail to assess pupils' abilities to bring together different aspects of their mathematical knowledge and apply it in new and unfamiliar situations' (Ofsted, 1995).

Such observations recur in more recent reports, although the inspectors take great pains to highlight exceptional instances of good practice. In a recent major survey of secondary education, a general trend is noted towards close alignment between in-course teacher assessment and end-of-course national assessment. At lower secondary level: 'The quality of formal tests, which are the mainstay of assessment ... is improving and increasingly reflects the quality and style of the ... national tests.'

At middle secondary level: 'Assessment approaches ... are strongly influenced by the requirements of the GCSE.' And at upper secondary level: '[A]ssessment is similarly generally well geared to the requirement of examination courses.' At the higher levels, the inspectors judge that national assessment has a positive influence on assessment practice: 'by ensuring attention to all aspects of the syllabuses, providing explicit assessment objectives, and drawing on a range of evidence throughout the course'; and on the reliability of the resulting assessments by 'ensur[ing] that consistency of assessment is enhanced through moderation procedures'. However: '[P]upils see assessment and marking as a process which is done for them, and to them, and they are not greatly aware of, or involved in that process' (Ofsted, 1988a). These observations are amplified by a report on assessment at lower secondary level. This points to a premature emphasis on assigning levels or grades: 'Many departments determine the National Curriculum level achieved by each pupil at [regular] intervals.' Given the expectation that a pupil will advance by only one level every two years – and the lack of interpretability of raw test marks – such practice encourages pupils towards group-referenced rather than self-referenced assessment: 'The frequent testing undertaken in mathematics ... focuses pupils' attention on the issue of how well they are doing, although they more often see progress in terms of the ability sets they are in than the extent to which they have mastered the work covered' (Ofsted, 1998b).

This section has illustrated how an assessment system, which drives the evaluation of schools, teachers and pupils, exerts an important influence on teaching, studying and learning. Appraised in terms wider than its own, current systemic assessment is effective in focusing attention on immediate objectives of mastering specified mathematical material. However, the strategies that schools, teachers and pupils have generally adopted to achieve these objectives have a hidden cost, in giving insufficient attention to overarching objectives – which are not directly assessed – of developing pupils' independent capacities for problem solving and studying, and the cognitive and metacognitive capabilities underpinning these.

Conclusion

The major sections of this chapter have focused on the place of assessment in studying, teaching and schooling. They have shown how pupil self-assessment plays a central part in reflexive studying, and formative assessment a central part in responsive teaching. Together, these indicate important ways in which the quality of pupil learning in mathematics can be enhanced. Equally, this chapter has examined how systemic assessment shapes classroom teaching and assessment; and how these, in turn, shape pupil studying and self-assessment. Here, it seems that predominant features of current assessment practice are reducing the effectiveness of schooling in developing the overarching capabilities of all pupils to study mathematics and think mathematically.

References

Anthony, G. (1996) 'Active learning in a constructivist framework', *Educational Studies in Mathematics* 31(4): 349–69.

Bell, A. (1993) 'Some experiments in diagnostic teaching', *Educational Studies in Mathematics*, Special Issue on Design of Teaching, 24(1): 115–37.

Black, P. and Wiliam, D. (1998) *Inside the Black Box: raising standards through classroom assessment*, London: King's College.

Bromme, R. (1994) 'Beyond subject matter: a psychological topography of teachers' professional knowledge', in R. Biehler *et al.* (eds) *Didactics of Mathematics as a Scientific Discipline*, Dordrecht, The Netherlands: Kluwer: 73–88.

Brophy, J. (ed.) (1998) 'Expectations in the classroom', *Advances in Research in Teaching* 7, London: JAI.

Crooks, T.J. (1988) 'The impact of classroom evaluation practices on students', *Review of Educational Research* 58(4): 438–81.

Dearing, R. (1994) *The National Curriculum and its Assessment: final report*, London: School Curriculum and Assessment Authority.

Good, T.L. and Biddle, B.J. (1988) 'Research and the improvement of mathematical instruction: the need for observational resources', in D. Grouws (ed.) *Effective Mathematics Teaching*, Reston, VA: NCTM/Lawrence Erlbaum Associates: 114–42.

Johansson, B. (1993) 'Diagnostic assessment in arithmetic', in M. Niss (ed.) *Investigations into Assessment in Mathematics Education*, Dordrecht, The Netherlands: Kluwer: 169–84.

Leal, L.C. and Abrantes, P. (1993) 'Assessment in an innovative curriculum project', in M. Niss (ed.) *Cases of Assessment in Mathematics Education*, Dordrecht, The Netherlands: Kluwer: 173–82.

Leinhardt, G. (1988) 'Expertise in instructional lessons: an example from fractions', in D. Grouws (ed.) *Effective Mathematics Teaching*, Reston, VA: NCTM/Lawrence Erlbaum Associates: 47–66.

Maher, C.A., Davis, R.B. and Alston, A. (1992) 'A teacher's struggle to assess cognitive growth', in R. Lesh and S.J. Lamon (eds) *Assessment of Authentic Performance in School Mathematics*, Washington, DC: American Association for the Advancement of Science: 249–64.

Marton, F. and Saljö, R. (1976) 'On qualitative differences in learning', *British Journal of Educational Psychology* 46: 4–11 and 115–27.

Mason, J. (2001) 'Minding your Qs and Rs: effective questioning and responding in the mathematics classroom', in L. Haggerty (ed.) *Aspects of Teaching Secondary Mathematics*, London: RoutledgeFalmer.

Mathematics Working Group (1988) 'Final report', in *Mathematics for ages 5 to 16*, London: DES.

Ofsted (1993) *Mathematics: Key Stages 1, 2, 3 and 4: fourth year, 1992–93*, London: HMSO.

Ofsted (1995) *Mathematics: a review of inspection findings, 1993–94*, London: HMSO.

Ofsted (1998a) *Secondary Education: a review of secondary schools in England, 1993–97*, London: HMSO.

Ofsted (1998b) *How Teachers Assess the Core Subjects at Key Stage 3*, London: Ofsted.

Ruthven, K. (1994) 'Better judgement: rethinking assessment in mathematics education', *Educational Studies in Mathematics*, Special Issue on Assessment, 27(4): 433–50.

Ruthven, K. (1995) 'Beyond common sense: reconceptualizing National Curriculum assessment', *The Curriculum Journal* 6(1): 5–28.

Stobart, G. (1999) 'The validity of national curriculum assessment', *Education-line*.

Swan, M., Bell, A., Phillips, R. and Shannon, A. (2000) 'The purposes of mathematical activities and pupils' perceptions of them', *Research in Education* 63: 11–20.

Task Group on Assessment and Testing (1987) *Report*, London: DES.

Watson, A. (2000) 'Mathematics teachers acting as informal assessors: practices, problems and recommendations', *Educational Studies in Mathematics* 41(1): 69–91.

Wiliam, D. (2001) 'Formative assessment in mathematics', in L. Haggerty (ed.) *Aspects of Teaching Secondary Mathematics*, London: RoutledgeFalmer.

13 Culture, class and 'realistic' mathematics tests

Barry Cooper

Introduction

A recent report on English mathematics education claims, 'Maths education in this country is in crisis ... . For decades now England and Wales have been caught in a spiral of decline' (Wolf, 2000). It is difficult to attract mathematicians into teaching. This, it is argued, coupled with the recent stress on arithmetic, has led to a decline in the quality of school mathematics learning. This will further exacerbate the problem of teacher supply. To anyone familiar with English mathematics education, this sounds very familiar, being the argument used in the 1960s by Bryan Thwaites and others to justify fairly radical changes in the nature of secondary school mathematics (Cooper, 1985a). Those individuals were successful in gaining financial and political support to 'modernise' school mathematics. This reform, they argued, would reduce the discontinuity between school and university mathematics, thereby reducing the difficulties students experienced in moving from the 'traditional' mathematics of their schooling to the increasingly 'modern', or abstract, mathematics of university courses. Significant changes were made in curriculums. Such schemes as the Schools Mathematics Project 11–16 (SMP, 1969, 1970) introduced a new degree of abstraction into school mathematics, together with topics illustrating newer applications of mathematics. Sets, operations and groups, for example, were introduced into the O level course for 'more able' secondary school pupils (SMP, 1969, 1970). There was work on such applied topics as linear programming. A renewed attempt was made to demonstrate the relations between different areas of mathematics. Elements of investigational and project work were introduced. This particular mix of the pure and applied, representing a compromise between the wishes of different interest groups, held sway for a time (Cooper, 1985a). However, in the 1970s, as some elements of this 'modern mathematics' began to be taught to 'less able' children, it was vigorously attacked. Many thought that much of the work in abstract algebra was, at best, irrelevant to the interests and expected futures of most children and, at worst, positively harmful. Margaret Hayman, President of the Mathematical Association, argued that 'Much of the disorder in schools is because children are being asked to do work in all subjects, but particularly in mathematics, which is beyond their inherent capabilities' (Hayman, 1975). Her proposed solution was to prioritise arithmetic, rather than mathematics, for the majority. Such views produced pressure for further reform, culminating in the influential Cockcroft Report (Cockcroft, 1982). Alongside a renewed stress on the differentiation of the mathematics curriculum by 'ability' (Cooper, 1985b; Ruthven, 1986), this report argued for the importance of 'problem-solving, including the applications of mathematics to everyday situations' (para. 243). Through the rest of the 1980s and 1990s the *use* of mathematics became, at least rhetorically, a key concern for mathematics educators. This was recognised in the various incarnations of the attainment target *Using and Applying Mathematics*.

It is, of course, important to note that what actually occurs in classrooms often bears a tenuous relationship to the rhetoric and recommendations of textbooks, teachers' guides and official recommendations. Wolf (2000) notes, of the passion for 'real-life' contexts, that 'mostly aren't real at all'. Nevertheless, this brief account of change reminds us that school mathematics is not some unchanging body of knowledge and practice. As the content, as well as the teaching and learning strategies, of school mathematics changes, there will also be changes in the form and content of assessment. An obvious example has been the increased emphasis on extended coursework over the past quarter of a century. Given the importance of mathematics achievement in selection for higher education and jobs, it would seem worthwhile to ask questions about the ways in which various versions of mathematics and, in particular, various forms of assessment might favour some cognitive or affective characteristics of children over others. It is often claimed, for example, that coursework favours girls while timed examinations favour boys. Indeed one philosopher, during the recent panic concerning the relative performance of boys and girls in public examinations, has suggested that 'Boys and girls need to be assessed differently' (Grayling, 2000). He argues that males and females should be assessed by both examinations and coursework, with the better of the child's two results determining their future progress.

In this chapter I shall examine one possible way in which some forms of assessment may favour particular groups of pupils. My focus will be on items in timed tests, where the mathematical operation is presented in some 'realistic' context. These items will be discussed against the background of some research on cultural differences in orientations towards problem-solving. The key issues to be considered are whether the use of such items might lead to an underestimation of the mathematics some children actually know, and whether such effects are likely to be similar across social classes. In technical terms, are some items differentially valid? I shall also illustrate the mixed messages national curriculum (NC) items send to teachers and pupils about what the nature of 'realistic' problem-solving *ought* to be in mathematics. However, we need to consider first what the documents surrounding the various revisions of the NC have said about 'realistic' problems. We shall then be able to judge whether what has been recommended to teachers matches what has appeared in the annual tests and marking schemes.

Real-life problems

In all of the versions of the national curriculum, teachers have been encouraged to teach pupils to 'use and apply mathematics'. Early on, in *Mathematics for ages 5–16*, it was noted that 'real-life problems ... of their nature, do not come forward with a clear indication of the particular mathematics that they will require for their solution, nor will they necessarily draw on a narrow range of mathematics only' (DES/WO, 1988, p. 49). In using mathematics to 'tackle real-life problems', pupils should be able to decide whether there is enough information – and, if not, to decide what they need and where to find it; to distinguish between important and irrelevant information; to apply common sense and reasoning skills and to recognise that the 'best' mathematical solution may not be the best 'real' solution. This list was followed by a discussion of the role of modelling in using mathematics for 'practical purposes'. The subsequent curriculum document echoed this advice. Under Attainment Target (AT) 1, *Using and Applying Mathematics*, we find, 'Pupils should use number, algebra and measures in practical tasks, in real-life problems, and to investigate within mathematics itself' (DES/WO, 1989). In *Mathematics Non-Statutory Guidance*, we find, 'It is a characteristic of "real-life" problems that they frequently do not have unique solutions' (NCC, 1989, D4 2.2). Because 'applying mathematics to real problems does not come naturally or easily to many pupils, even when their grasp of the relevant knowledge and skills is sound', pupils therefore needed experience of tackling 'real-life' problems in the curriculum. Most recently, after earlier revisions in 1991 and 1994, the 1999 NC states that pupils, at Key Stage 2, should be able to 'identify the information needed to carry out the tasks', 'present and interpret solutions in the context of the problem' and 'estimate answers by approximating and checking that their results are reasonable by thinking about the context of the problem' (DEE/QCA, 1999). At Key Stage 3 they should be able to 'identify exceptional cases when solving problems' and 'recognise the importance of assumptions when deducing results; recognise the limitations of any assumptions that are made and the effect that varying the assumptions may have on the solution to a problem'. This summary indicates that elements of the mathematical modelling of 'realistic' problems have been recommended since the late 1980s. Deciding what information is relevant, carefully considering assumptions, considering solutions against the context, are all important aspects of 'modelling' (Edwards and Hamson, 1989).

During the 1990s, *Using and Applying Mathematics* has been assessed via teacher assessment rather than in the annual externally marked timed tests. However, a cursory inspection of annual test papers shows that many items employ 'realistic' contexts. It might be argued that children should apply what they may have learned about 'real-life' problems to such test items. If not, why not? Must they instead learn to think in terms of two different 'mathematics', with only one being applicable in tests? The next section considers four examples of 'realistic' items in order to illustrate the difficulties raised for teachers and pupils – and for the validity of assessment – by the ambiguity surrounding 'real-life' problems in the NC. It will also show that there is a mismatch between the various official recommendations made since 1988 and some of these test items.

Some contrasting examples

Consider the Key Stage 3 item below. This appeared in Tiers 3–5, 4–6 and 5–7 (QCA, 2000). What is a child to make of it? We are told that a 'special person' will be chosen to open the new canteen. Initially, the reader may think of a celebrity as a possibility, but the next sentence appears to indicate that the 'special person' is to be a pupil, a teacher or a member of staff. The pupil may now wonder whether any or all of these three might qualify as 'special persons'. If it assumed is that they might, and if the pupil draws on everyday personal experience of schools to postulate some possible counter-examples to the assumption of equal numbers in the three groups, this pupil will be able to move towards producing an acceptable explanation by referring to the probable different numbers in the three categories. The marking scheme also allows as an alternative explanation, 'It would be true if there were 20 pupils, 20 teachers and 20 dinner people' (QCA, 2000). Leaving aside the potential confusion surrounding the reference to a 'special person', the key point is that the child is expected to consider the number of persons of each type as a variable. They may do this by reference to everyday experience. This approach will not hinder their successful completion of the item. Here, a range of possible answers is allowed and thinking in a realistic 'modelling' perspective will allow success.

14.   A school has a new canteen.

A special person will be chosen to perform the opening ceremony.

The names of all the pupils, all the teachers and all the canteen staff are put into a box.

One name is taken out at random.

A pupil says:

> There are only three choices.
> It could be a pupil, a teacher or one of the canteen staff.
> The probability of it being a **pupil** is ⅓

This pupil is **wrong**. Explain why.

Source: QCA, 2000

Now consider the item below. What might a similar approach, realistically considering variable features of the situation, lead to here? A pupil might reason along the following lines. If the lift were always full with exactly 14 people, *because* there were always people waiting *and* nobody used stairs *and* nobody broke the rule about 14 being the maximum *and* no wheelchairs, etc. reduced the lift's carrying capacity below 14, then it would need to ascend 20 times, since 269/14 is approximately 19.21, and a lift must ascend a whole number of times. Of course, a child who reasoned like this might realise that it was unlikely in 'real-life' that this would be the answer, since either people would become impatient and use the stairs if there were too many queuing or, on the other hand, the lift would not always be full if there were too few people queuing. Since the correct answer, according to the marking scheme, is 20 – and no other – we must assume that the designers of this item thought that the reference to the 'morning rush' and the absence of any reference to stairs would warrant the *implicit* assumptions required to produce an answer of 20. Here, a realistic 'modelling' perspective would lead not to success, but to failure.

(a)   This is the sign in a lift at an office block:

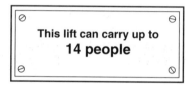

In the morning rush, 269 people want to go up in this lift. How many times must it go up?

Source: SEAC, 1992

These two items, with their marking schemes, send quite different messages to children and teachers. In the first case, the child should contemplate fully the variable features of the context; in the second they should not. What is particularly ironic is that the lift item does in fact require the child to introduce a realistic consideration – that lifts ascend in whole numbers – but bars any others such as people using stairs or breaking rules (Cooper, 1992). In both items, an assumption is made by test designers that certain things are obvious. The child needs to share this sense of the obvious in order to succeed.

We can ask what is an *intelligent* response to the lift item. Intelligent activity has been described as grasping the essentials in a situation and responding appropriately to them (Heim, 1970). Clearly, this leaves much room for disagreement about whether some performance is intelligent or not. Who determines what is essential, what counts as an appropriate response, and in just what situations? In the case of the lift item, it could be argued that the intelligent response, given the sometimes absurd nature of school mathematics, is 20. We all know, it might be claimed, that in school mathematics, 'real-life' problems have tended, unlike real 'real-life' problems, to have one correct answer. It is therefore intelligent, in the context of school tests, to respond on this assumption, whatever rhetoric may have been around concerning the importance of learning about realistic problem-solving. This response, instead of considering the implications of the 'real-life' context represented in the item, responds to the encompassing context of the cultural situation represented by school mathematics itself. Others might not be so happy to 'play the game', given its absurdity. For them, intelligent activity would mean taking the represented context seriously and failing to give the answer 20 as the single outcome.

To see how a failure to share the sense of the obvious – of what is intelligent – might threaten the validity of testing, consider the *level* 6 item below, concerning a tennis tournament.

Organising a competition

David and Gita's group organise a mixed doubles tennis competition. They need to pair a boy with a girl.

They put the three boys' names into one bag and all the three girls' names into another bag.

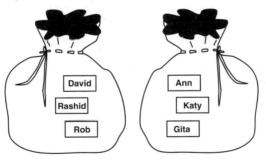

| David |
| Rashid |
| Rob |

| Ann |
| Katy |
| Gita |

Find all the possible ways that boys and girls can be paired.
Write the pairs below. One pair is already shown.

Rob and Katy

Source: SEAC, 1993

At the period when abstract algebra was in favour, this item might have been displaced by *Find the Cartesian product of the sets {a, b, c} and {d, e, f}*. The underlying operation here is that of combining elements, one from each of two sets, to produce all possible pairs. The mark scheme gives as its example of the correct nine pairs:

Rob and Katy

Rob and Ann

Rob and Gita

Rashid and Katy

Rashid and Ann

Rashid and Gita

David and Katy

David and Ann

David and Gita

This systematic arrangement suggests that the tennis context did not matter to the test designer. Clearly, an alternative arrangement of the three groups of three pairs – with each group using all six names – would be a more realistic one. However, it can be seen that the context might matter to pupils by referring to children's likely experience of televised draws for such competitions as the Football Association Cup, where the draw is made without replacement (Cooper, 1994). Here, once a team is paired with an opponent that is the end of the matter. The draw is not rerun to produce different pairings. In fact, exploratory research with Year 6 children found that children often offered just three pairs, sometimes coupled with an account of the *methods* by which pairs could be generated (Cooper, 1998a, 1998b). Crucially, some of these children proved themselves capable of generating nine pairs when asked whether three really were all the possible pairs. Mike, having stopped after writing three pairs, was asked whether there were any more to be found:

BC: … if I said, here, write down all the pairs you think you could get, of boys and girls – all the possible ones – do you think there are more than three? Or just three?

Mike: There'd be nine.

He proceeded to write them down. Mike seemed able to carry out the mental operation required by the Statement of Attainment (SoA) given for the item, *identify all the outcomes of combining two independent events*, once he had *recognised* that it was required. However, because he failed to interpret the intended meaning of the item, his initial performance did not reflect this underlying competence. He initially produced a realistic three pairs, after first considering methods of generating the pairs. The invitation to reflect further led to the production of nine, along with an account of why nine boy–girl pairs exist (Cooper, 1998a).

Subsequent research on a larger scale, funded by the Economic and Social Research Council (ESRC) and carried out with Máiréad Dunne and Nicola Rodgers, has shown the production of three pairs to be a common response to this item. In interviews, when children who had produced three pairs then were asked to consider whether all possible pairs had been found, six further pairs were frequently produced (Cooper and Dunne, 2000a, 2000b). Some ten per cent of a sample of 125 10–11-year-olds produced an initial three pairs followed by a subsequent nine. Furthermore, this pattern is more frequent amongst children from the lower-middle and working-classes than amongst upper middle-class children (Cooper and Dunne, 2000a, 2000b). I have already noted that some children took the clause 'find all the possible ways' to indicate that *methods* were required either instead of, or in addition, to actual pairs. Amongst 13–14-year-olds a greater proportion of children seemed to understand what was required, though working-class children were still more likely to respond realistically than others, and four of the ten Year 9 children producing three pairs switched to nine when asked to reconsider, while one produced eighteen (Cooper and Dunne, 2000b).

I want to suggest that some of the children who produced three pairs, even though they subsequently showed they knew how to generate nine, may share a particular orientation towards 'realistic' problems. We saw with the lift item that a child needed to have enough of a 'feel for the game' (Bourdieu, 1990) to see that only a homoeopathic dose of realism – but no more – was required. Children who produce three pairs may be failing to operate on this assumption. They may instead be assuming, perhaps tacitly, that a 'realistic' context should be responded to with realistic considerations. They might therefore, in responding, draw on their everyday experience of sport. If tennis were to be played in 'real-life' we would need three pairs, not nine. For some of these children, this item will fail to assess validly their mathematical competence. While they can do what the SoA requires, they might not demonstrate this in a written test. Of course, if the SoA were to be reworded to include a reference to carrying out the operation *in this sort of context*, we might have to revise this conclusion. However, it is not obvious that *mathematical competence* should be so defined. This matter can only be decided on the basis of a clearer view than currently seems to exist as to what should count as mathematics in school.

Interestingly, children who gave three pairs as their initial answer to this item were also more likely to respond realistically to another item. In the figure overleaf, children are asked to judge the likelihood of a car or lorry going by in the next minute on the basis of given tabulated data. Acceptable answers were 'unlikely' for the lorry, and 'likely' or 'very likely' for the car. It became clear in interviews in which children explained their choices, that many drew on their actual experience of roads around schools to answer this question, often ignoring the given data completely (Cooper, 1998a; Cooper and Dunne, 2000a). Others drew on the given data and their everyday knowledge.

In the larger project a correlation was found between the child's social class and the nature of the proffered explanation, with working-class children being much more likely to rely on their everyday experience than others (Cooper and Dunne,

The children in Year 6 conducted a traffic survey outside the school for 1 hour.

Type	Number that passed in one hour
car	75
bus	8
lorry	13
van	26

When waiting outside the school they try to decide on the likelihood that a **lorry** will go by in the next minute.

Put a ring round how likely it is that a **lorry** will go by in the next minute.

| **certain** | **very likely** | **likely** | **unlikely** | **impossible** |

They also try to decide on the likelihood that a **car** will go by in the next minute.

Put a ring round how likely it is that a **car** will go by in the next minute.

| **certain** | **very likely** | **likely** | **unlikely** | **impossible** |

Source: SEAC, 1993

2000a, p. 103). Because the given data matched most children's everyday experience, 'realistic responders', relying on their knowledge of real traffic flows, could still gain marks. However, it is easy to see that, had the data not matched typical everyday experience, they might not have done so. Unless they were to change their mode of response, realistic responders, faced with given data in which, say, lorries were most common, would have produced incorrect answers. As I have noted, there was a correlation between responses on the tennis and traffic items. Children who responded realistically on one tended to do so on the other (Cooper and Dunne, 2000a, p. 116). This supports the idea of an underlying orientation comprising a disposition to behave in a consistent manner towards 'realistic' problems. Some children are more likely than others, *whether they are intended to or not*, to respond to 'realistic' mathematics items in terms of everyday considerations and experience. Furthermore, the Year 6 children who respond 'realistically' to both of

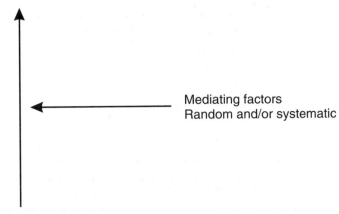

Child's performance in some context

Mediating factors
Random and/or systematic

Child's mathematical competence
Knowledge, understanding, skills

Figure 13.1 Competence and performance

these items are more likely to be working-class (Cooper and Dunne, 2000a). In the next section I will describe some sociological research bearing on this finding, but I end here with some comments on the simple model of the assessment process that has been used implicitly so far (Figure 13.1).

This model posits the existence of something – competence – which the child carries around from situation to situation. This enables us to ask questions about the ways in which the demonstration of competence is constrained or enabled by particular situations or contexts, or is mediated by various factors. For example, we would readily accept that a severe cold might act as a mediating factor in preventing a child from demonstrating her mathematical knowledge (competence) in some examination (performance). We would be making, implicitly, the predictive claim that, without the cold, this child would have performed better. My earlier remarks about children's differing dispositions to draw on their everyday experience when faced with 'realistic' looking items can be framed in the same way. Here the disposition is seen as a mediating factor and, analytically at least, as separable from mathematical competence per se. Children who produced three pairs in the tennis item often proved to be capable of providing nine, but a disposition to think realistically appeared to be mediating – here constraining – the expression of their competence in performance.

However, it is not always easy in practice to make the distinction between an underlying competence and performance in particular contexts. I have already noted, in discussing the tennis item, that a choice could be made between the original SoA and a revised one which refers to the capacity to carry out the combinatorial operation in a 'real-life' setting. The choice perhaps reduces to a debate about what is to count as *mathematical* thinking in schools. Furthermore, it has been shown that people can often carry out arithmetical operations in the context of their everyday life, in work or consumption settings, that they cannot reproduce in the context of school problems (e.g. Lave, 1988; Nunes *et al.*, 1993). Should these people be seen as having an arithmetical competence or not? The answer here might depend on whether we regard some sort of deep understanding as a necessary criterion for the competence or, instead, are willing to accept some sort of rule of thumb as adequate. It also clearly depends, however, on which situations we choose to regard as relevant for inferring competence from performance. These are difficult questions. As one philosopher of education has argued, we are 'often unable to identify independently from particular social contexts individual cognitive traits or competencies which may be thought of as persisting over time and [are] manifestable in a range of future circumstances' (Davis, 1998, p. 103). In order to do this we need, amongst other matters, to decide what are going to count as cases-in-context of such capacities as *identify all the outcomes of combining two independent events*. Should the relevant cases include both 'find the Cartesian product of the sets {a, b, c} and {d, e, f }' and the tennis item? The first demands knowledge of esoteric terminology, the second necessitates the disposition to ignore the invitation provided by the 'realistic' context to respond with just three pairs. Perhaps, for our purposes, we should just note that the use of the language of competence/performance in a discussion of assessment involves (i) a philosophically realist claim that something relatively enduring in the mind/brain enables successful performance in various contexts and (ii) that in claiming that a child has a competence, we are effectively predicting, on the basis of performances in a range (often very limited) of assessment contexts, that this child will demonstrate the competence in some future, yet to be experienced, contexts. How similar these future contexts need to be to the assessment contexts is a critical question, but often ignored (Davis, 1998). Let us return now to the issue of social class. Why might different social origins be associated with different responses to 'real-life' problems in tests?

Sociocultural differences and education

Before the 1970s the relative lack of educational success of working-class children was frequently understood in terms of some aspect of cultural, or subcultural, difference between social classes. Sometimes different values, sometimes different perspectives on the future, sometimes linguistic differences, were picked out as potential candidates to explain class differences in achievement. Many of these substantive issues became lost in debates over whether concepts of cultural deficit or difference provided a better, or perhaps more politically acceptable, account of the relations between children from various social backgrounds and the demands made of them in schools. For my purposes, it is perhaps adequate to note that the key term in the last sentence is *relations*. If curriculum, pedagogy and assessment in schools reflect the ways of life and thinking of some social groups more than others, then it seems likely that children from the latter groups will find success at school harder to achieve, as a result of the greater discontinuity between what the school demands and what these children initially bring with them from home. A simple example can illustrate this. If some children in a society speak one language at home, and some a second, but mathematics testing is carried out only in the first, then children speaking the second language are likely to find the tests more difficult than the others, irrespective of their mathematical competence. This example is of a type where a solution is relatively easy to imagine. Testing could take place in the two languages, with a choice available. This might also apply to schooling itself. Of course, in a society where one language is of higher social status than the other, this solution would raise other difficulties concerning subsequent opportunities.

The case of some cultural differences is less straightforward, because some of these differences are often thought to be less arbitrarily related to what education *ought* to comprise, than is mother tongue. We can see what this means by considering a well-known example. Luria (1976), in the 1930s, studied unschooled adults in 'remote' villages in Central Asia. In the context of post-revolutionary Russia, he was interested in the relation between 'social systems', 'cultural and historical advances', absence of schooling and 'patterns of thinking'. Here is one of the problems that were given to individuals. The respondent is an illiterate 37-year-old.

Researcher: Cotton can only grow where it is hot and dry. In England it is cold and damp. Can cotton grow there?
Respondent: I don't know.
Researcher: Think about it.
Respondent: I've only been in the Kashgar country; I don't know beyond that ...

Luria notes that, in this case and many others, individuals do not enter into the closed and abstract inferential system of the syllogism. Instead, personal experience is relied upon. It is easy to see that *if* the sort of abstract reasoning represented by classical syllogisms were thought to be a necessary component of any education, then these individuals, and children raised in this cultural environment, would be disadvantaged, at least initially, compared to children whose cultural environment has already introduced this sort of logical framework. Luria also asked people to classify various objects, for example: hammer, saw, log, hatchet. Here is an example of an attempt to persuade a 39-year-old illiterate peasant to see three of these as tools, with the log as the odd one out. He had already argued that all four were needed together.

Researcher: Which of these things could you call by one word?
Respondent: How's that? If you call all three of them a 'hammer', that won't be right either.
Researcher: But one fellow picked three things – the hammer, saw and hatchet – and said they were alike.
Respondent: A saw, a hammer, and a hatchet all have to work together. But the log has to be here too.
Researcher: Why do you think he picked these three things and not the log?
Respondent: Probably he's got a lot of firewood, but if we'll be left without firewood, we won't be able to do anything.

Researcher: True, but a hammer, a saw and a hatchet are all tools.
Respondent: Yes, but even if we have tools, we still need wood – otherwise we can't build anything.

Luria points out the situational, practical nature of this thinking. It was very difficult to persuade these respondents to undertake what the researchers termed abstract classification. Similar results were found in studies of the Kpelle people of Liberia in the 1960s and 1970s (Cole, 1996). Clearly, the children of the people in these studies were likely to experience difficulty with schooling in the Western tradition, and indeed they did, though they were very skilled in processes of measurement and thinking relevant to their own way of life (Cole, 1996, pp. 72–5).

Is there any evidence that this sort of functional, practical thinking tied to experienced material contexts characterises some social groups more than others in our own society? Holland (1981), working with Bernstein, presented primary-age children from various socio-economic backgrounds with a set of 24 coloured photographs of food items. These could be organised through 'context-independent principles':

- *animal* roast beef, pork chop, sausages, hamburgers, sardines, fishfingers
- *vegetable* lettuce, green beans, peas, boiled potatoes, chips, baked beans
- *animal products* milk, butter, cheese, ice-cream, boiled egg, fried egg
- *cereal* bread, cakes, biscuits, rice, Rice Krispies, spaghetti rings

As part of the work, children were asked to group the items and explain their grouping. The instruction was: 'Here are some pictures of food. What we would like you to do with them is put the ones together you think go together. You can use all of them or you can use only some of them' (Bernstein, 1996, p. 33). Social class differences were found in the initial responses of children. Middle-class children were more likely to use general principles of classification, e.g. 'The same kind of thing, both made from milk' or 'Those two you get from the sea'. Working-class children were more likely to refer to their everyday life, e.g. 'That's what we have for Sunday dinner'. Given a second chance to classify the pictures, middle-class children often switched to a classification derived from everyday life, while working-class children remained in the everyday mode of response. The similarity of the working-class responses to those of Luria's unschooled adult respondents is noteworthy, though it should be stressed that the differences between the social class groups in Holland's work were not differences of kind, but of tendency. Some working-class children did use non-everyday classifications.

The patterns of response in Holland's study can be understood in terms of Bernstein's theory of pedagogic codes (Bernstein, 1996). One aspect of this concerns the ways in which boundaries are drawn within knowledge transmitted in schools and similar institutions. Bernstein uses the concept of *classification* to refer to what meanings can be put together legitimately (Bernstein, 1996). Strong classification of knowledge, meaning more impermeable boundaries between, for example, school subjects, would be associated with keeping meanings from different disciplines apart or, on some readings of his work, keeping meanings from academic disciplines and everyday life apart. The associated concept of a *recognition rule*, possessed or not by a person, refers to the means 'by which individuals are able to recognise the speciality of the context that they are in' (Bernstein, 1996, p. 31) and, therefore, which meanings are relevant. We can see that children in Holland's study operated with different recognition rules for judging which meanings were relevant in the pictures task. Some initially saw their everyday experiences as relevant, some did not (for accounts of why these differences exist see Bernstein, 1996; Bourdieu, 1986).

We can now apply these ideas to the case of 'realistic' mathematics items. On the surface all of the four we have considered, certainly when compared to the Cartesian product item, seem to reflect a weakening of the boundary between school mathematics and everyday matters. We are not presented with sets of algebraic elements but with canteens, lifts, traffic and tennis. An examination of the marking schemes, however, shows that the boundary between the mathematical and the everyday has not been weakened as much as at first appears. Children have to interpret successfully this rather confusing set of signs. What is required by the tennis item is that children recognise that, in the context of a mathematics test, they should operate in an abstract mode, notwithstanding the 'real-life' context. Practical, situational or functional thinking relevant to the real problem of creating pairs to play tennis should be put to one side. As we saw, many children seem, in Bernstein's terms, to lack the required recognition rule. However, unlike Luria's and some of Holland's respondents, many of these schooled children, including those from the working class, did respond to a simple cue to reconsider their response. This showed that once they had recognised what was required, they could produce the required pairs. However, their capacity to demonstrate the combinatorial operation was blocked initially by their failure to recognise the context as one requiring a non-practical response. Similarly, the children who responded to a request to explain their choices in the traffic item by referring to everyday experience were also demonstrating a disposition to recognise such 'realistic' items as warranting practical responses. They lacked a legitimate 'feel for the game'. Given the mixed messages that children and their teachers have received about 'real-life' problems, alongside the cultural orientations of some children, developing this 'feel' might prove quite a challenge.

Conclusion

The Year 6 children discussed earlier were soon to enter secondary school. There they would, after a further three years, be faced by Year 9 tests containing further potentially confusing 'realistic' items. The ESRC projects found that, in the Key Stage 2 Year 6 tests, there were larger differences in performance between the social classes on 'realistic' test items than on non-'realistic' items (Cooper and Dunne, 2000a). Controlling, for the measured ability of children, the word count of items or the difficulty level of items did not lead to the disappearance of this effect. I have argued here that a partial explanation for this finding may be that working-class children are less sure how to read *legitimately* the intended boundary between purely mathematical and everyday considerations when confronted by 'realistic' items that are not really real.[1] Ironically, in 1996 at least, the proportion of 'realistic' items decreased as one moved from Tiers 3–5 through to Tiers 6–8 of the Key Stage 3 tests. Working-class children were more likely to be entered for the lower tiers (Cooper and Dunne, 2000a, p. 137). As a consequence, they were more likely to be tested via the type of item that, amongst the researched Year 6 children, working-class children found relatively more difficult. We can ask whether this is the most appropriate basis to assess both what they know and the quality of the teaching they have received.

I have shown how realistic items can produce difficult problems of interpretation for pupils, and why these difficulties are likely, for cultural reasons, to be greater for working-class pupils than others. Such interpretative difficulties are a threat to the validity of the assessment process. As a consequence of assessment based on such items, working-class children in particular may achieve test results that fail to reflect their actual mathematical understanding. Since Key Stages 2 and 3 results will be taken into account in allocating children to teaching sets, some children may receive a less rich mathematics curriculum than they should. Furthermore, their opportunities for future study, and ultimately job placement, may be adversely affected by such set allocation. I have also shown that NC 'realistic' items send contradictory messages to teachers concerning the role and nature of modelling in school mathematics. Clearly, if it is thought that 'realistic' items are educationally worthwhile then much more time needs to be given to designing items and marking schemes that are less absurd than the lift item and less confusing than the tennis item. Only greater attention to the quality of items will make them fair measures of what working-class children know and can do. It might also, one hopes, produce items which do not so obviously contradict the official messages set out for teachers over the past ten years concerning the study of 'real-life' problems.

Note

1   A further important issue addressed in Cooper and Dunne (2000a) concerns the tendency of working-class children to provide less linguistically explicit answers than other children – a difference also predicted by Bernstein's theoretical work – with the result that, as in the tennis item, they fail to demonstrate understanding they actually have. The book also analyses sex differences comparable to the social class differences discussed in this chapter.

References

Bernstein, B. (1996) *Pedagogy, Symbolic Control and Identity: theory, research, critique*, London: Taylor & Francis.

Bourdieu, P. (1986) *Distinction: a social critique of the judgement of taste*, London: Routledge and Kegan Paul.

Bourdieu, P. (1990) *In Other Words*, Cambridge: Polity.

Cockcroft, W.H. (1982) *Mathematics Counts*, London: HMSO.

Cole, M. (1996) *Cultural Psychology*, Cambridge, MA: Belknap/Harvard University Press.

Cooper, B. (1985a) *Renegotiating Secondary School Mathematics: a study of curriculum change and stability*, Basingstoke: Falmer.

Cooper, B. (1985b) 'Secondary school mathematics since 1950: reconstructing differentiation', in I.F. Goodson (ed.) *Social Histories of the Secondary Curriculum*, Barcombe: Falmer: 89–119.

Cooper, B. (1992) 'Testing National Curriculum mathematics: some critical comments on the treatment of "real" contexts for mathematics', in *The Curriculum Journal* 3(3): 231–43.

Cooper, B. (1994) 'Authentic testing in mathematics? The boundary between everyday and mathematical knowledge in National Curriculum testing in English schools', *Assessment in Education: principles, policy and practice* 1(2): 143–66.

Cooper, B. (1998a) 'Assessing National Curriculum mathematics in England: exploring children's interpretation of Key Stage 2 tests in clinical interviews', in *Educational Studies in Mathematics* 35(1): 19–49.

Cooper, B. (1998b) 'Using Bernstein and Bourdieu to understand children's difficulties with "realistic" mathematics testing: an exploratory study', in *International Journal of Qualitative Studies in Education* 11(4): 511–32.

Cooper, B. and Dunne, M. (2000a) *Assessing Children's Mathematical Knowledge: social class, sex and problem solving*, Buckingham: Open University Press.

Cooper, B. and Dunne, M. (2000b) 'Constructing the "legitimate" goal of a "realistic" mathematics item. A comparison of 10–11 and 13–14 year-olds', in A. Filer (ed.) *Assessment – social practice and social product*, London: RoutledgeFalmer: 87–109.

Davis, A.J. (1998) *The Limits of Educational Assessment*, Oxford: Blackwell.

DfEE/QCA (1999) *Mathematics: the national curriculum for England*, London: DfEE/QCA.

DES/WO (1988) *Mathematics for Ages 5 to 16*, London: HMSO.

DES/WO (1989) *Mathematics in the National Curriculum*, London: HMSO.

Edwards, D. and Hamson, M. (1989) *Guide to Mathematical Modelling*, London: Macmillan.

Grayling, A. (2000) 'Just change the marking', *The Guardian* 24/8/00.

Hayman, M. (1975) 'To each according to his needs'. *Mathematical Gazette* 59: 137–53.

Heim, A. (1970) *Intelligence and Personality*, Harmondsworth: Penguin.

Holland, J. (1981) 'Social class and changes in orientation to meaning', in *Sociology* 15(1): 1–18.

Lave, J. (1988) *Cognition in Practice: mind, mathematics and culture in everyday life*, Cambridge: Cambridge University Press.

Luria, A. R. (1976) *Cognitive Development: its cultural and social foundations*, Cambridge, MA: Harvard University Press.

Mason, J. (2001) 'Minding your Qs and Rs: effective questioning and responding in the mathematics classroom', in L. Haggarty (ed.) *Aspects of Teaching Secondary Mathematics*, London: RoutledgeFalmer.

NCC (1989) *Mathematics: non-statutory guidance*, York: NCC.

Nunes, T., Schliemann, A.D. and Carraher, D.W. (1993) *Street Mathematics and School Mathematics*, Cambridge: Cambridge University Press.

QCA (2000) *Mathematics Tests: teacher pack*, London: QCA.

Ruthven, K. (1986) 'Differentiation in mathematics: a critique of *Mathematics Counts* and *Better Schools*', *Cambridge Journal of Education* 16(1): 41–5.

SEAC (1992) *Mathematics Tests 1992, Key Stage 3*, London: SEAC/University of London.

SEAC (1993) *Pilot Standard Tests: Key Stage 2: mathematics*, Leeds: SEAC/University of Leeds.

SMP (1969) *Book 5*, Cambridge: Cambridge University Press.

SMP (1970) *Book 3T*, Cambridge: Cambridge University Press.

Wiliam, D. (2001) 'Teaching for understanding', in L. Haggarty (ed.) *Aspects of Teaching Secondary Mathematics*, London: RoutledgeFalmer.

Wolf, A. (2000) 'Countdown', *The Guardian* 5/9/00.

Social and contextual issues in Mathematics

14 Issues of equity in mathematics education

Defining the problem, seeking solutions

Peter Gates

Introduction

It is often assumed that the responsibilities of the mathematics teacher are, in the main, to teach mathematics so that all students can achieve their full potential. However, what do we do when the needs of different pupils are diverse and conflicting? How do we ensure equity in our teaching when the curriculum, the teaching styles and assessment procedures fundamentally favour the white middle-class male? How do we ensure that pupils from disadvantaged backgrounds achieve highly when the mathematics we present is intended, organised and structured to advantage the more prosperous student? How do we satisfy the needs of pupils from diverse cultural backgrounds when the mathematics we present is fundamentally white and Eurocentric? I will begin my chapter with a quote from Claudia Zaslavsky:

> It is the content and methodology of the mathematics curriculum that provides one of the most effective means for the rulers of our society to maintain class divisions.
>
> (Zaslavsky, 1981, p. 15)

Notice here she maintains that not only is there a problem for those of us concerned about equity in mathematics education, but that the culpability lies both with what we teach as well as how we teach it. Consequently we all bear some of the responsibility for the failings of mathematics education and therefore need to consider what we can do to change things. Before I go on to consider what we might do, I need to consider in some detail just what I see as the problem.

The social role of Mathematics

It can hardly be contested that we live in an uneven and unjust society where access to education and to justice depend on the capital one can appropriate and accumulate – particularly through the benefits the education system bestows on some individuals. There is ample evidence in the academic and research literature in education to support this contention such that it is hardly now contentious.

Unfairness is felt through the disappointment, hopelessness and frustrations of ordinary people as they go through their everyday lives. It exists in the knots in the pit of the stomach and the tears in the eyes. Injustice exists in the disappointments many children face when they are not endowed with financial resources to have what other children have and take for granted. Injustice exists in the frustration, anger and self-depreciation when a pupil is placed in a low set for mathematics based on some assessment procedure over which they have no control and which they feel is unfair. Injustice is a process that goes on all around us, even when – and arguably especially when – we do not look for it or recognise it.

Mathematics thus acts as a 'gatekeeper' to social progress. A qualification in mathematics seems to be considered as vital for many jobs as it is for entry to university, even when the subject to be studied bears little connection to mathematics. Furthermore, a qualification in mathematics results in higher salaries in later life so what we do in schools actually does affect not only the here-and-now existence of our pupils, but also their future prospects too (Cotton, 2001). So …

What is the problem?

One of the most politically charged statements one can make is to claim that politics ought to be kept out of education, and, furthermore, that mathematics education is neutral and value free. As Claudia Zaslavsky says in the quote above, mathematics and mathematics education provides a means for the stratification of our society, not just *arbitrarily* – but in a *particular* fashion. Clearly any activity could serve to demarcate between those who can and those who can't. The particular strength of mathematics education is the way in which it encourages us to think that the divisions between those who can do mathematics and those who can't is perfectly natural and, moreover, that it is legitimate (see also Skovsmose and Valero, 1999). Unfortunately, mathematics education is not blind – it does not undertake this stratification and enculturation in a random fashion, but as I shall go on to argue, it does it in a deliberative fashion, drawing on particular forms of stratification resulting in specific social groups being differentially disadvantaged.

As a start I will re-pose five questions that John Costello presented in his book *Teaching and Learning Mathematics 11–16*, since these will help position myself and will also help you to begin to locate my arguments.

- Mathematics is generally taught in a narrow context, with little concern for its historical and cultural setting. Would the subject be enriched by such concern?
- Is the mathematics curriculum in Britain racist, in the sense of discriminating against the needs, values and best interests of certain ethnic groups?
- To what extent can and should school mathematics be used politically, to promote certain values or social developments, and is it being used in this way?
- It is a common complaint that school mathematics is remote from the familiar

experiences of many pupils. Could it usefully be more closely based on the pupils' culture, however that might be identified?

- Is studying the mathematics of a particular culture or society a reasonable and productive way of understanding that society?

(Costello, 1991, p. 158)

You will no doubt have your own considered responses to these questions, my own responses to them are: yes; yes; considerably, no; yes; not entirely but it can help.

As a teacher of mathematics, one holds certain values and one articulates values through the forms of classroom organisation and the nature of interactions we have. In other words we hold implicit and explicit values and these explicit values might convey a set of implicit values or 'worth' which may even be contrary to those we hold. Some values may be deeply embedded in the accepted practices of a school. Such values would impinge also on the values we held to be important in and through the study of mathematics – and we give out these messages all the time.

I have spent many years in a variety of classrooms and what I see often upsets me. I feel uncomfortable when I see children labelled as 'less able' placed into 'bottom sets' and fed diets of, at worst, tedium or, at best, irrelevant and uninteresting exercises. I feel uncomfortable when the majority of pupils in those bottom sets seem to have had very similar life experiences. I feel angry when I can see them realise that there really is no point in working hard to learn mathematics because the structure of the school means they cannot achieve high GCSE grades whatever they do. I feel frustrated when I see mathematics envisaged by pupils, parents and teachers as little more than a collection of techniques to be captured rather than an approach to understand and to tackle society's ills. But this is not about me; this is about those children who give up on mathematics, since those who give up on mathematics – or, rather those whom mathematics gives up for sacrifice – give up on society. Okay, so that is a bit extreme, but it is my contention that *mathematics* education in schools plays a significant role in organising the segregation of our society and, conversely, as a mathematics teacher you will play your part too. As Sue Willis cogently argues:

> Mathematics is not used as a selection device simply because it is useful, but rather the reverse.

(Willis, 1989, p. 35)

In other words, mathematics education plays its part in keeping the powerless in their place and the strong in positions of power. It doesn't only do this through the cultural capital a qualification in mathematics endows on an individual. It does this through the authoritarian and divisive character of mathematics teaching – it is often supposed that one can do maths or one can't, but an accusation or admission that you 'can't do maths' is more than just plain fact of capability; it is a positioning strategy – something that locates one in particular relations with others. It locates you as unsuccessful, and lacking in intellectual capability; it locates you on the edge of the employment and labour market, as virtually unemployable. Mathematics education thus serves as a 'badge of eligibility for the privileges of society' (Atweh, Bleicher and Cooper, 1998, p. 63). How do these badges get given out – or more importantly, what hurdles are there in the race to collect the badges? I will look at several hurdles – the first being that of rationality.

Hurdle 1 – rationality, the apparatus of reason

I shall begin by looking at rationality – or the nature of reason and reasoning, and I will draw on the notion that rationality is both a social construct as well as another of those misrecognition mechanisms. Underpinning our western culture and philosophical approach to reason and rationality, is the belief, derived centuries ago, that decisions should be made based upon 'abstract, rational principles – that is, principles that are seen as separate from and independent of the circumstances in which those decisions are taken' (Paechter, 2001). Surely a perfectly reasonable approach? Yet, it is far from reasonable. Such a position arises because of the position of power that males have exercised over females in the western world for centuries. Carrie Paechter puts it this way:

> Although we now recognise that women and girls are as capable of rational thought as are men and boys, it remains the case that females are more likely to use alternative methods of making decisions. Girls and women are more likely to argue that strictly reasoned conclusions are not always an appropriate way to approach certain situations; in this they could be described as using emotional, rather than logical intelligence (Goleman, 1996). Carol Gilligan (1982) and her collaborators (Gilligan and Attanucci, 1988), for example, have found that when it comes to moral decision-making, males have a tendency to use strictly rational criteria for moral choice, focusing in particular on moral rules. They tend to see moral choices as being founded on general ethical principles that are followed whatever the circumstances. Females, on the other hand, tend to focus on the particular situation in which the moral decision is being made. Although each gender can take the other perspective when prompted, each has a tendency to concentrate on one as the decision-making method of first choice; males are more likely to use the rationalistic, 'justice' perspective that emphasises moral principles, females to take a non-rationalistic, 'caring' approach that focuses on the support and preservation of human relationships.
>
> (Paechter, 2001)

Now, I have to make a serious and central point about what is being claimed here. I do not want to claim that there is something 'essentially' rational about the male, and something 'essentially' emotive about the female. What we have instead is the social construction of identity with the result that some groups or sections of society are forced, encouraged or constrained to adopt preferred ways of behaving, interacting and responding to challenges that go on to be undervalued by the education system.

Hence, reason and 'cold' rationality *tend* to be features the male of the species becomes conditioned to prefer. The female *tends* to be conditioned to experience a predilection for more caring, collaborative, 'warm' relationships as a way of interacting and solving the problems encountered in life. Of course these are only *tendencies* and we all know people who negate any tendency we can identify. Yet it does not require strict uniformity of practice or predilection for a stratification process to become effective. It only requires a tendency, which then becomes a self-generating inclination. Now, in order for the male of the species to continue to be dominant, the next step, is to misrecognise *rationality* as something that was intrinsically valuable. This process would provide a mechanism for the continuance of male domination, as well as providing a smokescreen for that domination. What can we use? Why, mathematics of course!

> Success at Mathematics is taken to be an indication of success at reasoning. Mathematics is seen as *development* of the reasoned and logical mind.
>   (Walkerdine and The Girls and Mathematics Unit, 1989, p. 25)

Hence mathematics can – and does – act as a filter, gradually tapping off those who do not conform to the standards of rationality that have come to be perceived as more valuable. However, we must not get bogged down here into thinking that this is merely an issue about girls' lamentable attainment. The position in the 1970s and 1980s of girls significantly underachieving at mathematics is gradually being reversed. Now the problem is officially seen as the underachievement of boys, since girls are apparently doing much better. So why should we continue to be concerned about the gender effect in mathematics education?

> The answer to this question is that it has increasingly become apparent that performance is not the only issue with which we should be concerned when looking at the relationship between gender and mathematics at the school level. Girls' enjoyment of and engagement with mathematics does not seem to have increased with increased success. While boys and girls are gaining roughly equivalent numbers of A*–C passes at GCSE, this is not translating into equal numbers of GCE A level entries. In 1999, for example, the female entry among 16–18-year-olds was only 57.6 per cent of the male entry. This translates into GCE A level passes for 31,065 male pupils as against 18,512 for females in this age group.
>
>   (Paechter, 2001)

The result filters down into the success girls feel at mathematics, the alienation they experience in thinking of the subject, and the rates of study at *higher* levels – all tied up with their developing self-image as adolescents. Significantly fewer girls than boys continue on to do mathematical sciences at university level, and fewer still go on to become professional mathematicians. The 'glass ceiling' may be a little higher, but it is still there. Yet is does appear that girls successively come to enjoy mathematics less than boys even though they achieve at least as highly. The twist is that not only are more career paths open to those with mathematics qualifications, but a qualification in mathematics brings with it generally higher salaries and all which that implies.

Hurdle 2 – the delimitation of acceptability

One way in which this stratification shows itself in mathematics *pedagogy* is the tendency for mathematicians – and teachers of mathematics – to value the neutral, cultural-free, decontextualised world that inhabits the mathematics textbook. There is a game played in the teaching of mathematics. We claim most strongly that mathematics is a real-world discipline, that it is useful to solve real-world problems, and we construct real-world problems for pupils to solve in the comfort of the classroom, away from the real realities of everyday life. Yet in the problems we offer, pupils are only supposed – or, only allowed – to take the reality so far. Beyond the limits placed on the 'mathematised' worlds it just gets silly. The example discussed by Barry Cooper (Chapter 13, p. 196) is a good example here. Look back to it before reading on.

Of course the answer is 20! If you stray too far from the pattern of rationality, the rules of the game (which go '29 divided by 14 is 19.2, rounded up is 20'), then it just gets silly. This is the Goldilocks principle of the reality behind mathematical problems – not too much, not too little – just enough. But just enough to what? Well, enough to put off a lot of people. What sort of people will be put off – or will be reluctant to see the rules of the game? How about those people who tend to feel the actual context is important, those who feel that it is important to consider the need to find a real solution to people's problems, those people who feel that the practicalities of everyday life are what is important. Where is this going? Well, the people who will tend to be successful at such problems will be those who can take a contextualised problem and strip away the context to focus on abstracted techniques – yes, boys (Gripps and Murphy, 1994). Research has shown that in both mathematics and the sciences boys tend to be more comfortable in ignoring the contrived contextualisation surrounding 'mathematised' problems, whereas girls tend to be more comfortable understanding the nature of the problem. This of course results in girls 'wasting' their time focusing on the irrelevant aspects (Paechter, 2001).

Yet, this goes further, as Barry Cooper argues, since those who are more likely to be comfortable ignoring the everyday reality, focusing instead on the esoteric decontextualised nature of mathematical problems, are those who inhabit the upper social classes. So not only does mathematics serve to misrecognise the alienation of girls, it also serves to misrecognise the alienation of working-class pupils. To most mathematics teachers, and most top-set, high-flying mathematically successful pupils, it is pretty obvious that the answer to the lift problem is 20. Unfortunately, those who think otherwise will not get into the inner sanctum of educational achievement and neither will it get them a good GCSE pass in mathematics.

You have to learn your place and your role, whether you are a teacher or a pupil. Pupils have to learn to be learners but, more than this, they have to learn the limitation of what they have to learn. In achieving this, children learn the rules of social order – what Basil Bernstein calls 'hierarchical rules'. Basil Bernstein argues that the way in which pedagogical practices organise the educational experiences for different children separates the *local* from the *less-local*. The children who tend to fall through this net are often those children from lower working-class families who become constrained into the local, context dependent skills. This process is further explained by the diverse influences of the two sites in which their learning takes place – the school and the home. Where the home situation forces attention on the local context, pupils will be at a disadvantage in a school site demanding a focus with less context specificity. Children will thus be limited in the level of success they can achieve through schooling since they fail to fit the model of an ideal successful pupil.

> In this way children's consciousness is differentially and invidiously regulated according to their social class origin and their families' official pedagogic practice.
>
> (Bernstein, 1990, p. 77)

Consequent practices and forms of organisation in schools will reinforce this process, through stratification and separation – setting, streaming, banding and other means of diversifying their population. This then separates out the pupils whose knowledge is localised, labelling and pathologising them as educational failures. Pupils who have access to the linguistic structures privileged by the school will thus be themselves privileged – school for them will be a means of gaining credibility and worth. Those who do not will experience school life as relative or absolute failures, will reject and be rejected by the value systems in place.

The official and dominant argument for social class variation in educational success goes something like this. There are clear differences in all sorts of arenas between pupils from different social classes. They are linguistically deprived, and tend to have lower IQs. They tend to have shorter concentration spans and their behaviour is more disruptive and disrespectful of the values of the school. This is possibly due to a deficit in material conditions in the home and a paucity of intellectual stimulation.

However, the evidence from many studies fails to substantiate this argument. The counter argument then goes like this. There are differences between cultural outlooks partly because of the differential material conditions imposed upon different social classes by the current prevailing social order. So that the privileged social classes can remain privileged we need a system that will value the culture of the privileged and devalue that of the disadvantaged. Furthermore, we need to do this in a way that conceals this process and makes the segregation look both natural and justified. And that is where schools enter the equation. Schools are set up to value the dominant culture – and award certificates to those who share its values most. Conversely, schools devalue the subservient culture, labelling its proponents as deviant and failures. You might think I am little more than a conspiracy theorist. This will possibly depend on which side of the conspiracy you gravitate toward – or whose side you are on – largely because we cannot separate an individual's orientation to the teaching of mathematics from a deeper set of political and ideological values (see Gates, 2000 for more on this).

Consider some of the evidence. Four major studies of language use and social class (Tizard and Hughes, 1984; Labov, 1969; Bernstein, 1971; Heath, 1983) have shown that working-class children are as competent at conceptual and logical thinking as middle-class children. Furthermore, working-class children have a language capability that is no less deficient than any other social class – different in many respects, but not deficient. Children from working-class backgrounds can thus perform as well, but do not achieve as much success. What schools and teachers therefore interpret as deficiency or underachievement can also be seen as a differential privileging of different cultural backgrounds.

So there are three issues here – the *inclusion of context*, the *appropriateness of response*, and *the relevance of everyday reality* and these result in a tendency for females and children from socially disadvantaged backgrounds to be placed at a particular disadvantage in respect of mathematics. This is because of the way in which our mathematics education places limits on acceptability – by limiting the utility of the context, by limiting the forms in which pupils are expected to respond to mathematical problems and by limiting the attachment to pupils' everyday reality. I will now go on to suggest that this social injustice does not stop here.

Hurdle 3 – ethnicity

In the UK, the Government Office for Standards in Education has recently published a damning report entitled *Educational Inequality: Mapping Race, Class and Gender* (Gillborne and Mirza, 2000), which provides a clearer picture of the ways in which pupils from ethnic minority groups fall behind in relation to their white peers. Black and ethnic minority youngsters are disadvantaged in the classroom by an education system that perpetuates existing inequalities. Despite the UK Government's commitment to tackling racism, black children failed to share in the dramatic rise in attainment at national examinations in the 1990s to the same degree as their white peers. How does this relate to mathematics education? The report itself goes on to illustrate one way this disadvantage becomes institutionalised through the allocation of pupils to different groups, preparing for the different tiers at the GCSE examination.

> Black pupils were significantly less likely to be placed in the higher tier, but more likely to be entered in the lowest tier. This situation was most pronounced in mathematics where a *majority* of Black pupils were entered for the

Foundation Tier, where a higher grade pass (of C or above) is not available to candidates regardless of how well they perform in the exam.

(Gillborne and Mirza, 2000, p. 17)

So we are again culpable for pragmatically disadvantaging yet another social grouping. The reasons for the failure of pupils from ethnic minority backgrounds can be traced back to the introduction of the National Curriculum (NC) in the 1980s, where the Government's report on its implementation stated:

> We are concerned that undue emphasis on multi-cultural mathematics, in these terms, could confuse young children. Whilst it is right to make clear to children that mathematics is the product of a diversity of cultures, priority must be given to ensuring that they have the knowledge, understanding and skills that they will need for adult life and employment in Britain in the twenty-first century. We believe that most ethnic minority parents would share this view. We have not therefore included any 'multi-cultural' aspects in any of our attainment targets.
>
> (HMI, 1985, para 10.20, p. 87)

Derek Kassem points out that the discussion stopped there; for the next ten or more years there was no real discussion about giving the NC a multicultural dimension (Kassem, 2001). The new NC effectively states that mathematics 'transcends cultural boundaries' (DfEE/QCA, 1999a, p. 14). In its favour it does remind us that 'different cultures have contributed to the development and application of mathematics' (DfEE/QCA, 1999a, p. 14), yet fails to give this a socially or historically critical qualification.

Slightly more chilling is the superficially attractive pronouncement that learning mathematics can promote pupils' cultural development. We read:

> Mathematics provides opportunities to promote *cultural development*, through helping pupils appreciate that mathematical thought contributes to the development of our culture and is becoming increasingly central to our highly technological future.
>
> (DfEE/QCA, 1999a, p. 8)

But whose culture? Whose highly developed future? There is certainly no mention here of how mathematics also contributes to the defence industry, to the eradication of other cultures through the destruction of the rainforests, to the poverty and starvation of children in developing countries due to the mathematics of interest payments on Third World debt. It is surely not *mathematics* that contributes to the development (or destruction) of culture, but *those who use* the mathematics. We might have hoped to have seen some mention of how useful mathematics is in helping us explore the extent and roots of poverty, or to ask critically searching questions about the world in which we live – which includes those countries and cultures with which many pupils from ethnic minority backgrounds share some history. Naturally a response to this argument is that it is biased and value ridden, whereas mathematics is neutral, culturally independent and value free. The reality is that mathematics is not value free; it is a product of the range of cultures as well as socio-economic systems. What counts as mathematics, and who does mathematics is fairly contentious. From America, George Stanic points out that the question of 'Whose mathematics?' is fairly clear.

> All current statistics indicate that those who study advanced mathematics are most often white males.
>
> (Stanic, 1989, p. 58)

This poses the central question of how it is that this comes about; what contribution does the content of the actual mathematics curriculum make to this and what influence do mathematics classroom practices have? It is this I come on to now.

Hurdle 4 – authoritarianism

As a classroom teacher one easily becomes steeped in the routines of the everyday classroom cultures and practices to such an extent that, in the same way that a fish does not notice the water, one does not notice the ordinary everyday strategies that might be contributing to exclusion and disadvantage. I will start by presenting a group task I was offered as a student teacher. In small groups we had to discuss whether a teacher of mathematics should be '*an* authority or *in* authority'. The task was posed in a way that seemed to indicate that in some fashion these two could be separate, yet both are about adopting a position on the place of control in the classroom. The two are basically interconnected. Control over the mathematics by being an authority in the subject implies not only that I know *better* (not just more), but also that my knowledge counts *more* than others. Either way there is little room for democratic practices or for pupils to be critically engaged in their learning.

Tony Cotton has suggested that in order to establish a classroom environment in which pupils are critically engaged in their learning, there are some practical questions to work on:

- How can mathematics teachers help to develop an ethos of mutual respect?
- How can we support the development of maths teachers as good role models?
- How can children's views of learning and their expectations of mathematics be valued?
- How can we enable pupils to be more involved in the decisions we take over their learning?

> (Cotton, 2001)

Now of course, this does not mean that pupils are asked to vote on whether they should undertake each activity, exercise or homework task. But it might involve teachers working on their classroom practices and forms of classroom organisation such that if pupils *were* asked to vote, they would vote in favour.

A way forward

Looking for a way forward might usefully be first attacked by setting out some contexts in which we might view mathematics education.

Organisation of the school

The organisation of school mathematics within the school as an institution is hampered by the various forms of external control imposed upon pupils and teachers, and these form a complex network of interrelated themes. We have policy imperatives from Government, expectations from parents and pupils, and so on.

If we claim that schools as institutions and we as teachers are there to help children realise and achieve their full potential, then surely this must include the full range of potentialities that they have. One of these is to live in a socially just world in which equity is argued for and over, if not fully achieved. If we want a socially just world then we ought to organise socially just classrooms – and consider the meaning of democracy in the mathematics classroom. This is not a simple 'let's take a vote on whether we do this exercise / do this homework / listen to the teacher'. But it does involve a whole range of possible strategies and forms of organisation (see particularly Cotton, 1998).

Teachers can involve themselves here by reorienting themselves to the notion of authority. Mathematics classrooms are most commonly characterised by their dependency on a variety of notions of authority – the authority of the teacher to be in control of the space and in control of the mathematics, the authority of the assessment system to dictate what is to be learned unquestioningly. Where we can't change, we can question.

Of course, any discussion of equity in the mathematics classroom has to include the rather insidious practice of ability discrimination – more usually termed 'setting'. Again, all the evidence points to one rather stark fact. Setting in mathematics does not raise standards – a statement which contradicts the widely held perception that ability discrimination enhances attainment (See Boaler Chapter 7 in this volume; Boaler, 1997; Boaler *et al.*, 1998). Indeed it is this perception that leads to the almost universal application of ability grouping in mathematics at secondary level. The widely held professional logic is that in by placing pupils in ability groups, teachers can better match work to the ability levels of pupils since the spread of ability is narrower than would otherwise be the case in all attainment groups. One argument, which may explain findings that setting restricts attainment, can be found in the paradoxical claim that when teaching setted groups, teachers actually respond less to pupils' individual needs than they do when teaching all attainment classes (Boaler, Wiliam and Brown, 1999, p. 374).

The significance of these findings at secondary level draws the authors to claim something very powerful, challenging and disturbing:

> The strength of the curriculum polarisation, and the diminution of the opportunity to learn that we have found in the current study, if replicated across the country, could be the single most important cause of the unacceptably low levels of achievement in mathematics in Great Britain. The traditional British concern with ensuring that *some* of the ablest students reach the highest possible standards appears to have resulted in a situation in which the vast majority of students achieve well below their potential.
>
> (Boaler, Wiliam and Brown, 1999, p. 380)

A review of the research literature on grouping by ability across all school subjects, carried out by the National Foundation for Educational Research (NFER) has suggested that:

> ... it is possible to identify a general trend which suggests that setting, compared with mixed ability teaching, has no significant effect on pupil achievement.
>
> (Sukhnanden, 1999, pp. 6–7)

So why is setting an issue in a chapter on equity? Well, the answer to this will be obvious if you spend any time looking at the make-up of the different ability groups in any comprehensive school. Furthermore, setting is a mechanism for legitimising the very process of differential privileging of cultural background. We know that setting does not actually have an effect on raising overall standards – though the likelihood is that you will not accept my argument here. However, I don't expect any chapter in any book to radically alter deeply held beliefs. What is important is that you at least recognise the controversy, and enter it with an awareness of what is at stake. This brings me on to ...

Organisation of the relations

Engaging in mathematics is engaging in life. It reflects a part of that life and consequently reflects how we want to interact and engage with others, and how we actually interact, treat and relate to others. School life, and mathematics classrooms in particular (though not especially) are just a part of that wider set of interactions we engage in and part of the competencies we develop and which we call life. So to teach mathematics effectively requires a sense of citizenship. It requires a belief in the power of mathematics to explain and to expose. It develops a propensity to use mathematics, to feel empowered to use mathematics, to tackle social questions, to challenge and critique. The American National Research Council see a direction in which change needs to take place.

Teachers' roles should include those of consultant, moderator and interlocutor, not just presenter and authority. Classroom activities must encourage students to express their approaches, both orally and in writing. Students must engage in Mathematics as a human activity; they must learn to work cooperatively in small teams to solve problems as well as to argue convincingly for their approach amid conflicting ideas and strategies.

(National Research Council, 1989, p. 61)

Mathematics classrooms therefore could be seen more as communities, and as in any community, different individuals have different roles (teacher, learner, helper, carer, facilitator) which need not all be age or experience related.

There are some clear messages here for how we ought to organise our classroom and our teaching of mathematics. Which brings me to ...

Organisation of the curriculum

What mathematics do we teach? Perhaps more importantly in terms of transformations we might want to undertake, how might we see mathematics as usefully employed to solve real problems. What is a real problem? There are two possibilities:

1   Developing mathematical tools – calculation techniques, data handling techniques, etc., that are useful to interrogate real life situations.
2   Developing the feeling of taking control is very real for adolescents. Hence making the problems we work on with pupils more purposeful is not only making mathematics more meaningful and its study more important and relevant, but is also contributing to the personal and social development of our pupils.

Using and applying Mathematics with a social responsibility

It is not often easy to find examples of ideas, resources and activities to use with children in the classroom that reflect different orientations to equity and social justice. One area to look into is what is often termed 'critical mathematics' – usually describing the use of mathematics to provide a critique of local, national or global issues and questions (see, for example, Ernest, 2001). However, this is not just an approach that is limited to a small band of politically motivated teachers, but is now deeply integrated in the Government's approach to the curriculum where the NC documentation for *Citizenship* provides encouragement for including such approaches in secondary schools. For pupils aged 14–16 years we have the following two objectives (reformulated by Ernest (2001) and included in this form for brevity) now introduced as legal requirements.

1   Pupils should gain knowledge and understanding about becoming informed citizens, including human rights, the diverse national, regional, religious and ethnic identities in the United Kingdom, the media's role in society, including the internet, wider issues and challenges of global interdependence and responsibility, including sustainable development and Local Agenda 21.

2   Pupils should develop the skills of enquiry and communication including researching political, moral, social issues, problems or events by analysing information from different sources, showing an awareness of the use and abuse of statistics; expressing, justifying and defending orally and in writing personal opinions about them, and contributing to group and exploratory class discussions and debates.

(Ernest, 2001, from DfEE and QCA, 1999b, pp. 15–16)

Hence there is now a requirement that teachers – and mathematics teachers are included – widen the scope of their teaching to include such broad issues. Of course Government pronouncements are never enough on their own. First, teachers need the will to adapt their teaching – and naturally I hope that by reading this chapter you will be stimulated and encouraged to find the will. Second, teachers need to have the ideas, context, tasks, etc. to formulate classroom activities that offer opportunities to pupils – and here I shall try to offer a small sample of suggestions. A very good source of global issues, tasks and activities can be found in the book *Multiple Factors* (Shan and Bailey, 1991). Here are some more starting points:

Context	Traditional approach	Equity approach
Best buys		
Some products are available in a range of sizes or quantities. For a number of different produces find out which is the 'best buy' in terms of value for money.	Choose some different sizes of a product – e.g. breakfast cereals – and work out the cost per unit (either in weight of number). Identify the best buy. Which cereals are most expensive? (Bear in mind that weight alone is not sufficient – a bowl of Ricicles weighs a lot less than a bowl of Weetabix.)	Consider how fair it is that larger sizes cost less. Since traditional mathematics will unsurprisingly discover that food is cheaper if bought in larger sizes, it raises the question of why they make small sizes. Who actually buys the small sizes? What reason do people have for buying small packets rather than large ones? Is there any correlation between the shopper's income and the sizes of cereals purchased? How much does the packaging cost when you buy various foods?

Context	Traditional approach	Equity approach
Defence A considerable amount of money each year is spent on the defence industry.	During a recent war, a tank was positioned on a cliff aiming at an enemy gunship. What is the angle of projection that gives the greatest range?	Compare the defence budget with that of the education budget and the third world aid budget. What conclusions might be drawn? Find out the cost of a Scud missile, chieftain tank, helicopter gunship, nuclear submarine. Compare with the cost of an X-ray machine, … (find out what other machines are used or needed by your local hospital). How much does it cost your local hospital to do a bone marrow transplant on a child? How is this cost broken down? Where does the money end up? How many bone marrow transplants could be carried out for the cost of each Scud missile?
Gambling The National Lottery is a good source of data and has its own website.	Is the National Lottery fair? What numbers come up most and least often? Do they come up as expected? What are the best and worst combinations of numbers to choose?	Is the National Lottery fair? What proportion of disposable income do punters from different social classes spend on lottery tickets? Who spends more? Who wins more? Where do the lottery funds go? Who benefits most from lottery grants? Before 1997? After 1997? Has the election of a Labour Government made any difference? You won't find this data on the National Lottery website.
Elections In order to form representative bodies to undertake the administration and government at local, regional and national levels, systems of elections are designed to find out who is to belong to those bodies.	Look at the data from the last general election. Are all constituencies the same size? How many MPs are there? How many are female? What is the largest and smallest majority?	Is the system of electing MPs fair? Why? Is there a fairer system? Explore Single Transferable Vote, Alternative Transferable Vote, 'first past the post', etc. What reasons are there for the continued use of our current system? Why are there many more male MPs than female MPs? What percentage of people vote in your local council elections? What reasons do people have for not voting? Do we live in a democracy?

Now let me justify that list of suggestions. I suspect there might be many criticisms. They are not really mathematics; they are politics. They are more like PSE (Personal and Social Education) or humanities issues. In order to respond to these sorts of criticisms I'll offer a quote from Jan Winter, a former mathematics teacher now working at Bristol University:

> I believe that we cannot teach children to be numerate if we do not pay attention to the broader experience of their learning. The mathematical skills that are so highly prized are meaningless if a pupil does not have the personal, social and moral education to make sense of the world and thus know when to use them. So, at all levels, mathematics and real life are all part of the whole experience of children and it is up to us to find ways of making our teaching of mathematics reflect that.
>
> (Winter, 2001)

Quite. Responding to the very real equity issues in mathematics education requires us to consider a fairly comprehensive reorientation to the way mathematics is introduced and used and to the way mathematics is taught. In this chapter I have tried to describe some of the ways in which mathematics conveys social injustice and how it achieves this in respect of different disadvantaged social groups. In addition I have given some suggestions for how one might work to offer a challenge to many of the current sources of injustice. In concluding, I do not want to leave you with the impression that I believe mathematics teaching holds the key to solving all societies ills. It's a start though.

Some useful resources

Christian Aid (1999) *The Debt Game*, London: Christian Aid (www.christian-aid.org.uk).
Christian Aid (1999) *The Trading Game*, London: Christian Aid (www.christian-aid. org.uk).
Collins, J. (1992) *Maths and the Tropical Rainforests Set 1* and *Set 2*, Pearson Publishing, London.
Gates, P. (ed.) (2001) *Issues in Mathematics Teaching*, RoutledgeFalmer, London. (All royalties from sales of this book are going to a children's charity).
Shan, S and Bailey, P. (1991) *Multiple Factors. Classroom mathematics for equality and justice*, Trentham Books, Stoke-on-Trent.
Wright, P. (ed.) (1999) *The Maths and Human Rights Resource Book*, Amnesty International, London.

References

Atweh, B., Bleicher, R. and Cooper, T. (1998) 'The construction of social context of mathematics classrooms: a sociolinguistic analysis', *Journal for Research in Mathematics Education* 2(1): 63–82.
Bernstein, B. (1971) *Class, Codes and Control. Volume 1. Theoretical studies towards a sociology of language*, London: Routledge and Kegan Paul.

Bernstein, B. (1990) *The Structuring of Pedagogic Discourse. Volume 4. Class, codes and control*, London: Routledge.

Boaler, J. (1997) *Experiencing School Mathematics. Teaching styles, sex and setting*, Buckingham: Open University Press.

Boaler, J., Wiliam, D. and Brown, M. (1998) 'Students' experiences of ability grouping – disaffection, polarisation and the construction of failure', *Proceedings of the First Mathematics Education and Society Conference*, Centre for the Study of Mathematics Education, Nottingham: 367–82.

Costello, J. (1991) *Teaching and Learning Mathematics 11–16*, London: Routledge.

Cotton, T. (1998) 'Toward a mathematics education for social justice', unpublished Ph.D. thesis, University of Nottingham, Nottingham.

Cotton, T. (2001) 'Mathematics teaching in the real world', in P. Gates (ed.) *Issues in Mathematics Teaching*, London: RoutledgeFalmer.

DfEE/QCA (1999a) *Mathematics. The National Curriculum for England. Key Stages 1–4*, London: DfEE/QCA.

DfEE/QCA (1999b) *The National Curriculum for England: citizenship*, London: HMSO.

Ernest, P. (2001) 'Critical mathematics education', in P. Gates (ed.) *Issues in Mathematics Teaching*, London: Routledge.

Gates, P. (2000) 'A study of the professional orientation of two teachers of mathematics', unpublished Ph.D. thesis, University of Nottingham, Nottingham.

Gates, P. (2001) *Issues in Mathematics Teaching*, London: RoutledgeFalmer.

Gillborn, D. and Gipps, C. (1996) *Recent Research on the Achievements of Ethnic Minority Pupils*, Ofsted Reviews of Recent Research, London: HMSO.

Gilborne, D. and Mirza, H. (2000) *Educational Inequality: mapping race, class and gender*, London: Ofsted.

Gilligan, C. (1982) *In a Different Voice: psychological theory and women's development*, Cambridge, MA: Harvard University Press.

Gilligan, C. and Attanucci, J. (1988) 'Two moral orientations: gender differences and similarities', *Merrill-Palmer Quarterly* 34: 223–37.

Gipps, C. and Murphy, P. (1994) *A Fair Test? Assessment, achievement and equity*, Buckingham: Open University Press.

Goleman, D. (1996) *Emotional Intelligence: why it can matter more than IQ*, London: Bloomsbury.

Heath, S. (1983) *Ways With Words*, Cambridge: Cambridge University Press.

HMI (1985) *Mathematics from 5 to 16, Curriculum Matters 3*, London: HMSO.

Kassem, D. (2001) 'Ethnicity and mathematics education', in P. Gates (ed.) *Issues in Mathematics Teaching*, London: RoutledgeFalmer.

Labov, W. (1969) *A Study of Non-standard English*, Washington: ERIC Clearinghouse for Linguistics.

National Research Council (1989) *Everybody Counts. Report to the nation on the future of mathematics education*, Washington, DC: National Academy Press.

Paechter, C. (2001) 'Gender, reason and emotion in secondary mathematics classrooms', in P. Gates (ed.) *Issues in Mathematics Teaching*, London: RoutledgeFalmer.

Shan, S. and Bailey, P. (1991) *Multiple Factors. Classroom mathematics for equality and justice*, Stoke-on-Trent: Trentham Books.

Skovsmose, O. and Valero, P. (1999) *Breaking Political Neutrality: the critical engagement of mathematics education with democracy*, Report No. 17, Roskilde, Denmark: Centre for Research in Learning Mathematics.

Stanic, G. (1989) 'Social inequality, cultural discontinuity, and equity in school mathematics', *Peabody Journal of Education* 66(1): 57–71.

Sukhnandan, L. (1999) 'Sorting, sifting and setting: does grouping pupils according to ability affect attainment?' *NFER News* Spring 1999, Slough: NFER: 6–7.

Tizard, B. and Hughes, M. (1984) *Young Children Learning. Talking and thinking at home and at school*, London: Fontana.

Walkerdine, V. and The Girls and Mathematics Unit (1989) *Counting Girls Out*, London: Virago.

Willis, S. (1989) *Real Girls Don't Do Maths. Gender and the construction of privilege*, Geelong, Australia: Deakin University Press.

Winter, J. (2001) 'Personal, spiritual, moral, social and cultural issues in teaching mathematics', in P. Gates (ed.) *Issues in Teaching Mathematics*, London, RoutledgeFalmer.

Zaslavsky, C. (1981) 'Mathematics education: the fraud of "Back to Basics" and the socialist counter-example", *Science and Nature* 4: 15–27.

15 Social and critical mathematics education

Underlying considerations

Marilyn Nickson

Over the past decade and a half, sociocultural factors have come to dominate mathematics education at a variety of levels. At the broader level, the society in which a given mathematics classroom is situated affects the teaching and learning that takes place as well as the mathematics that is taught (Scott-Hodgetts, 1992). At the level of the individual, pupils have their particular view of what mathematics is all about (Winter, 1992) and the cultural diversity within a class may mean that some of them bring a different first language to the learning situation (Clarkson and Dawe, 1997) as well as different approaches to understanding concepts such as number, that are culturally determined (Ginsburg *et al.*, 1997). At the same time, teachers struggle with their own view of mathematics and how to get it across in the classroom in such a way as not to conflict with the pupils' world (Adler, 1997). This world is essentially the community in which they live and forms much of their reality, and mathematics will be meaningful (or not) if children see its relevance to their world (Skovsmose, 1994). Accordingly, mathematics has to be 'realistic' to be accessible to them (Gravemeijer, 1997). It is possible for at least a large majority of children to gain access to acceptable levels of mathematics and to be properly numerate (see below) only if factors of this kind are paid some attention. This chapter will draw on factors such as these, which are imbedded in current theory, in order to establish why it is important that (a) the social aspects of the teaching and learning of mathematics need to be emphasised and (b) the critical aspect of mathematics education needs to be stressed in the application of mathematics.

Shifts in theoretical perspectives

A concern with a more social perspective of mathematics education has necessarily brought with it new theoretical perspectives, or, in some instances, the adaptation of existing theoretical positions. It is important that the judgement and choices of teachers are informed and the guidelines provided by such theories help to fulfil this function. For many years, the theoretical underpinning of much of the teaching and learning of mathematics has been heavily influenced by Piagetian thought, with some lingering influences from behaviourism. As a result, much of past research tended to focus on the individual child learning-specific concepts in an isolated situation. The shift away from the dominance of this approach has been brought about partly by the recognition that there were certain limitations in Piaget's work, one of which is that the experimental work that informed his theory did not take the social and cultural context of the learning into account, as well as other factors (Hughes, 1986). This is not to say that Piaget's work has been discounted but rather that it has been tried, evaluated, adapted and has provided the basis for new theories in the way in which theories grow (Popper, 1979). These in turn have provided the springboards for many of the newer approaches used in mathematics education as we shall see in what follows.

The most fundamental change, which Piaget's concept of a genetic epistemology has brought to education, is identified by von Glasersfeld (1991) as a redefinition of the concept of knowledge and the way in which knowledge becomes established and accepted. This redefinition has influenced mathematics education in particular, and has redirected us towards a more pragmatic view of how knowledge comes into being, bringing with it an adaptive function that has the following effect:

> ... this means that the results of our cognitive efforts have the purpose of helping us to cope in the world of our experience, rather than the traditional goal of furnishing an 'objective' representation of a world as it might 'exist' apart from us and our experience.
>
> (von Glasersfeld, 1991, p. xv)

This reminds us that not only is learning a purposeful activity but that if we want children to learn in a meaningful way, the purpose must be relevant to their growth and adaptation to the world around them. Children will learn when they are motivated to do so and their interest is aroused because they can see the point of what they are being asked to do. Thus, the somewhat mechanistic approach of behaviourism has been overtaken by one with an emphasis on cognition, i.e. on 'knowing' and on learning as 'coming to know' through links with their reality, as opposed to 'coming to do' certain things with which the learner can make no connections.

Concurrently with this shift from the psychologically-oriented view to a more socio-psychological interpretations of how learning takes place, there has been a similar shift in philosophical issues related to mathematics education. This has involved a change in perceptions of the nature of mathematics from a 'given', abstract body of knowledge that exists 'out there', to one that is seen as social in its origins and its applications (Lerman, 1990; Ernest, 1991; Nickson, 1992; Nickson and Lerman, 1992; Restivo, 1993). It is recognised that mathematics, just as any other subject, has evolved as a result of human activity and, as a subject, it grows and changes through problem solving, trial and error and the interpersonal exchange of ideas. A mathematical idea may start with one person but ultimately the idea has to be communicated to others, shared with and applied by them, during which process it may be disproved or adapted. Sometimes a long-standing mathematical idea may be discarded or some new mathematical idea may be discovered (e.g. the recent solution to Fermat's last theorem), so that the mathematical body of knowledge is not static and inert but changing and expanding. At the same time as this new emphasis on the social nature of mathematics has arisen, mathematics education researchers have become more aware of the difference in demands made by mathematics as a way of thinking and education as a discipline (Brown, 1997) and of the need to accommodate the two. Political concerns have also become prevalent, (e.g. Julie *et al.*, 1993; Kjægård *et al.*, 1996) with the recognition of the prime importance of mathematical knowledge as a powerful social tool without which individuals will not achieve personal autonomy in a technological world.

These phenomena, taken together, have led research in mathematics education to move away from an emphasis on experimental situations where children's mathematical thinking is studied in an artificial situation with controlled variables, to one where children's mathematical thinking is more likely to be studied in classroom or group situations and the process of learning mathematics becomes one of discussion, negotiation and shared meanings. In this way, the aim is not just for the pedagogy to be effective but it will also convey messages about the nature of mathematics itself, its relevance to everyday life and its foundation in human activity. The intention is that the subject comes to be perceived as social in its foundations as well as its uses (Nickson, 1992). Conjecture, hypothesis, testing ideas, trial and error, all become part of the taken-for-granted aspects of mathematics. The focus on the child is retained but it is on the child-in-context, i.e. the child as learner who has had considerable experience in the context of the social world before entering the classroom, experience that is continuous and contiguous with their experience at school, and that will affect what and how they learn in the context of the classroom. In a sense, each child brings their own individual context with them.

Theoretical interpretations underlying a social/critical perspective on the teaching and learning of Mathematics

The approaches to teaching Mathematics that have been developed in order to address concerns of a more social nature are founded in *cognitivism*, which essentially focuses on 'how we come to know'. Examples of some of these approaches are briefly described below. The notion of *constructivism* is pervasive since it has evolved from the basic Piagetian notion that individuals *construct* their knowledge as they interact with the reality of their world. (It is important also, however, to recognise the work of sociologists of knowledge such as Berger and Luckman (1966) and their notion of the 'social construction of reality'.) There is recognition of the fact that children do not learn in a vacuum but by exchange with others and through contact with the physical world around them. The subtle differences between constructivist approaches lie in (a) the perspective of personal *construction* of mathematical knowledge or (b) the personal *reconstruction* of mathematics that already exists (Gravemeijer, 1997). The former is sometimes referred to as the 'bottom up' approach in which mathematical ideas are 'constructed' by the child and the teacher's role becomes one of structuring situations so that this can happen. The latter is known as 'top down', where the existence of mathematical concepts is recognised in a sense as 'pre-specified', and the role of the teacher is to enable the child to come to know these in a meaningful way. We shall now look at some of these approaches and the different emphases each of them has and in considering such theories, bearing in mind 'the reality of the pedagogic situation in which each of us works' (Nickson, 1995). It is arguable that the 'bottom up' approach, for example, may be difficult to adopt fully if one were dealing with classes of forty or more as is the case in many countries.

Constructivism

A large proportion of current research literature in mathematics education is given over to discussions of constructivism (see Jaworski, Chapter 5) and studies related to it. The term has taken on a global meaning which, with frequent and uncritical use, could very easily have negative effects in the classroom if the underlying ideas are over-simplified in their use. (In an attempt to redress this potential it is frequently referred to as socio-contructivism or social constructivism, e.g. Cobb, 1991; Ernest, 1991.) As some of the research reported here will indicate, 'This new model of learning has yet to be situated properly in the totality of mathematics education' (Nickson, 1995, p. 165). Noddings (1993) refers to it as 'a movement growing in influence and popularity' and warns that it may come to be seen as a 'method' as opposed to a theoretical perspective. Constructivism, however, is not a methodology, rather it is a way of interpreting how children come to know or make sense of something. It is important to bear these factors in mind when considering the ways in which constructivism exerts an influence in the mathematics classroom. In referring to constructivism as an epistemology, Cobb *et al.* (1991) note that:

> Its value to mathematics education will, in the long run, depend on whether this way of sense making, of problem posing and solving, contributes to the improvement of mathematics teaching and learning in typical classrooms with characteristic teachers. If it eventually fails to do so, then it will become irrelevant to mathematics educators.
>
> (p. 158)

A central theme of the constructivist approach is an acceptance of the fact that the reality of one individual is different from that of another and that individuals 'construct their own mental representations of situations, events, and conceptual structures' (ibid.). This construction is individual to each child. Children clearly already have many such representations when they begin schooling, and recognition of this fact is paramount in the constructivist perspective of what should go on in the classroom. What becomes accepted generally as 'knowledge' is the result of shared consensus over the years, as, for example, our number system has become. What is 'knowledge' for an individual child as they enter school is what they have experienced and stored and made their own. They extend that knowledge as a result of new experiences when they have to use what they already know to interpret the new situation in which they find themselves, and one of the ways of doing this is through discussion and sharing their experience with others. Thus, negotiation and discussion are characteristics of a classroom in which a constructivist approach is adopted. Where the number system is concerned, for example, a teacher may allow the class to develop their own symbols to represent different quantities and the children will discuss the merits of one system versus the other. The notion is that ultimately they will understand better the reasons for having the number system as it exists. This is an example of how the social aspect of learning becomes vital to the development of knowledge (Jaworski, 1994).

On the whole, the idea of the individual child constructing its own knowledge does not convey an impression that promotes the social aspect of learning. However, Cobb *et al.* (1991) write that:

> Because mathematical meaning is inherently dependent on the construction of consensual domains, the activities of teaching and learning must necessarily be guided by obligations that are created and regenerated through social interaction.
>
> (p. 165)

The idea of social interaction may go some way towards acknowledging the social nature of mathematical knowledge-making but for some it is not far enough. Lerman (1998) writes:

> A psychology focused on the individual making her/his own sense of the world does not engage with social and cultural life: other theoretical discourses, such as approaches to sociology which merely describe are not adequate for mathematics education either.
>
> (p. 1–77)

Argue against

Lerman advocates what he calls a 'discursive psychology for mathematics education', which he envisages incorporating 'action, goals, affect, power and its lack, based on sociocultural origins'. In other words, constructivism as a theory, in itself, is not an adequate basis for explaining and guiding the child's sense-making of the world in which they live.

It is important to recognise the variations of the constructivist perspective and to be aware of the effect of the different interpretations of the way in which mathematics is taught and learned. There are three major implications of this theoretical approach for the effective teaching and learning of mathematics. The first is that children are no longer seen as 'receivers' of knowledge but *makers* of it, in that they are actively engaged in selecting, absorbing and adjusting what they experience in the world around them. It follows, then, that to learn mathematics children must be put in situations where they have to 'mathematise' and so be involved in doing it. The second major implication of constructivism follows from this, which is that, in order to 'mathematise', children need to experience mathematics in a context other than a purely mathematical one. In order to make sense of the mathematics they meet in school, to access it and make it their own, they have to link it with the reality of their world and what they already know (Aubrey, 1993). The teaching of mathematics must therefore be linked with contexts that are 'real' to children and with which they can identify. The third major implication is that each child's contribution in a mathematics lesson needs to be acknowledged and considered, not just by the teacher but also by other members of the class. This follows from the unique nature of each child's perception of a situation and the experience they bring to it. Aubrey suggests that every child must be helped to extend their range of mathematical strategies and mathematics teaching should not undermine 'their natural inventiveness by a struggle to find the single, convergent and acceptable response' (ibid. p. 39). This encapsulates one of the fundamental aspects of what constructivism is about and emphasises the importance of discussion and negotiation within the teaching/learning situation that adopts this perspective, as noted earlier.

Gravemeijer (1997) points out that, 'Educationalists attach different consequences to the recognition of the importance of informal strategies and situated cognition' (p. 319). A child's individual way of solving a mathematical problem is valued because it is their method, that has been successful for them, in their particular circumstances. As a result of this importance attached to the individual's perceptions of mathematics it is held that:

> ...mathematics education should acknowledge idiosyncratic constructs and foster a classroom atmosphere where mathematical meaning, interpretation, and procedures are explicitly negotiated.
>
> (Gravemeijer, 1997, p. 320)

This is reflected in the extension of the concept of constructivism either to socio-constructivism or social constructivism (Cobb *et al.*, 1991; Ernest, 1991). The children's strategies and solutions in solving problems are the focus of the teaching. They are shared with each other and discussed and in the process, become justified and accepted or not, as the case may be, and the meaning develops in the process of this reflection and discussion.

Cognitive apprenticeship

Another approach within the cognitivist paradigm is the 'cognitive apprenticeship' model (Brown, Collins and Duguid, 1989) where knowledge is seen as 'situated, being in part a product of the activity, the context, and culture in which it is developed and used' (p. 32). By acknowledging the 'situation' in which individuals learn, we as teachers gain some insight into 'where they are coming from' and the kind of experience they are bringing to the teaching and learning of the classroom. The situation will affect what they have learned and how. The notion of situated learning developed by Brown *et al.* (1989) and Lave and Wenger (1991), plays a strong part in current research in mathematics education generally (e.g. Boaler, 1993; Nunes *et al.*, 1994). Because of linking mathematical learning with experience in the 'real world', a major implication of this perspective for learning and teaching mathematics is that to be meaningful, new mathematical knowledge and skills are most effectively learned in situations where they are applied. In their discussion of situated learning, Fennema and Franke (1992) note that 'Knowledge acquired in school is not situated in the broader life of an individual because the activities, contexts, and culture of the school are not related by the learner to his or her out-of-school culture' (p. 160). The teacher's role becomes one of helping children to make connections between the learning that takes place in the classroom and their experience in the 'real world'. In a somewhat blunt comparison, the difference between this approach and constructivism would be that it is seen as a 'top down' perspective, where the mathematics is taken as 'given' and children do not actually construct it themselves. However, there is commonality between the two in the importance given to making use of the children's prior knowledge and experience, and to the teacher's role of acting as a mediator of that experience so that mathematics is learned in a meaningful way. An example of the results of not building on informal knowledge is given by Ginsberg *et al.* (1997) who studied the informal pre-school mathematical knowledge of children from across several countries (Japan, China, Colombia, Korea and the US). Within the US sample (which included African-Americans, Hispanics, Koreans and Whites) they found that children 'with the possible exception of the Hispanics, possess reasonable competence in informal mathematical thinking' (op. cit. p. 191). While some children go on to do well they note that in particular, the African-Americans do not, even though their pre-school performance is not very different from other groups, including the Japanese. They begin school with an 'adequate intellectual ability but do not go on to realise their potential in school' (op. cit. p. 201).

Realistic mathematics education

Yet another approach is known as 'realistic mathematics education' which has developed from Freudenthal's view of mathematics as a form of activity and of mathematics education as a process of 'guided reinvention' (Freudenthal, 1973). 'Mathematising' is seen as the goal of mathematics education and involves solving problems, looking for problems and organising subject matter. 'Mathematising' may be done within mathematics itself or within the sphere of the 'real world'. In other words, problems may be non-contextualised mathematics, e.g. straightforward 'sums' to be done or equations to be solved, or they may be everyday problems such as finding the cost of a number of items at a given price . Realistic mathematics is mainly concerned with helping children to come to recognise, understand and apply mathematical processes such as generalising and formalising (Gravemeijer, 1997). Five educational principles implicit in realistic mathematics education have been identified by Streefland (1991):

1   the source of concept formation is reality;
2   pupils are given the opportunity to be constructors and actively contribute to the learning process by this involvement;
3   the learning process must be interactive so that in the course of constructing

knowledge about fractions from real life situations, pupils discuss and collaborate when necessary;

4   different lines of learning (e.g. fractions, ratio and proportion) are entwined so that both vertical and horizontal 'mathematisation' can take place;

5   the various tools used in the process of coming to understand mathematics symbols, diagrams and visual models, should result from the need to describe and use what they have found out for themselves.

Clearly, this has much in common with other constructivist approaches but as noted earlier, it has a 'top down' connotation in that it acknowledges the 'giveness' of mathematics at the outset while at the same time, it aims to build on children's strategies and previous learning to gain access to it. Implicit in this approach is an acknowledgement of 'the importance of *knowing* number facts' and that emphasis on children's mental strategies does not, in itself, necessarily strengthen the learning of basic number (Beishuizen, 1997, p. 18). It acknowledges that children, one way or another, have to have basic number facts in order to progress mathematically. Stressing the fact that different children have different ways of coming to know what these facts are is, in itself, not enough to ensure that such facts are learned.

Critical Mathematics education

The increase in the development of social considerations related to mathematics education noted earlier are exemplified by Skovsmose's (1994) work in developing a philosophy of what he calls 'critical mathematics education'. This philosophy has implications for the nature of the mathematics curriculum, in terms of aims, content and pedagogy that can be seen in much of current mathematics education thinking (e.g. Restivo, 1993; Noddings, 1993; Gates, 1997; Lerman, 1998). It is based on the notion arising from developments in critical theory and summarises the relationship of critical theory to education in this way: '*If educational practice and research are to be critical, they must address conflicts and crises in society*' (Skovsmose, 1994, p. 22, author's italics). Thus it becomes highly important that the role that mathematics plays in solving social and world problems should be emphasised. By doing so, Skovsmose sees mathematics education as playing a strong role in developing 'critical citizenship' so that it does not 'degenerate into a way of effectively socialising students into a technological society and at the same time annihilating the possibility of them developing a critical attitude towards precisely this society' (p. 59). It is important for students to be critically aware of the ways in which mathematics is used to inform decision-making at all levels, to reflect upon the processes and outcomes when it is used in this way and to be able to participate in critical decision-making of this kind themselves.

The examples given by Skovsmose of the implications for the mathematics curriculum that this theory holds are not unlike the approach used in realistic mathematics education and are in the form of project work. However, the importance of the reflective aspect of what is entailed is emphasised to a greater extent, both in depth and breadth of scope. Pupils are not only asked to reflect upon the mathematics inherent in the project; they are invited to reflect upon (a) the social issues implicit in the situation that forms the context of the project, (b) how the mathematics they have engaged in has helped to inform the judgements they have made and (c) the *consequences* of certain actions being taken as a result of the judgements they have made. Skovsmose refers to the use of a 'thematic approach' to the mathematics curriculum and he describes some of the work that has been undertaken in Danish high schools that exemplify this (see also Nielsen *et al.*, 1999). One example is a project dealing with 'Economic Relationships in the World of a Child' which is made up of units dealing with the immediate world of the individual child (starting with the pocket money they get each week), then the child as part of a family and finally, as a member of society. (See also Skovsmose, Chapter 8 in this volume.)

While the notion of critical mathematics education may be new to many, there has been a growing acknowledgement (as noted earlier) of the power that mathematical knowledge brings to the individual in a technological society, and how important it is for all mathematics educators to be aware of this whatever the age of the children they teach (e.g. Mellin-Olsen, 1987; Knijnik, 1995; Julie, 1998). Noddings (1993) hints at this when writing about constructivism, and says, 'Unless it is embedded in an encompassing, moral position on education, it risks categorisation as a method, as something that will produce enhanced traditional results' (p. 158). In other words, the status quo will be maintained; the mathematics educators' aim of educating children in mathematics not just more effectively in the sense of being numerate, but more meaningfully in the sense of being aware of the part it plays in everyday decision-making, will not happen. Skovsmose's work provides a theoretical perspective from which this can happen.

A Vygotskian perspective

The work of Vygotsky has been invoked in a variety of research studies related to mathematics education in recent years (e.g. Bartolini-Bussi, 1991; Lerman, 1998; Bocro *et al.*, 1995). Mellin-Olsen (1987) describes Vygotsky's notion of *activity theory* as embodying both society and the individual: 'The individual acts on her society at the same time as she becomes socialised [into] it' (p. 33). It is the involvement of the social dimension in the child's education that has made Vygotsky's work of particular relevance to the study of the teaching and learning of mathematics. Vygotsky's (1962) interpretation of the notion of imitation in connection with education is a way into understanding how the social nature of education arises in the first place. He notes that:

> To imitate, it is necessary to step from something one knows to something new. With assistance, every child can do more than he can by himself – though only set by the limits of his development.

The idea of imitation by definition involves someone else – it cannot take place in isolation; also it takes place in the immediate environment of the child and the act of imitation results in extending the child's repertoire in some way. Vygotsky goes on to develop the importance of this interpretation in the education of children and, having noted the importance of both imitation and instruction in the child's development, he says:

> What the child can do in cooperation today he can do alone tomorrow. Therefore the only good kind of instruction is that which marches ahead of development and leads it; ... instruction must be oriented towards the future, not the past.
>
> (Vygotsky, 1962, p. 104)

He suggests that in more traditional methodologies when we have asked children to do a particular task that they are unable to do without help, we have:

> ... failed to utilise the zone of proximal development and to lead the child to what he could not yet do. Instruction was oriented to the child's weakness rather than his strength, thus encouraging him to remain at the pre-school stage of development.

The zone of proximal development (ZPD) is described in terms of the discrepancy between what a child is able to do at the point of entry into a problem situation and the level reached in 'solving problems with assistance' (ibid. p. 103). Even if a child is unable to solve a set task entirely on their own, in this view, with the help of either peers or the teacher or both, they will have extended their repertoire of knowledge to some extent at least and will be able to build on this by developing new strategies to help them eventually reach a solution to the problem.

Lerman (1998) elaborates on this Vygotskyan perspective and relates it to current developments in mathematics education. He notes that many tend to view ZPD as 'a kind of force field which the child carries around, whose dimensions must be interpreted by the teacher so that activities offered are within the child's range' (p. 71). Drawing on the work of Davydov (1988, 1990), he suggests that the intended meaning of the ZPD is in fact 'a product of the task, the texts, the previous networks of experiences of the participants, the power relationships in the classroom' (idem). Lerman uses this Vygotskyan stress on social considerations to develop the notion of a 'discursive psychology for mathematics education' referred to earlier.

Numeracy

As well as being aware of new theoretical perspectives, it is also important to be aware of current interpretations of numeracy since these also have social connotations. One definition of basic numeracy is given as 'the ability to operate flexibly with numbers in solving real problems, and especially in operating efficiently either mentally or using a calculator' (Dickson *et al.*, 1984, p. 250). A broader and more recent working definition for a numeracy project states that 'Numeracy is the ability to process, communicate and interpret numerical information in a variety of contexts' (Askew *et al.*, 1997). More recently still, the document issued to primary schools in the UK that underpins the Numeracy Hour introduced in all primary schools says the following:

> Numeracy in Key Stage 1 and Key Stage 2 is a proficiency which involves confidence and competence with numbers and measures. It requires an understanding of the number system, a repertoire of computational skills and an inclination and ability to solve number problems in a variety of contexts. Numeracy also demands practical understanding of the ways in which information is gathered by counting and measuring, and is presented in graphs, diagrams, charts and tables. This proficiency is acquired through giving a sharper focus to the relevant aspects of the programmes of study for mathematics.
>
> (DfEE, 1999)

There is a shift here from an ability merely to solve numerical problems to acknowledging the contextual implications inherent in numeracy. To understand number is to be able to use it and apply it in a meaningful way. Communication and interpretation of information as well as 'practical understanding' (which suggests application, in the description above) imply a social context that has not received the attention due to it in the past. This is implicit in the cultural model for numeracy advocated by Baker (1995) who argues that this is an appropriate perspective from which to view numeracy because mathematics is both the product of and basis for, the science, commerce and technology of a society. This shift in perspectives on numeracy is further evidence of the acknowledgement of the social concerns embedded in mathematics education and in this case, at the most basic level of its learning and use.

Implications of social/critical considerations for classroom practice

Shifts in theory, which accommodate social/critical issues, necessarily broaden the aims of mathematics education and the methodology used to achieve them. We have seen that there is an emphasis on the 'child in context' and that the notion of context is viewed holistically from the level of the individual to the level of society as a whole of which the individual is a part. In order to project mathematics so that children are enabled to access it in a meaningful way, at least two things are necessary: (a) mathematics must be seen as social in its origins, and (b) it must be applied in a socially critical way. For the subject to be characterised as 'social' in the classroom implies that it needs to be approached 'socially', i.e. it should be talked about and shared, open to negotiation and discussion, conjecture and hypothesis. For the application of mathematics to be socially critical, the contexts in which children learn it and apply it need to be meaningful in terms of their reality. Children need to be put into situations where they have to 'mathematise' about issues that are relevant to their world and not about matters that are false in the sense that they have no bearing whatsoever on their reality or the world in which they live.

Popkewitz (1984) writes that:

> Contrary to prevailing belief, the potency of social science is not in the utility of knowledge but in its ability to expand and liberate the consciousness of people into considering the possibilities of their human conditions.
>
> (p. 8)

The potency of mathematics education is as strong as any other social science in this respect. To realise this potency, it is vital that the social and critical nature of mathematics education is acknowledged in classroom practice.

References

Adler, J. (1997) 'The dilemma of transparency: seeing and seeing through talk in the mathematics classroom', *Proceedings of the 21st Conference for the International Group for the Psychology of Mathematics Education* 14–19 July 1997, 2: 1–8.

Askew, M., Brown, M., Rhodes, V., Wiliam, D. and Johnson, D. (1997) 'Effective teachers of numeracy in UK primary schools: teachers' beliefs, practices and pupils' learning', *Proceedings of the 21st Conference of the International Group for the Psychology of Mathematics Education* 14–19 July 1997, 2: 25–32.

Aubrey, C. (1993) 'An investigation of the mathematical knowledge and competencies which young children bring into the school', *British Educational Research Journal* 19(1): 27–41.

Baker, D. (1995) 'Numeracy as a social practice: primary school numeracy practices', *Proceedings of the Third British Congress of Mathematics Education (Part 1)* 13–16 July 1995, 1: 128–35.

Bartolini Bussi, M.G. (1991) 'Social interaction and mathematical knowledge', *Proceedings of the Fifteenth Annual Meeting of the International Group for Mathematics Education* 1: 1–16.

Beishuizen, M. (1997) 'Mental arithmetic: mental recall or mental strategies', *Mathematics Teaching* 160: 16–19.

Berger, P.L. and Luckman, T. (1966) *The Social Construction of Reality*, Middlesex: Penguin Books Ltd.

Boaler, J. (1993) 'The role of contexts in the mathematics classroom: do they make mathematics more "real"?' *For the Learning of Mathematics* 13(2): 12–17.

Boero, P., Dapueto, C., Ferrari, P., Garuti, R., Lemut, E., Parenti, L. and Scali, E. (1995) 'Aspects of the mathematics-culture relationship in mathematics teaching-learning in compulsory school', *Proceedings of the Nineteenth Annual Meeting of the International Group for the Psychology of Mathematics Education* 1: 151–66.

Brown, J.S., Collins, A. and Duguid, P. (1989) 'Situated cognition and the culture of learning', *Educational Researcher* 18(1): 32–42.

Brown, S.I. (1997) 'Thinking like a mathematician', *For the Learning of Mathematics* 17(2): 36–7.

Clarkson, P.C. and Dawe, L. (1997) 'NESB migrant students studying mathematics: Vietnamese students in Melbourne and Sydney', *Proceedings of the 21st Conference of the International Group for the Psychology of Mathematics Education* 2: 153–60.

Cobb, P., Wood, T. and Yackel, E. (1991) 'Learning through problem solving: a constructivist approach to second grade mathematics', in E. von Glasersfeld (ed.) *Radical Constructivism in Mathematics Education*, Dordrecht, The Netherlands: Kluwer: 157–76.

Davydov, V.V. (1988) 'Problems of developmental teaching', *Soviet Education* 30: 6–97.

Davydov, V.V. (1990) 'Soviet studies in mathematics education: volume 2. Types of generalization in instruction', in J. Kilpatrick (ed.) J. Teller (trans.) *Education* 14–21 July 1996, National Council for Teacher of Mathematics, Reston, VA: 142–58.

DfEE (1999) *The National Numeracy Strategy*, Cambridge: Cambridge University Press.

Dickson, L., Brown, M. and Gibson, O. (1984) *Children Learning Mathematics*, London: Cassell Educational Limited.

Ernest, P. (1991) *The Philosophy of Mathematics Education*, Basingstoke: The Falmer Press.

Fennema, E. and Franke, M.L. (1992) 'Teachers' knowledge and its impact', in D.A. Grouws (ed.) *Handbook of Research on Mathematics Teaching and Learning*, New York: Macmillan: 147–64.

Freudenthal, H. (1973) *Mathematics as an Educational Task*, Dordrecht, The Netherlands: Reidel.

Gates, P. (1997) 'The importance of social structure in developing a critical social psychology in mathematics education', *Proceedings of the 21st Conference of the International Group of Mathematics Education* 2: 305–12.

Ginsburg, H.P., Choy, Y.E., Lopez, L.S., Netley, R. and Chao-Yuan, C. (1997) 'Happy Birthday to you: early mathematical thinking of Asian, South American, and US children', in T. Nunes and P. Bryant (eds) *Learning and Teaching Mathematics: an international perspective*, Hove: Psychology Press Limited.

Gravemeijer, K. (1997) 'Mediating between concrete and abstract', in T. Nunes and P. Bryant (eds) *Learning and Teaching Mathematics: an international perspective*, Hove: Psychology Press: 315–45.

Hughes, M. (1986) *Children and Number: difficulties in learning mathematics*, Oxford: Blackwell.

Jaworski, B. (1994) 'The social construction of classroom knowledge', *Proceedings of the Eighteenth Conference of the International Group for the Psychology of Mathematics Education* 3: 73–80.

Julie, C. (1998) 'The production of artefacts as goals for school mathematics?', *Proceedings of the 22nd Conference of the International Group for the Psychology of Mathematics Education* 1: 49–65.

Julie, C., Angelis, D. and Davis, Z. (eds) (1993) *Political Dimensions of Mathematics 2: curriculum reconstruction for society in transition*, Cape Town: Maskew Miller Longman.

Kjærgård, T., Aasmund, K. and Lindén, N. (eds) (1996) *Numeracy, Race, Gender and Class*, Landås, Norway: Caspar Forlag A/S.

Knijnik, G. (1995) 'Intellectuals and social movements: examining power relations', *Numeracy, Race, Gender and Class: Proceedings of the Third International Conference of the Group for the Political Dimensions of Mathematics Education*, Bergen: Caspar Forlag A/S: 90–113.

Lave, J. and Wenger, E. (1991) *Situated Learning: legitimate peripheral participation*, New York: Cambridge University Press.

Lerman, S. (1990) 'Alternative perspectives of the nature of mathematics and their influence on the teaching of mathematics', *British Educational Research Journal* 16: 15–61.

Lerman, S. (1998) 'A moment in the zoom of a lens: towards a discursive psychology of mathematics teaching and learning', *Proceedings of the 22nd Conference of the International Group for the Psychology of Mathematics Education* 1: 66–84.

Mellin-Olsen, S. (1987) *The Politics of Mathematics Education*, Dordrecht, The Netherlands: Kluwer.

Nickson, M. (1992) 'The culture of the mathematics classroom: an unknown quantity?', in D.A. Grouws (ed.) *Handbook of Research on Mathematics Teaching and Learning*, New York: Macmillan: 100–14

Nickson, M. (1995) 'Mathematics education as an international marketplace', in T. Kjærgård, A. Kvamme and N. Linden (eds) *Numeracy, Race, Gender and Class: Proceedings of the Third International Conference of the Group for the Political Dimensions of Mathematics Education*, Bergen: Caspar Forlag A/S: 150–68.

Nickson, M. and Lerman, S. (1992) *The Social Context of Mathematics Education*, London: Southbank.

Nielsen, L., Patronis, T. and Skovsmose, O. (1999) *Connecting Corners: a Greek-Danish project in mathematics education*, Copenhagen: Forlaget Systime A/S.

Noddings, N. (1993) 'Politicising the mathematics classroom', in S. Restivo, J.P. van Bendegem and R. Fischer (eds) *Math Worlds: philosophical and social studies of mathematics and mathematics education*, Albany: State University of New York: 150-61.

Nunes, T., Light, P., Mason, J. and Allerton, M. (1994) 'The role of symbols in structuring reason: studies about the concept of area', *Proceedings of the Eighteenth Conference of the International Group for the Psychology of Mathematics Education* 3: 255–62.

Popkewitz, T. (1984) *Paradigm and Ideology in Educational Research: the social functions of the intellectual*, London: The Falmer Press.

Popper, K. (1979) *Objective Knowledge – an evolutionary approach*, Oxford: Oxford University Press: 88–95.

Restivo, S. (1993) 'The social life of mathematics', in S. Restivo, J.P. van Bendegem and R. Fischer (eds) *Math Worlds: philosophical and social studies of mathematics and mathematics education*, Albany: State University of New York: 247–78.

Scott-Hodgetts, R. (1992) 'The National Curriculum: implications for the sociology of the classroom', in M. Nickson and S. Lerman (eds) *The Social Context of Mathematics Education: theory and practice*, London: South Bank Press: 10–25.

Skovsmose, O. (1994) *Towards a Philosophy of Critical Mathematics Education*, Dordrecht, The Netherlands: Kluwer.

Streefland, L. (1991) *Fractions in Realistic Mathematics Education: a paradigm of developmental research*, Dordrecht, The Netherlands: Kluwer.

von Glasersfeld, E. (1991) (ed.) 'Radical constructivism in mathematics', Dordrecht, The Netherlands: Kluwer.

Vygotsky, L.S. (1962) *Thought and Language*, Cambridge, MA: MIT Press.

Vygotsky, L.S. (1978) *Mind in Society*, Cambridge, MA: Harvard University.

Winter, R. (1992) 'Mathophobia, Pythagoras and roller-skating', in M. Nickson and S. Lerman (eds) *The Social Context of Mathematics Education: theory and practice*, London: South Bank Press: 81–93.

Section 7

International perspectives

16 Different cultures, different meanings, different teaching

Birgit Pepin

Introduction

> Every child in every society has to learn from adults the meaning given to life by his society; but every society possesses with a greater or lesser degree of difference, meanings to be learned. In short, every society has a culture to be learned though cultures are different.
>
> (Levitas, 1974, p. 3)

If one went into any mathematics classroom in the world, apart from obvious language differences, what would one expect to see? Would the mathematics be the same? Would teachers be trying to achieve the same sorts of things, and would they be doing the same sorts of things? Why might things be different, and in which ways does this make one reflect on one's assumptions, concepts and beliefs concerning teaching and learning of mathematics? These questions lie at the heart of what is presented in this chapter.

The literature contends that the culture of each mathematics classroom is the product of what the teacher and pupils bring to it in terms of knowledge, conceptions and beliefs, and how these affect the social interactions within the particular context. Culture is viewed here as 'the invisible and apparently shared meanings that teachers and pupils bring to the mathematics classroom and that govern their interaction in it' (Nickson, 1993, p. 102). However, the particular context of the classroom is also part of the larger institutional (e.g. school) and societal context of a particular education system, with its embedded values, beliefs and traditions, which may be manifested in adopted curriculums, educational practices, systemic features, to name but a few. These institutional and societal features represent a second source of influence on teaching and learning cultures and set the frame for the social interaction in the mathematics classroom. Thus, teaching and learning cultures of mathematics classrooms may vary according to the actors within them (e.g. teachers and pupils), and to the institutional and societal context in which lessons take place.

In this chapter the intention is to develop an understanding of the ways in which cultures of teaching and learning mathematics are shaped by and shape the different contexts in England, France and Germany. The findings reported are primarily based on a study of mathematics teachers' work in England, France and Germany (Pepin, 1997, 1999a, 1999b, 1999c). Whilst acknowledging that it is difficult and untimely here to generalise about a country's teaching population and the context in which mathematics teachers work, it is nevertheless helpful to 'paint a picture of what it is like' in the respective countries (and that is what is intended when talking about mathematics teachers' work in the three countries). Therefore, 'profiles' of working conditions, of mathematics teachers' tasks and responsibilities, and of their classroom practices, are presented, in order to develop an understanding of the 'culture' of their work.

Why compare?

This question seems relevant for any comparative view and it is important to demonstrate the value of comparing cultures of different countries. By stepping outside a particular set of cultural traditions and observing classroom practices in other countries, we may question our own traditional practices, norms and expectations that are so widely shared and familiar, so much so that they become nearly invisible to members within a culture (Kawanaka *et al.*, 1999). Thus, by comparing we may become aware of the choices we have made in constructing the educational process (Stigler and Perry, 1988).

However, when comparing it is important to realise and acknowledge that what we see in the mathematics classroom is culturally embedded: the mathematics, the teaching and the learning of mathematics. Not only is teaching an activity embedded in culture, but so is what is taught, and countries have developed their own ways of engaging students in the process of learning mathematics (Cogan and Schmidt, 1999). Kawanaka *et al.* (1999) contend that 'Teaching and learning, as cultural activities, fit within a variety of social, economic and political forces in our society. Every single aspect of mathematics education, from a particular teacher behaviour to national policy, must be considered and evaluated within a socio-cultural context' (p. 103).

Whilst it might be exciting to view, or read descriptions of, mathematics lessons of different countries, we have to find possible explanations for the similarities and differences that we see and experience. How can we understand teachers' practices in the light of what we know about the different countries? If we believe that the teaching and learning of mathematics is 'culturally embedded', what are the cultural and intellectual underpinnings that influence the teaching and learning of mathematics? Where do the cultural and educational traditions stem from, and how do they feed into the classroom? These and more questions have to be posed and answered, if we want to benefit from comparing teaching and learning mathematics in different countries.

What is different about the school context?

Most French and English mathematics teachers work in comprehensive schools, whereas German teachers can be either working in a *Gymnasium* (Grammar school), a *Realschule* (Technical school) or a *Hauptschule* (Secondary Modern school), all state-run schools, depending on the school form for which their teacher education course has prepared them. Whilst the *Realschule* and the *Hauptschule* have a vocational orientation towards education, the *Gymnasium* has a distinctive academic tradition and prepares pupils for university entry. About 40 per cent of an age cohort attend the *Gymnasium*. German teachers have to (and are educated to) teach at least two subjects (e.g. mathematics and physics, or mathematics and information technology, or mathematics and physical education).

Teachers in France and Germany know exactly how many hours they have to teach each week and each year and, if they teach more than that, they are paid overtime. In England, there is a notion of what the teacher is supposed to be doing per year ('1265 hour rule') and this is a nominal figure, neither aggregated by teachers nor considered to be realistic in terms of contractual hours. In addition, the statutory number of hours taught by a teacher in France is less than that even notionally suggested in England. French and German teachers have to be in school for their timetabled lessons and perhaps some meetings and parents' evenings, whereas an English teacher is expected to be present in school throughout the day, in addition to meetings and parents' evenings.

Regarding salaries, German teachers' salaries are the highest (with differences in salaries between teachers of different school forms), followed by the English and then the French. In addition, teachers in Germany and France enjoy civil servant status, with its attached job security, fixed number of weekly periods and pension rights.

In the lower secondary years in French mathematics classrooms, pupils are taught in mixed-ability classes, based on their form groups. These groups are generally put together on the basis of catchment area, meaning that pupils who come from the same primary school or village are grouped together. There are also different 'option' groups, i.e. where form groups are put together based on their choices of foreign languages. There is no grouping of pupils by perceived ability. Rather, all pupils in a particular class are given the opportunity to study and learn the same mathematics, with each topic studied for the same amount of time by all pupils (though not according to the clock, which is the stereotyped view of teaching in France by 'outsiders'). In Germany, pupils are allocated, according to parents' wishes and teachers' recommendations, to one of the three school forms (*Hauptschule*, *Realschule* or *Gymnasium*). Once streamed into the three school forms, pupils are generally taught in form groups, and these form groups are generally put together on the basis of catchment area. Although the core curriculum for mathematics all over Germany is similar for all pupils, the mathematics is treated in different ways, with logical thinking and proof being emphasised in the *Gymnasium*. The majority of pupils in England are taught in the same school form, the comprehensive schools. However, most are setted for mathematics during their first year in secondary school, according to their results in National Curriculum tests. Once in those sets, they follow the same National Curriculum, but from different starting points and with different envisaged end points. These end points determine, to a large extent, the depth and breadth of the mathematics studied.

What is different about the mathematics?

At first glance, mathematics is the same in whatever country it is taught. Curriculums of England, France and Germany only vary slightly in their content. However, a country's perceptions of the nature and role of mathematics have a major influence on the development of school mathematics curriculums and on the ways in which teachers approach teaching their subject (Pepin, 1999b).

In Germany, mathematics teachers, and in particular *Gymnasium* teachers, hold a relatively formal view of mathematics. Here mathematics is, by and large, seen as an abstract and unified body of knowledge that needs to be passed on to pupils, a static discipline developed abstractly and to be transmitted appropriately. It is considered to consist of symbols and rules that are immutable and 'true' – a defined system waiting to be discovered. In short, the emphasis is on the abstractness of mathematics and its structure in helping to educate pupils. Although their environment makes it very difficult for them (see below), *Hauptschul* teachers nevertheless aspire to this formal view of mathematics. More realistically, however, they view mathematics as a 'bag of tools', made up of an accumulation of facts, rules and skills to be used by the apprentice or skilled artisan.

In France, the 'formal' view of mathematics has been traditionally held and it is still recognisable in what teachers say about their view of the subject. However, there has been, perhaps, not a shift but overlay of perspective from the formal to a more dynamic view of mathematics. This view emphasises developmental and social aspects of mathematical knowledge that needs to be carried out by individuals or groups of individuals, that is open to question, challenge and discussion, that needs to be explored and investigated, in order to grow as knowledge in pupils. But there is also a third 'utilitarian' view recognisable in the French mathematics classroom. Mathematics has to be useful and accessible for all.

In England, this last aspect is probably most emphasised, the view that mathematics is a 'tool' for doing other things. In many ways, mathematics here appears to be a set of unrelated but utilitarian rules and facts. However, there is also the view of a dynamic, problem-driven mathematics where patterns are generated and then transformed into knowledge. In 'investigation lessons', for example, teachers see the doing of mathematics as the central characteristic of the subject (rather than its content) and may encourage problem-solving and investigational work as a major focus of their lessons.

What is different about what teachers do?

Teachers in the three countries have many tasks and responsibilities in the school. Beside the task of form tutor, teachers hold positions of responsibility within mathematics or of responsibility in administration or staff councils in the school. In France, the emphasis is on the teaching of mathematics with little or no responsibilities for the pastoral care of pupils or for the wider school community. The expectation for French teachers' role in the classroom is concerned with the teaching and learning of mathematics and children's academic performance in school.

The responsibility of the teacher could be said to start from the moment the pupils enter the mathematics classroom and ends when they leave it. In Germany, there are different responsibilities of teachers for different school forms. Whilst *Hauptschul* teachers tend to be heavily involved with the pastoral care of their pupils, *Gymnasium* teachers are regarded first as subject specialists, although they have some pastoral care duties. In general, German teachers are responsible for the academic side of teaching, with the involvement of a moral dimension and with some defined tasks in terms of pastoral care. In England, mathematics teachers have many more responsibilities in terms of pastoral care than their French and German colleagues. To a large extent, they are responsible for the pastoral as well as the academic side of schooling. It appears here that a climate has developed where the pastoral care and other non-teaching responsibilities are at least as important as the preparation and teaching of the subject.

In terms of classroom practices, mathematics teachers in all three countries use whole-class teaching to a large extent, but there are important differences (Pepin, 1999a). English teachers spend relatively little time explaining concepts to the whole class, whereas French and – in particular – German mathematics teachers devote a substantial proportion of the school day to whole-class teaching. When English teachers use whole-class teaching, they typically explain a concept from the front in a relatively didactic way. Unless the lesson takes the form of an 'investigation', English mathematics teachers mostly introduce and explain a concept or skill to pupils, give examples on the board and then expect pupils to practise on their own or in small groups while they attend to individual pupils. Looking at mathematics teaching in more detail, in English mathematics classrooms there are few situations where pupils discover multiple solutions or investigate new solutions that require reasoning, and these are usually reserved for 'investigation' lessons. The major aim seems to convey a mathematical concept and let pupils get as much practice as possible. The emphasis appears to be on the skill side of mathematics and on 'getting it right'.

In France, teachers tend to focus on developing mathematical thinking, which includes exploring, developing and understanding concepts, and mathematical reasoning. They attempt to forge links between skills and 'cognitive activities' (small investigations) on the one hand, and concepts on the other. Pupils have to reason (sometimes with rigorous proof) their results and they are given cognitive activities to discover notions of mathematics for themselves. Relatively little time is spent on routine procedures. The most intriguing problems are treated in class, whereas the routine questions are left for homework.

In Germany, where the view of mathematics is relatively formal and includes logic and proof, the teacher's role is that of the explainer who teaches the structure of mathematics through an 'exciting' delivery and by adapting the structured textbook approach meaningfully. In particular in the *Gymnasium* where expectations are high, topics are discussed in great depth and teachers spend a large amount of their time in discussion with children in order to challenge their mathematical thinking. Logical thinking is regarded as most important. However, the invention of new solutions or procedures is not usually encouraged, and lessons appear relatively formal and traditional in terms of their mathematical content.

What is it that is important in the three countries?

In terms of conditions of work, in one system mathematics teachers can go home between lessons, whereas in another they have to stay in school for the whole day. Working in a system where teachers are not obliged to stay in school implies that teachers might not feel the same collegiality as those who are expected to stay. On the other hand, teachers who work in a system where they are expected to stay in school all day are more likely to be involved in non-teaching tasks, such as administration or pastoral care of pupils. Furthermore, there are differences in the amount of time teachers are asked to spend teaching their subject, and the amount and nature of other tasks they are expected to do. In particular English mathematics teachers are generally asked to do many tasks beside their teaching-related responsibilities, whereas French teachers, for example, are expected to focus on tasks directly related to the teaching of their subject. It appears that English mathematics teachers do not seem to be left enough time to reflect on and prepare their mathematics lessons. There are 'hundreds' of other things that need doing during a school day. In Germany and France, lesson preparation and marking, for example, are usually done at home, because teachers are only expected to stay in school for their timetabled lessons. In England, teachers usually try to fit in their work (marking 'every pupil's book at least once a week'), whenever they are not timetabled to teach (but are in school). This includes some of their break times, which in turn can become 'frantic', so that little time is left for relaxation between lessons. They claim that they are busy all day, all the time.

Although in all three countries there are meetings, such as faculty or class council meetings that teachers have to attend, in England teachers complain about too many – and too frequent – meetings. English teachers are involved with different responsibilities in the school, so they attend more meetings because of their respective tasks and commitments. It appears that the actual frequency of meetings related to mathematics teaching is no greater than in the other two countries but, because English teachers have so many other responsibilities beside their subject teaching, the overall number of meetings is greater. Moreover, English teachers' perception of the high frequency of their meetings is also likely to be a result of the fact that they feel generally so pressurised in terms of time that they complain about things that are in fact not much different for their French and German colleagues. Indeed, it appears that English teachers are always short of time and the teachers themselves recognise this, and they want more time for various projects or improvements to their work.

In both France and England, pupils are taught in state-run comprehensive schools, in mixed-ability groups in France, and in 'sets' in England. An outside observer might ask how this can work in France. One of the reasons might lie with a feature of the French (and German) system concerning the ways pupils are 'treated' if they fall behind expected levels of learning. In France (and Germany) pupils are expected to reach a certain target at the end of every academic year, otherwise they have to repeat the year (*redoublement*). In France there are national targets, 'required skills', in every year (in Germany there are different targets for different school types, for every year). Teachers can advise parents and ask pupils to repeat the year, if they have fallen behind expected levels of learning. However, in every class (form group of about 28 to 30 pupils), there are usually only about two or three pupils who are required (or advised) to repeat the year. On the other hand, in England pupils reach levels of the National Curriculum and some might progress further than others within the same year. The focus in England is on the individual, on how individual pupils advance within their capabilities, and there are expected levels for each set. Pupils who do not achieve expected levels (of a set) are put into sets where the targets are lower. For French mathematics teachers this means that they have a larger range of ages in any one year but mathematically, allegedly, they have a more homogeneous class. Mathematics teachers in England, on the other hand, have to provide a different mathematical 'diet' for different sets and ages, whichever level and set they are.

In terms of classroom practices, there are several features that are important to note. In Germany, mathematics teachers talk to pupils about the mathematics in a more or less conversational style – this is part of their craft knowledge. They are keen to involve their pupils in discussions and explorations about mathematical topics, to 'problematise' pupil experiences and what they already know and to lead them to the notion to be acquired. Textbooks help them to consolidate this with exercises. This is a strong feature of a German mathematics lesson, in particular in the *Gymnasium*. In the German *Hauptschule* and *Realschule*, the situation is different. Although teachers there would also like to teach mathematics in a conversational style, they acknowledge that the children in these school forms need more support and practical help, they will not be able to 'wander in the realms of abstract mathematical structures'. This, in their view, is provided by presenting a relatively short explanation, followed by exercises from the textbook. In addition, these exercises are fairly short and not very 'wordy'. It is quite significant that *Gymnasium* teachers relish the challenge of an exciting and well-structured delivery of mathematical topic and intriguing exercises – they are the subject specialists. *Hauptschul* teachers, on the other hand, see their task as that of establishing an atmosphere in which they can help children learn, for them, difficult mathematics and to make this experience as successful and comfortable as possible. In addition, it might be important to note that once streaming has taken place into one of the three school forms, all pupils follow the same curriculum and little differentiation is practised in lessons by teachers. This is particularly evident in the *Gymnasium*, where pupils are expected to follow the rhythm of the class, otherwise they have to repeat the year, or leave the school for another school form.

In France, the traditional *cour magistral* – lecture-type lesson – has been replaced almost entirely by lessons organised in three parts: the *activité* (cognitive activities that are to lead and help students understand the main notion to be studied); the *cours* (the essential part of the lesson, to be written down in the *cahier de cours*) and the exercises. This lesson structure is supported by textbooks and mathematics inspectors, and thus reflects the pedagogical 'priorities' of mathematics teaching in the country. It can be argued that it is in teachers' interest to follow the inspectors' advice, because they determine, partly on the basis of such inspections, the speed at which teachers move up the salary scale. However, teachers also see the 'outdatedness' of the *cours magistral* and are keen to offer a 'softer' way to teach and understand the mathematics, and this is provided by suitable *activitiés*. One outstanding feature of a French mathematics lesson is – and it has to be remembered that they teach in mixed-ability classes in state-run comprehensive schools – that for the teacher it is about the mathematics to be learnt, how to present mathematics in an interesting way, how to 'attack' it from different angles and perspectives, and how to understand and express the logical lessons learnt from it.

In England, unless the lesson is intended for investigational activities, teachers usually give short explanations to introduce the topic or skill to be learnt, and the majority of lesson time is spent on exercises selected by teachers. Pupils work on exercises provided by textbooks or worksheets, with the individual help of teachers. Mathematics teachers claim to have little time for lesson planning, and because of this lack of time they want a plan 'off the shelf' that they can follow 'with confidence'. However, commercial mathematics textbooks offer little in terms of mathematical variety or structure, intellectual challenges or linguistic complexity. Furthermore, mathematics departments have limited funds available for textbooks, which means that often only top sets or only older pupils are provided with textbooks. On the whole, teachers see their role of being in charge of what to teach to individual sets (within school and National Curriculum constraints), how to teach it (according to perceived ability) and the extent and nature of practice needed. In fact, a striking feature of an English mathematics lesson is that the teacher is the 'absolute controller'. Teachers decide on the criteria on which sets are organised, with which mathematical diet pupils are provided according to their sets, what is taught and to what 'depth', which exercises to leave out and which mathematical language to use.

Why are things different (or similar) in different countries?

What is interesting about all of this is that mathematics teachers across the three countries teach similar curriculums and work, and within two of them under similar conditions, but act very differently. This can partly be understood in the light of the national cultural tradition of the three countries (Pepin, 1999a). In England individualistic views and the principle of morality expect teachers to spend a considerable amount of time on pastoral responsibilities – all approaches that could be said to derive from (English) humanistic principles. It is difficult, however, to identify educational traditions that account for all aspects of their classroom practices. The fact that mathematics teachers in England spend little time on whole-class explanation, but rather concentrate on letting pupils practise on exercises where they can attend to the needs of the individual pupil, might be traced back to individualistic traditions. However, the lack of time for lesson preparation cannot be so easily understood. Indeed, it seems that in recent years cultural traditions, such as the English liberal-humanistic and individualistic traditions, have been overridden by a more technocratic approach. Teachers are left no longer to practise within the old tradition of attending to the needs of individual pupils, but are forced to abide by a newer tradition of competition and accountability of schools. With justifications such as economic performance, parental expectations and the idea of raising standards, teachers are being pushed to 'produce results', rendering teaching into a technical exercise in an 'Audit Society' (Power, 1997), failing to account for the sources of educational values that teachers (and learners) hold. Teachers' original concern for more individualistic and child-centred approaches to teaching and learning mathematics is overridden by concerns for examination results and departmental or school league tables.

In general, French mathematics teachers are expected to prepare and teach their lessons, and the secular tradition frees teachers from major pastoral duties. Moral education and pastoral care duties are left to the Church and the parents. The principle feature of French mathematics lessons is the concentration on challenging mathematics activities and exercises that can be understood in terms of traditional (encyclopaedic) views of, and high regard for, rationality. Teachers try to pose thought-provoking problems and expect students to struggle with them. They draw together ideas from the class and write them down in the form of a *cours*, reflecting their expectation of keeping the whole class together and moving pupils forward together, which is an egalitarian view. There is also the mixed ability teaching underpinned by the concern for pupil entitlement to the whole curriculum, another egalitarian principle, where it is considered vital to give every pupil access to the entire curriculum. Whether and how learning takes place is left to the teacher's skills. Every child brings a different set of assumptions and experiences to which the teacher has to attend, and French teachers talk about the 'classroom reality', which is of heterogeneous rather than homogeneous groups, and talk about the need to apply more individualistic approaches in their classrooms. This, however, has not been part of their education and traditional perceptions of teaching. It is left to the skill of the individual teacher to 'bridge the gap' between 'theories of equality' and a heterogeneous audience to be brought up to examination standard.

In Germany, liberal-humanistic views encourage mathematics teachers to combine academic teaching and the moral side of education. Depending in which school type of the tripartite system teachers are working, their responsibilities in terms of pastoral care are greater (*Hauptschule*) or lesser (*Gymnasium*). In terms of educational traditions, the liberal-humanistic customs (of Humboldt, see Pepin, 1999a, 1999b) are still detectable and upheld in the pedagogic approaches of German *Gymnasium* teachers and influence to a large extent the pedagogic culture of perceived 'good' mathematics teaching. A German (*Gymnasium*) lesson is typically characterised by a conversational style where teachers try to involve the whole class in discussion, and sometimes over a considerable period of time. The emphasis is on a well-structured approach and pupil understanding, all reflecting part of humanistic ideals, and often pupils' mistakes in homework or class exercises are used to check and deepen pupil understanding. Typically, a teacher brings pupils to the board and discusses their mistakes and understanding with the whole class. The tradition of the country encourages teachers to teach the class as a whole, an egalitarian principle, and they are expected to move pupils (possibly the whole class) to a different level of cognition. The main task of the mathematics teacher is to provide an interesting introduction and explanation of the mathematical notions, in the most 'stimulating' way, but at the same time adhering to perceptions of mathematics as a logical construct to develop mathematical thinking. However, no support is given on how to tackle this coherence and logic of mathematics, or to bring it into line with pupil experiences, in particular for pupils of the *Hauptschule*. Teachers are left as mediators here in their attempt to make mathematical constructs coherent for learners. The *Hauptschul* teachers find themselves in a difficult situation: how to teach the highly structured (but watered-down grammar school) mathematics to a low achieving and demotivated audience of children, where about one third have difficulties reading German, and have had life experiences (for example, as refugees) that teachers feel they cannot attend to in class.

However, mathematics teachers in all three countries, but particularly in England, want to have more time: time to spend with pupils in their classrooms and time to think about and discuss pedagogical issues with colleagues. The most important group of reference is the pupils, not headteachers, parents or inspectors; they want to close their doors and teach their subject. Teachers' most important rewards are related to pupil understanding and the relationships they have with their pupils. In particular English mathematics teachers claim that more and more tasks and responsibilities are laid on them, which not only keep them away from what they really want to do – be in the classroom with their pupils – but it also results in an intensification of their work. Teachers feel more and more driven by 'external' expectations and pressures relating to tasks they do not value. It appears that the 'technocratic' moves of recent curriculum implementation in England, where teachers are told what and, increasingly, how to teach, overlay the traditional 'liberal-humanist' traditions where teachers used to be at the centre of decision-making in schools.

In terms of pupil organisation, the different practices can be seen as examples of areas where cultural and structural traditions go hand in hand. One example is the grouping of pupils, in different school types and 'streamed' (as in Germany), or in 'mixed ability' groups (as in France) or 'setted' (as in England). In addition, there are perceived egalitarian traditions in Germany and France about taking everybody in the class forward (which in turn necessitates the repeating of the year, if a pupil has not reached the expected level of the year). In England, pupils are allowed to go up the year groups working at a pace that is perceived to be appropriate to them – possibly a reflection of individualistic views. These practices are, arguably, underpinned by philosophical beliefs about education (individualism or egalitarian views), but once established it becomes part of the structures of the system and mathematics teachers have to work within them.

Teachers' principles and beliefs show many similarities. Mathematics teachers in the three countries want to concentrate their main efforts on the core task of teaching. Interestingly, what all teachers want most is to teach, to 'reach' pupils and help them to understand mathematics. They feel satisfaction when pupils are successful, whatever their perception of pupil success, and when pupils show teachers that they are interested and involved. Teachers want to be preoccupied with classroom matters and they do not want to be pulled away to tasks that have nothing to do, as they see it, with teaching. Although administrative responsibilities (such as those of headteachers) are better remunerated and generally have a higher status than classroom related tasks, teachers see their main responsibilities within the classroom and generally with their work with children. They enjoyed mathematics at school and they want to impart that enthusiasm and knowledge of mathematics to their pupils. This seems to be a very strong guiding principle.

What are the challenges for us in this country?

Concerning mathematics teachers' work, the expectation for the French teachers' role in the classroom is concerned with the academic learning of mathematics and children's academic performance in school. The English teachers' tasks encompass the whole child and they are responsible for the academic, as well as the pastoral side of pupil development. For German teachers it depends on the school type, but in general teachers are responsible for the academic side of teaching with the involvement of a moral dimension and with some defined tasks in terms of pastoral care. Regarding the ranges of demands on teachers in the three countries (demands by the system and demands by the schools on teachers), one can detect a spectrum with two extremes in terms of tasks and responsibilities. At one extreme, French teachers appear to be concerned with preparing and teaching their mathematics lessons. At the other extreme, English teachers regard as their tasks lesson preparation, teaching, marking, form tutor work and extra-curricular activities, to name but a few. English teachers are expected to participate in tutorial and pastoral programmes, whilst playing a full part in assisting departmental developments. Documents such as job descriptions and staff handbooks, for example, specify all those extra tasks for English teachers and many activities outside the formal timetabled curriculum are listed. So there is a wider range of demands on teachers in England than on those in France. Yet, however different the ranges of demands are in the three countries, all teachers see as the main objective of their job to teach their subject. They see the main purpose of their job as being in their own classrooms, on their own, with their class, teaching mathematics. However, the reality for English mathematics teachers is that although they want to focus on the same range of demands as their French and German colleagues, there are also other demands on them. English mathematics teachers feel that some of those demands that are made on them prevent them from fulfilling the tasks that they see as most important, the teaching of the subject. Although all teachers feel that a lot of things are asked of them and that the work load is increasing, in terms of the attention that they can give to mathematics teaching and learning, English mathematics teachers claim that they can actually give less attention to, and they can spend less time on, those, for them, crucial bits of their job (preparing and teaching of their lessons) than those who have fewer demands on them.

The concern for England lies in the fact that English mathematics teachers, realistically or unrealistically, perceive their workload as too high. They feel that they do not have enough time for lesson preparation, for reflection on the mathematics they teach and on pupil understanding of the mathematics. More money, either for initial teacher education or for performance-related pay, will not necessarily attract those who relish engagement in thinking about teaching and learning mathematics. The conditions of work also have to be right, and rewards must be provided for those who want to concentrate and specialise on classroom teaching. In terms of changes and implementation of curriculum, teachers regard themselves as professionals who have their own values and principles, which are in turn culturally determined, but these do not change as rapidly as some 'reformers' would like. It has to be borne in mind that teachers might become gatekeepers to change, perhaps holding on to conservative practices, perhaps adopting and adjusting the changes into their world of pedagogical practices in their own ways. Learning cannot be reduced to statements of learner behaviour, and the administration associated with examinations and test results must not become more important than the concerns about the learning process. Mathematics teachers want to be connected with and take part in the learning processes of their pupils, and not pressurised into a 'result mode' where they have to 'teach for the test'.

A second concern for English mathematics teachers relates to their perceptions of teaching and learning. One of teachers' explanations for their practice, and arguably one of the 'sacred cows' of Anglo-Saxon pedagogic theory, is 'child-centredness'. What do we actually mean by 'child-centredness'? Do we mean the 'progressive' approach where prominence is given to learning experiences, as advocated, for example, in the Cockcroft Report? Or do we refer to the 'child-centredness' of Piaget, where the child is assumed to progress through various levels of growth and sequential stages? How do these views go with a centrally designed curriculum, as for example in France or England? The issue here is that the meaning of 'child-centredness' can be 'lived' in different ways in the mathematics classroom, depending on the philosophical and educational underpinnings we adhere to.

This leads us to the central assertion that teachers' principles and classroom practices need to be understood in terms of educational and cultural traditions. To understand pedagogical styles in terms of the underpinning educational values of the respective country appears to make a transfer of 'good' teaching or learning strategies (however identified) across countries inappropriate. The identified 'good' practices are likely to work differently in different settings, because it is the underpinning educational values and philosophies that give meaning to pedagogic styles. This, in turn, has implications for the mobility of teachers across countries (Pepin, 1999c). It is not enough to 'moderate' the (European) countries' teaching degrees. A wider cultural view needs to be taken and it can be argued that teachers need a period of *enculturation*, before they can expect to become effective in any country. It seems necessary for teachers to become 'enculturated' into the cultural traditions of schooling within the country. Teachers need to understand and become familiar with the cultural traditions and practices of the country of their choice. This implies not only classroom practices, but also principles and perceptions of mathematics and of how mathematics should be taught and learnt. This is likely to take some time, with teachers working in classrooms, talking to colleague teachers and pupils, and trying to understand the systems and culture in which they work. Enculturation is likely to be a difficult undertaking. In practical terms it involves teachers suspending their own judgements about what they think are the correct ways of doing things and it necessitates open-mindedness. It involves tolerance of new ideas and approaches, and finally an acceptance that they work within a particular system. Thus, it seems that teacher mobility is rather more complex than might have been anticipated.

To conclude, it is argued that stepping outside a particular country's traditions may be appropriate in order not only to develop an understanding of the influence of particular traditions on mathematics teachers' practices, but also to explore new perspectives that were not considered before. It is claimed that teachers' pedagogical styles, and in particular their pedagogy in the classroom, are a personal response to a set of institutional and societal constraints (e.g. curricular organisation), to a set of traditions (e.g. educational traditions), and a set of assumptions (e.g. principles of teaching and learning). Mathematics teachers' work needs to be analysed and understood in terms of the larger cultural context, which will help us to reconsider our own taken-for-granted assumptions and practices. This, in turn, will prevent us from rendering teaching into a technical exercise concerned with mere skills, but lead us to successfully account for the sources of educational values and perceptions that mathematics teachers hold, in order to be aware of the 'hidden messages' that are likely to be conveyed to learners.

References

Cogan, L.S. and Schmidt, W.II. (1999) 'An examination of instructional practices in six countries', in G. Kaiser, E. Luna and I. Huntley (eds) *International Comparisons in Mathematics Education*, London: Falmer Press.

Kawanaka, T., Stigler, J. W. and Hiebert, J. (1999) 'Studying mathematics classrooms in Germany, Japan and the United States: lessons from TIMSS videotape study', in G. Kaiser, E. Luna and I. Huntley (eds) *International Comparisons in Mathematics Education*, London: Falmer Press.

Levitas, M. (1974) *Marxist Perspective in the Sociology of Education*, London: Routledge and Kegan Paul.

Nickson, M. (1993) 'The culture of the mathematics classroom: an unknown quantity?', in D.A. Grouws (ed.) *Handbook of Research on Mathematics Teaching and Learning*, New York: Macmillan.

Pepin, B. (1997) 'Developing an understanding of mathematics teachers in England, France and Germany: an ethnographic study', unpublished Ph.D. thesis, University of Reading, Reading.

Pepin, B. (1999a) 'The influence of national cultural tradition on pedagogy', in J. Leach and B. Moon (eds) *Learners and pedagogy*, London: Paul Chapman in association with The Open University.

Pepin, B. (1999b) 'Epistemologies, beliefs and conceptions of mathematics teaching and learning: the theory, and what is manifested in mathematics teachers' practices in England, France and Germany', in B. Hudson, F. Buchberger, P. Kansanen and H. Seel (eds) *Didaktik/Fachdidaktik as Science(s) of the Teaching Profession. TNTEE Publications* 2(1): 127–46.

Pepin, B. (1999c) 'Mobility of mathematics teachers across England, France and Germany', *European Educational Researcher* 5(1): 5–14.

Power, M. (1997) *The Audit Society*, New York: Oxford University Press.

Stigler, J. W. and Perry, M. (1988) 'Cross-cultural studies of mathematics teaching and learning: recent findings and new directions', in D.A. Grouws, T. J. Cooney and D. Jones (eds) *Perspectives on Research on Effective Mathematics Teaching*, Reston, VA: National Council of Teachers of Mathematics.

17 What can we learn from international comparisons?

Geoffrey Howson

The history of comparative studies

One of the first written records of education in English schools is that by Alcuin in the eighth century. In it, he tells how his predecessor, Aethelbert, at the school attached to the great church at York, 'more than once went … abroad … to see if he could find in those lands new books or studies which he could bring home with him,' (Sylvester, 1970). The desire, then, to find out what is happening in other countries and whether there are practices elsewhere that could be adopted with advantage in the UK is by no means a new one.

Kaiser would have labelled this type of investigation a 'travellers tale' belonging to the 'first phase of comparative education' (Kaiser *et al.*, 1999). Her descriptions will be used as a framework in this section in which we shall see how comparative studies affecting the UK have evolved.

Interest in comparative education has continued to grow through the centuries and was given an added impetus as a result of the spread of state education. England was slow to provide 'state' education: it was not until 1870 that school boards were established throughout England to provide elementary education up to the age of 13 (even then such education was neither compulsory nor always free). But the reformers of the early nineteenth century were quick to collect and use data from other countries to show how far behind England lagged educationally. So, for example, in 1831 the *Quarterly Journal of Education* contained articles on the syllabuses and curriculums of the French *École Polytechnique* and a typical German *Gymnasium*. These were intended to illumine the great differences that existed between these foreign institutions and, respectively, the two ancient English universities, and the old, established grammar schools, which still paid scant attention to mathematics and science. This provides an example of what Kaiser terms the 'second phase' of comparative studies.

Gradually, the two types of study already described evolved to create a third in which educators attempted not only to describe what they saw in other countries but also to identify the tenets of the philosophy of education which helped produce what they observed. Here, a suitable example might be the study carried out by Kay-Shuttleworth, who, before establishing what was, in effect, the first English teacher training college (Battersea, 1840), visited existing institutions in Germany and Switzerland. In Germany he found too much concentration on 'instruction rather than education'. It was the Swiss colleges that he decided to emulate; for them, 'formation of character' was 'the great aim of education'. Again, he decided that he would follow the Swiss pattern of having general academic education precede pedagogical training and teaching practice.

The fourth type of study identified by Kaiser refers essentially to the work of those who, in the twentieth century, came to be known as 'comparative educators': scholars who studied systems of education and, for example, sought to identify the social and political causes responsible for educational practices. Such work could undoubtedly help people better to understand their own and others' educational systems, how they had evolved and why they often had different priorities. However, it differed significantly in its aims from the studies of, say, Kay-Shuttleworth which, in a phrase we shall return to later, specifically aimed at 'value for use'.

What is important to notice is that all the studies so far mentioned were essentially qualitative (although, of course, they contained data on student numbers, hours of instruction, etc.). There was no attempt to compare student attainment by means of any standardised instruments. The latter was essentially Kaiser's fifth phase and it burgeoned in the 1960s following the establishment of the International Association for the Evaluation of Educational Achievement (IEA). This body superintended three large-scale international studies of mathematics attainment: the first, FIMS, in 1964, the second, SIMS (1980–2), and the third, TIMSS (which also included a study of attainment in science, 1992–). In addition to these major international studies, there have been, in recent years, a host of other studies, two of which will be described in the fourth part of this chapter, that focused attention on curriculums, teaching methods, textbooks, assessment procedures, etc.

The value of comparative studies: to whom?

That one can learn from comparative studies is not in dispute. What should be questioned, however, is the nature of their value, to whom a study will have value, and whether or not the resulting conclusions will convert into 'value for use'.

As we have seen, comparative studies were once of great value to individuals. However, with the growing centralisation of education, particularly in the UK, it might appear that nowadays they have little to offer to individual teachers. That this is not entirely the case is shown by a recent project (see Kaiser *et al.*, 1999, pp. 171–3), which took teachers from London schools to Switzerland to see what they could learn from observing class management and teaching methods there. (Indeed, observing classes in one's own country is still a valuable 'comparative study'.)

Nowadays comparative studies are more frequently seen as answering the questions of governments and their agencies. The coming of 'secondary education for all' after World War 2, permitted wide-scale comparisons of educational attainment. As expenditure on national educational systems began to rise, and the importance of a well-educated workforce was recognised, governments sought both to ensure that money was being well spent and also that they kept abreast of economic competitors in the 'educational race'. Their motivation to participate in large-scale international comparative studies increased.

Significantly, then, the vast sums required to mount TIMSS came almost entirely from North American and, in particular, US Federal sources.

The results of this were twofold. TIMSS was much better funded than its predecessors and so was able to engage in many activities that they had been denied (see the third part of the chapter). Inevitably, though, there arose a bias towards seeking answers to questions set by the principal funding agencies. Moreover, the teams established to answer these questions were, as might be expected, North American dominated (see Kaiser *et al.*, 1999, for reports by the various team leaders), which introduced other biases.

Governments were able to learn from TIMSS about relative standards of mathematical attainment, but could it provide guidance on how to raise standards? To know, for example, as every comparative study reveals, that students' performances are directly related to the educational standards reached by their parents (see, for example, Beaton *et al.*, 1996[1]) can provide explanations, but no help: the parents' standard of education cannot be raised retrospectively. One must, then, dig deep into the TIMSS data to find 'value for use'. National systems of education will not be changed overnight because of what is learned from a comparative study, yet such a study can have a significant effect. Indeed, the imposition of a National Curriculum in England was probably expedited by the country's poor showing in the Second International Mathematics Study (SIMS) and in similar, smaller, studies undertaken in the 1980s. Such studies, however, did not reveal how best to design and implement such a curriculum.

TIMSS,[2] though, despite its weaknesses, was a remarkable study and we shall now consider its work in more depth.

The Third international Mathematics and Science Study (TIMSS)

FIMS and SIMS were not well endowed financially and essentially comprised the testing of randomly chosen samples of students from two populations: 13-year-olds, and those in their last year of upper secondary school who had opted to take a specialist mathematics course (e.g. an English A level in mathematics). The first study was the subject of much criticism from those who complained of the problem of matching test items to curriculums. That all the items were multiple-choice led to further criticisms. SIMS, again, used only multiple-choice items, but tried better to match 'the' curriculum. Indeed, it distinguished clearly between three 'curriculums': the *intended*, established at a national level and studied by curriculum analysis; the *implemented*, what was actually taught in classrooms and investigated through questionnaires and the *attained*, what students actually learned as revealed by the various tests. An interesting aspect of SIMS was the inclusion of a longitudinal study: students were tested at the beginning and at the end of the school year. This yielded some particularly interesting data in the case of Japan. Initially, one saw only an increase in the percentage of students able to answer an item correctly. However, when the data were disaggregated to show how individual pupils had performed on the two occasions, then interesting questions about the 'stability' of a student's knowledge were raised. For instance, on one item 59 per cent of students answered correctly at the start of the year and 60 per cent at the end. Yet only 38.5 per cent answered correctly on both occasions – i.e. over 80 per cent answered correctly on at least one occasion. What does that tell us about the number of Japanese students who knew how to solve the problem? Did the use of multiple-choice items confuse the issue – and if so to what extent?

TIMSS differed from its predecessors in many respects. First it tested three populations (and in both mathematics and science):

- *Population 1*   All students in the two adjacent grades that contain the largest proportion of nine-year-olds (usually Grades 3 and 4, i.e. Years 4 and 5 in England).
- *Population 2*   All students in the two adjacent grades that contain the largest proportion of 13-year-olds at the time of testing[3] (usually Grades 7 and 8).
- *Population 3*   Students in their final year of secondary education who were tested on 'mathematical literacy'. In addition a further test, on advanced mathematics, was available for those students specialising in mathematics.

For the first time both multiple-choice and open-response items were used in the tests. In addition, a separate test, taken by fewer countries and available both to Population 1 and Population 2 students, consisted of 'performance assessment' items: tasks that would take a student 15–20 minutes each to complete.

The main tests took about an hour for Population 1 students and 90 minutes for those in Populations 2 and 3. All tests (except that for specialist mathematicians) tested both science and mathematics. In order to test across the whole curriculum, any one student was tested on only a subset of the items, but including some drawn from a central 'core'. Statistical adjustments then ensured that those students who received more than their fair share of what were found to be the more difficult items were not penalised for this.

Students were not only tested for attainment, but they and their teachers completed questionnaires on a variety of aspects affecting their learning and teaching. These included investigating such questions as:

- What educational resources do students have in their homes?
- What are the academic expectations of students, their families and their friends?
- How do students spend their time out of school?
- How do students perceive success in mathematics?
- What are students' attitudes towards mathematics?
- Who delivers mathematics instruction?
- What are teachers' perceptions of mathematics?

- How do teachers spend their school-related time?
- How are mathematics classes organised?
- What activities do students do in their mathematics lessons?
- How are calculators and computers used?
- How much homework are students assigned?
- What assessment and evaluation procedures do teachers use?

Clearly, such information can throw light on students' performances in the attainment tests and can help illustrate important differences between countries.[4] One also learns more about other factors that can affect students' progress. For example, that one-sixth of all final-year students in Canada, the Netherlands and Norway claimed to do paid work for more than five hours a day (the proportion rose to one quarter in the USA); not surprisingly, the average marks of such students were lower than those of their peers.

In addition to reports on these attainment tests and other publications, TIMSS also established four major additional studies:

- the TIMSS Videotape Study analysed lessons in Japan, Germany and the USA;
- the Case Study Project collected and compared qualitative information on the educational systems of Japan, Germany and the USA;
- the Survey of Mathematics and Science Opportunities, studied teaching in six countries;
- the Curriculum Analysis Study studied the curriculums and textbooks in many countries.

The first two of these studies were relatively small-scale and clearly the countries had been selected to enable comparisons to be made between the USA and 'leading' Asian and European countries.[5] The third study resulted in some interesting qualitative findings based on observations in classrooms. The fourth, an extremely large one, suffered from over-ambition, and an over-supply of data, not all of which was sufficiently specific to permit useful conclusions to be drawn.

This latter observation brings us to an outstanding problem for TIMSS. Mathematics is a major component of the curriculum in *all* countries from the very beginning of formal education. In that respect it is unique. As a result many countries wished to take part in TIMSS — over 40 in the Population 2 written test. But how does one adequately test the knowledge of students drawn from extremely diverse systems in the same test? On the test given, 45 per cent of Grade 8 Singapore students reached the standard of the top 10 per cent internationally and 74 per cent were in the top 25 per cent. The corresponding percentages for England and Portugal were, respectively, 7 and 20; and 0 and 2. This gives us a (not unexpected) ranking of countries but really what else? Certainly, we in England should be somewhat alarmed that 74 per cent of Singapore students were demonstrating the same level of mathematical competence as our top 20 per cent! Even then, though, we know little about the full extent of the Singapore students' knowledge, since the items were chosen (after a field trial), not to test this, but to ensure that the average score over all the countries – and Portugal was by no means the weakest – was reasonable.

In fact, by going back to the raw data on individual items and concentrating on the performances of students from countries with similar social and economic backgrounds, it is possible to draw out some valuable and/or interesting information, particularly with respect to curriculum emphases and the mathematical knowledge that students acquire outside the classroom (Howson, forthcoming). Nevertheless, even then, there are great dangers in taking country rankings by 'students attainment in TIMSS' at face value. Yet it is these rankings that are trumpeted by the media, who ignore the way in which these simplify matters. Let us consider some of the factors that make the interpretation of such rankings far from straightforward.

	Mean Grade 7	% below Grade 7	Mean age Grade 7	Mean Grade 8	Mean age Grade 8	% above Grade 8	% in top 10%	TCMA Mean score (Grade 8)
BFL	65 (2)	5.4	13.0	66 (2)	14.1	0.2	17	140: 65
CAN	52 (6)	8.1	13.1	59 (7)	14.1	0.6	7	147: 60
ENG	47 (9)	0.6	13.1	53 (8)	14.0	0.5	7	130: 57
FRA	51 (7)	20.5	13.3	61 (5)	14.3	1.3	7	140: 61
HUN	54 (4)	10.5	13.4	62 (3)	14.3	2.0	11	162: 62
JAP	67 (1)	0.3	13.4	73 (1)	14.4	0.0	32	153: 73
NET	55 (3)	9.8	13.2	60 (6)	14.3	0.4	10	116: 59
SCO	44 (10)	0.3	12.7	52 (10)	13.7	0.5	5	125: 55
SWI	53 (5)	8.3	13.1	62 (3)	14.2	0.2	11	133: 64
USA	48 (8)	9.0	13.2	53 (8)	14.2	0.2	5	162: 53

Source: Adapted from tables in Beaton *et al.* (1996)

This table provides data from ten educational systems/countries: Belgium Flanders, Canada, England, France, Hungary, Japan, the Netherlands, Scotland, Switzerland and the USA. Columns 1, 3, 4, 5 give the mean scores obtained on the TIMSS Population 2 written test by students in Grades 7 and 8[6] and the rankings of the countries, together with the average ages of students in those grades. We see that, if we ignore Scotland, then there is relatively little difference in the latter: 4–5 months at the most. Scotland's students, though, are significantly younger than their counterparts elsewhere: to what extent, then, are Scotland's rankings fair?[7] Moreover, Columns 2 and 6, headed '% below ...' and '% above ...' contain other, vital information. They tell us the estimated percentage of 13-year-olds who were in Grade 6 or below, and the number in Grade 9 or above. These data tell us much about how a country deals with probably the most difficult problem in the whole of mathematics education, that of 'differentiation'. Mathematics is a subject in which some students can soon display ability that is far above average. What is one to do with these? Should one move them on to new material either within their age-group or by promoting them to the next grade (accelerating them), or take the opportunity to deepen their understanding by giving them more taxing and complex questions on the shared curriculum, and/or provide them with mathematical enrichment not in the average student's curriculum? Similar questions can, of course, be asked about how to cope with weaker students. As the data in the table opposite suggest, not all countries follow the same course. Japan, England and Scotland are conspicuous for the way in which they promote almost all students so that they remain within their age group. Yet there are still important differences between these countries on differentiation. Japan has a curriculum set out year by year and all students are expected to cope with that. As a result, both high-attaining students who hope later to enter a prestigious university, as well as low-attainers who simply wish to survive, will probably attend evening tutorials in private institutions to seek help. In England, on the other hand, variations in the rate of students' progress are expected and teachers and schools are expected to cope with this. As is clear from the data, France makes considerable use of 'retention', i.e. making students who do not reach the required standard repeat a grade.[8] Yet, in theory, England, France and Japan all provide 'comprehensive' educational systems. This is not the case in, for example, the Netherlands, where, at the age of 12, students are split into four streams (with two or more catered for within the same school) that do not share mathematical goals. How does all this affect the 'rankings'? Because the lower-attaining 13-year-olds in many countries have been excluded from the samples, those countries' marks may be too high relative to those of England, Scotland and Japan. But in essence, we know very little about the effect of the use of 'retention' on students. Does it really help and motivate the low-attainer?[9] TIMSS has not thrown light on such questions. Indeed, it would require a specific study devoted to this topic to provide the evidence that might help administrators. What we can say is that, as a result of these national differences, the TIMSS data throw little light on whether or not, as it is often argued, England has a 'longer tail' of low attaining students than other countries.

Column 7 helps us to answer the question: 'Are our high attainers as good as those in our 'competitor' countries?' It shows the percentages of Grade 8 students who would have been counted amongst the top 10 per cent in TIMSS. It will be seen, however, that England's top 7 per cent perform slightly better, relative to their counterparts in other countries, than does the whole English cohort.

But to what extent is TIMSS fair? Were students always being tested on material they had been taught? In an attempt to answer this question, panels in each of the countries were asked to determine (TCMA – Test-Curriculum Matching Analysis) whether or not each item could have been expected to have been taught to the 'median student'. The total number of points available in the test was 162 and Column 8 gives the number of points each country thought were 'appropriate' for its 'median Grade 8 student', and also the percentage marks each country's Grade 8 students scored on these items. Again, the data reveal disparities in 'curriculum matching' – in particular, England, the Netherlands and Scotland found many of the arithmetic and algebra items inappropriate for their median students. This fact can be interpreted as 'TIMSS was unfair to these students.' However, since there would not appear to have been any mathematics left untested that these students would have covered and those from other countries would not, questions arise both about expectations in these three countries and also the desirability of excluding such material (see below) from these students' curriculums. It will also be seen that in many countries it appeared to make little difference whether or not a topic had been taught: indeed, students from Belgium scored more highly on items thought inappropriate than on those in their curriculum. Contributing to this were the high scores they obtained on the probability items. Probability had not been taught in the classroom, but students had obviously acquired knowledge of simple probability from elsewhere.[10]

TIMSS, then, is especially useful in bringing to attention specific weaknesses in a country's performance and in illuminating key curriculum decisions that have often been concealed. Let us consider three examples (others are dealt with in Howson, to appear). One open-response item asked students to multiply 0.203×0.56. The item was answered correctly by 71.6 per cent of Grade 8 French students, by 72.9 per cent of Hungarian students and by 8.1 per cent of English and Scottish Year 9 students (indeed, fewer than a further 9 per cent of English students got it correct apart from the positioning of the decimal point – and only 10 per cent chose to omit the question). Clearly, these days long multiplication is not as important as it once was, and it could be argued that attempting to teach this technique to all students is 'wasteful' – that the below-average French students could have been learning something more useful. Suppose one accepts that argument: then what percentage of English (or Scottish) 13-year-olds do you believe should be capable of dealing with such a problem? Is this a topic that should be delayed until Key Stage 4?

Another multiple-choice item asked students to identify the correct value of W given that $P = LW$, where $P = 12$ and $L = 3$. The correct answer was chosen by 49.6 per cent of Scottish and by 52.6 per cent of English Year 9 students against, for example, 88.1 per cent of Japanese or even 71 per cent of students from the USA (who, it will be noted, did not perform well overall). Should this be a matter of concern in England and Scotland?[11]

A further multiple-choice item asked students to find an average speed. This item was considered appropriate for Scottish students but not for English ones. The percentages of Year 9 students selecting the correct answer were: England, 26.5; Scotland, 22.8; Belgium Flanders, 42.6; Japan, 49 and Singapore, 72.3. Clearly, the item was found relatively difficult. Yet an understanding of 'rates' would seem essential for any school-leaver or any student of science. Are we in England putting sufficient emphasis on its learning, and does it make sense to delay its introduction to Key Stage 4?

It is, I believe, at the level of study of individual items that TIMSS Populations 1 and 2 results offer most to educators. Are these items that we think our students should be able to answer and, if so, can they? The results of TIMSS-R, a repeat of testing of Grade 8 students carried out in 1999, have now been published. Those for England were disappointing, and showed no real improvement relative to those countries listed in the table on p. 264 which also participated in TIMMS-R. Regrettably, the gaps between the scores of English males and females widened (in favour of the males), and the better English students no longer performed as well as their Canadian and US counterparts.

Attention, too, could also be directed at data relating to gender differences. In England and Scotland males scored more highly than females in both Years 8 and 9 (significantly so for English males in Year 8).[12] These data correspond to traditional findings relating to mathematical attainment. Yet it is valuable to contrast the results obtained from a TIMSS test that cannot be prepared for, with those obtained on the English Key Stage 3 SATs in mathematics.

The results of the Year 9 'Performance Assessment' tests (Harmon *et al.*, 1997) were more encouraging for both England and Scotland. For 'performing mathematical procedures', England averaged 77 per cent and Scotland 75 per cent, against Switzerland's 76 per cent and top-scoring Singapore's 80 per cent.[13] However, on 'problem-solving and mathematical reasoning' the results were not so good: England, 54 per cent; Scotland, 52 per cent; Switzerland, 60 per cent and Singapore, 62 per cent.[14]

In many ways, the most successful part of TIMSS was that which tested mathematical and scientific numeracy amongst all students in their final year of secondary education. Here, items were not designed to fit some 'central core' of the curriculum, but rather solely to test students on the mathematical and scientific knowledge they would require to meet the needs of everyday life and responsible, intelligent citizenship. Thus all items were set in context and tested the ability to use mathematics: not just to remember it. Students from the Netherlands, Switzerland and Sweden all performed well in the tests, whereas those from Germany, Hungary and the USA had disappointing results. To equip *all* students with the mathematics they will actually need to cope better with adult life is a key aim of mathematics education, and it was a pity that more countries, including England and Scotland, did not participate in this part of TIMSS. Preparing all students to tackle some of the items set to 13-year-olds pales into insignificance as an educational goal alongside that of ensuring they are mathematically literate.

The problem of designing a test for the specialist mathematicians is one that really justifies Husén's[15] statement (1983) that 'comparing the outcomes of learning in different countries is in several respects an exercise in comparing the incomparable'.

First we notice that the percentage of the age cohort enrolled on the 'specialist' mathematics course differs greatly from country to country – from 2 per cent in Russia to 75 per cent in Slovenia. How can one compare the attainments of a minority of specialists with those of the vast majority of the age cohort? Just to complicate the issue further, the average age of the Russians was 16.9 and that of the Slovenians 18.9. (There is considerable variation between countries concerning the age at which students move on from school to university or elsewhere.) Even if one restricts consideration of results to those countries enrolling between 10 and 20 per cent of their students on a 'specialist' mathematics course (which would rule out England, which, like Scotland, did not participate in these tests), then other big differences still remain. There are, for example, considerable differences between countries relating to the degree of specialisation permitted and the number of subjects students must continue to study. Accordingly, for example, 48 per cent of Czech, 46 per cent of Italian and 64 per cent of Swedish students claimed to study 'specialist' mathematics for less than three hours per week. On the other hand, 97 per cent of French and Cypriot students and all those from Greece said that they had five or more hours of mathematics a week. Other data suggest that in some countries extra mathematics teaching was supplied to the more able students, but in Sweden to those requiring additional help: yet another policy difference.

The main conclusion from the study of specialist mathematics students would appear to be that little is to be gained from consulting the ranking lists of countries published in Mullis *et al.* (1998). Indeed, their deceptive simplicity may well prove a trap into which politicians might fall. There are some clear warnings in these tables of which heed should be taken, but they, by themselves, do not provide 'value for use'. A country wishing to improve its mathematics teaching, must carry out a careful study of responses to individual items, to the validity and significance they attach to these, and to the way that students' successes or failures can be linked, not only to specific topic areas, but, perhaps more importantly, to the varying cognitive demands of the individual items.[16]

To sum up, major international studies, such as those organised by IEA,[17] carry with them dangers, but can also add much to our knowledge of mathematics education and, especially, to the appropriateness of a country's educational expectations and performance. The rankings, and the way in which they are presented without qualification in the media, can be dangerous.[18] It is only too easy for these to be latched onto as an excuse for pursuing any educational policy. One must look further into the data to determine what might prove sound courses of action. Yet, nevertheless, rankings can be salutary. As any UK sports enthusiast will know, it is only international comparisons that alert one to weaknesses in one's own system! The effectiveness of an educational system, too, can never be judged solely by its own internal measures.

Two smaller studies

It is not only the large-scale studies such as TIMSS that are worthy of note. Indeed, although these tell us how a country is performing relative to others, it is the smaller, more focused study, which is likely to provide greater 'value for use'. In this section, then, we briefly describe two 'small' studies, both undertaken by individuals or small teams (but relying on much help from colleagues in the countries studied!). The first concerns primary school textbooks drawn from a variety of countries and the second is a study of the differences between primary and pre-school education in England and Japan.

A comparative study of primary school textbooks, with particular attention to the teaching of number, was commissioned by the Qualifications and Curriculum Authority (QCA) partly in response to the poor results obtained by English primary school students in TIMSS. It was carried out in two parts. Rosamund Sutherland and Tony Harries looked at textbook series, teachers' guides and curriculums from England, Singapore, Hungary, France and the USA, while I studied those from Canada, Ireland, Japan, the Netherlands and Switzerland, plus one from England. The two reports produced were extremely long and detailed and were not made publicly available. The criticisms they necessarily contained effectively ruled out publication by a Government authority. A summary was published (Howson *et al.*, 1999) and this presented some of the overall impressions the authors of the reports had gained after undertaking the study. We found, for example, that the big differences did not arise from the range of approaches used, for all countries made use of, say, the number line, the hundred square, and structural apparatus. The major differences appeared to be:

- The rate at which new ideas are introduced and the timing of this. (The summary report gives data which make it clear that we in England introduce *more* ideas at an early age and that these ideas are in general introduced *earlier* than in the other countries studied.)
- The time spent on a topic when it is first introduced and the extent to which any techniques are practised, revised and consolidated. (Again, data can be found in the summary report suggesting that there is far more chopping and changing of topics taking place in English classrooms than elsewhere.)
- The extent to which textbooks draw upon a clear understanding of the links between different aspects of mathematics and the manner in which these may be represented in text or illustrations.
- The place accorded to apparatus (either analogue or digital).
- The range and suitability of the applications of arithmetic employed, both as motivation and as sources for exercises.
- The relative emphasis placed on paper-based external representations, both as a way of communicating mathematics and as a means for supporting mathematical learning, and the use made of realistic contexts to generate multi-step mathematical situations.

Various recommendations were made for improving the situation in England. Here, we mention just one: that 'teachers' guides should offer teachers both an easy-to-use support that provides clear links with pupil texts and also a means of developing mathematical and psychological awareness'. English guides appeared very weak in these aspects compared to those available to teachers in several other countries. Here, of course, other factors come into effect, particularly financial – the emphasis governments wish to place on the provision of good texts, the financial support they will provide and the measures they are prepared to take to ensure that texts and accompanying guides are of a sufficiently high standard.

Such a study can have great value in drawing attention to problems and possibilities: whether actions are taken is another matter! This, though, is a constant factor affecting comparative studies.

The second study was carried out under the auspices of the National Institute of Economic and Social Research – again, witness to the importance that those concerned with the growth of national economies give to raising educational standards. This study by Julia Whitburn (2000) concerned early education in mathematics in England and Japan. Major components of the study were fieldwork, analysis of documentation and discussion. The fieldwork was carried out with classes of six- and seven-year-old children in three state schools in Tokyo and four in London. The schools were not selected by ministries or LEAs, but were selected at random from a list of schools satisfying requirements concerning size and geographical location, and permission was then asked to visit them. Schools in each country were observed over two periods each of two months and separated by a year. An objective test of numeracy/mathematical competence was administered to all the children in the study, to permit both cross-national comparisons and a measure of progress. Discussions were also carried out with classroom teachers regarding teaching methods and classroom practice. In both countries, national curriculums, textbooks and associated lesson materials, and the content and function of teachers' guides were also analysed. Finally, discussions were held with other educationists, academics and researchers on such issues as the sequencing of topics, the teaching of strategies for mental calculation, and ways in which to help slower children.

The results of the study are of considerable interest and it is impossible to summarise them adequately here. For example, results of tests showed that at age six the mathematical attainments of English children (average score 67) were superior to those of the Japanese – average score 37 (recall that formal education does not commence in Japan until age six). However, by age seven the Japanese children (92) had already overtaken the English (82). The main factors identified as being responsible for this were:

- societal attitudes and perceptions of the relative contributions of innate ability and perseverance;
- pre-schooling influences (these essentially relate to the way in which when children begin school their attitude to learning will have been greatly affected by pre-school experience);
- the way in which the central control of the educational system is manifested and the consequent effects upon children's classroom experience;
- the models of children's development and approaches to pedagogy adopted in the two countries;
- teachers' backgrounds and preparation; the management and climate of the classroom; teachers' attitudes; differences in classroom practice – teaching methods and approaches; pupil motivation and participation and expectations for pupils.

Clearly, a comparative study of this kind, although lacking the apparent objectivity[19] of the IEA studies, offers deeper insights into the workings of the two educational systems. Moreover, while exhibiting different standards of mathematical attainment it also provides 'value for use' in offering possible explanations for those differences. This does not mean that we should use comparative studies to find the currently 'highest achieving' country and seek to import its classroom procedures. Differing cultural, social and educational contexts rule out such simplistic solutions. Rather, the value of comparative studies lies in the way in which they challenge us to review and reconsider current aims, standards and practices and to realise that long-standing assumptions may be little more than local traditions urgently in need of re-examination and re-appraisal.

Notes

1 Beaton *et al.* (1996), does not provide data on parental education for England, but those for Scotland (typical of most participating countries) were 'one parent finished university' – average score of students 559, 'one parent finished upper secondary school' – 499, 'one parent finished lower secondary school' – 485. Wales and Northern Ireland did not participate in TIMSS.

2 A large selection of papers, both descriptive and critical, relating to the various aspects of TIMSS mentioned in this section and also to other comparative studies can be found in Kaiser *et al.* (1999).

3 The reason for this apparently odd wording will become clear when the reader studies Table 17.1.

4 Comparisons can, of course, also be made between data collected from FIMS and SIMS. Thus, for example, relative to other countries that participated in both SIMS and TIMSS, England's test performances (again at Population 2) declined in Geometry, Algebra, and Number and Proportion (the three subsets on which data are currently available).

5 Germany, however, performed weakly in TIMSS and so the two studies lost some of their apparent purpose. Any 'good practice' illustrated in the German videotapes simply illustrated that examples of good teaching can be found in most systems. One should not, however, then assume that such teaching is to be found in all of a country's schools.

6 In most countries formal education begins at age 6 rather then 5 as in England. Thus Grade 7 corresponds to our Year 8 and Grade 8 to Year 9.

7 The estimated median mark for Scottish 13-year-olds was actually higher than those for similar English and US students.

8 Even then there can be differentiation within a grade or class. A popular textbook series (see, e.g. Howson, 1995) divides exercises into two kinds. One type, 'savoir faire', tests basic knowledge of techniques and skills; the other, 'chercher', contains more open and contextualised problems drawing upon cross-curricular and societal links. One suspects the weaker students rarely progress to the second type of exercise.

9 Anecdotal evidence suggests it can provide a powerful incentive for those who are 'below average' but not really 'low' attainers.

10 This was true in other countries. Data are given in Howson (to appear) showing, for example, that on 'common sense' probability (i.e. that relating to the probability of single events) the Belgian and Japanese students scored more highly than their English counterparts (who had been introduced to probability in school). However, 'common sense' tended to let students down when the question related to independent, repeated trials, e.g. tosses of a coin, spins of a roulette wheel – indicating a topic that must be taught.

11 A marked feature in all the tests was the great difference in average scores on multiple-choice and open-response items. There is no suggestion that this would change rankings significantly, but it would appear to confuse our knowledge concerning the understanding students actually have of a topic. The general feeling one receives is that multiple-choice scores present a very rosy view of the situation.

12   The English and Scottish Year 9 gender differences were present on all types of items: multiple-choice, short answer, and extended-response (see Mullis *et al.*, 2000). English females matched the males on 'knowing and procedure' items but lagged behind them on 'reasoning and problem solving'. Scottish males led on both types of item.

13   Many leading countries, e.g. Japan, Belgium Flanders, and France, did not participate in these tests.

14   The English data are based on a sample of schools that did not meet the stringent TIMSS sampling requirements, whereas the Swiss data are for German-speaking cantons.

15   Husén was one of the leaders of IEA in its early days and played a considerable role in FIMS.

16   Thus, for example, French and Greek students performed extremely well on Population 3 items that required them to demonstrate skills and techniques, but considerably less well when asked to use their mathematics in context or to deal with out-of-the-ordinary items even though these made use of only relatively elementary mathematics. Again, Greek, students were appropriately proficient at supplying a formal proof in geometry, but less impressive at using simple logic to deal with a problem.

17   Others were organised in 1988 and 1990/91 by the US Educational Testing Services. A regular series of such tests, involving mathematics, is now promised from the Organisation for Economic Cooperation and Development (OECD).

18   Similar warnings apply to other, national rankings!

19   The word 'apparent' is used since although the data emerging from TIMSS might be 'objective', there is a great deal of subjectivity in the framing of items (and their balance), in the compilation of questionnaires, etc.

References

Beaton, A.E., *et al.* (1996) *Mathematics Achievement in the Middle School Years*, MA: TIMSS, Boston College.

Harmon, M., *et al.* (1997) *Performance Assessment Testing in IEA's Third International Mathematics and Science Study*, MA: TIMSS, Boston College.

Howson, A.G. (1995) *Mathematics Textbooks: a comparative study of Grade 8 texts*, Vancouver: Pacific Educational Press.

Howson, A.G. (forthcoming) 'TIMSS, common sense and the curriculum', in D.F. Robitaille and A.E. Beaton (eds) *Secondary Analysis of TIMSS Data*, Dordrecht, The Netherlands: Kluwer.

Howson, A.G., Harries, T. and Sutherland, R. (1999) *Primary School Mathematics Textbooks: an international summary*, London: QCA.

Husén, T. (1983) 'Are standards in US schools really lagging behind those in other countries?', *Phi Delta Kappan*: 455–61.

Kaiser, G., Luna, E. and Huntley, I. (eds) (1999) *International Comparisons in Mathematics Education*, Lewes: Falmer Press.

Mullis, I., *et al.* (1998) *Mathematics and Science Achievement in the Final Year of Secondary School*, MA: TIMSS, Boston College.

Mullis, I., *et al.* (2000) *Gender Differences in Achievement*, MA: TIMSS, Boston College.

Sylvester, D.W. (1970) *Educational Documents 800–1816*, Methuen: 2–4.

Whitburn, J. (2000) *Strength in Numbers*, London: NIESR.

Index